SPORTS FOR HER

A Reference Guide for
Teenage Girls

Penny Hastings

Greenwood Press
Westport, Connecticut • London

Library of Congress Cataloging-in-Publication Data

Hastings, Penny.
    Sports for her : a reference guide for teenage girls / Penny
Hastings.
        p.   cm.
    Summary: Discusses issues related to girls' participation in
sports and provides information on the rules, equipment, training,
and more for eight sports which high school girls are most likely to
play.
    Includes bibliographical references and index.
    ISBN 0-313-30551-X (alk. paper)
    1. Sports for women—United States Juvenile literature. 2. School
sports—United States Juvenile literature. [1. Sports for women.]
    I. Title.
GV709.18.U6H37   1999
796'.082—dc21   99-21279

British Library Cataloguing in Publication Data is available.

Copyright © 1999 by Penny Hastings

All rights reserved. No portion of this book may be
reproduced, by any process or technique, without the
express written consent of the publisher.

Library of Congress Catalog Card Number: 99-21279
ISBN: 0-313-30551-X

First published in 1999

Greenwood Press, 88 Post Road West, Westport, CT 06881
An imprint of Greenwood Publishing Group, Inc.
www.greenwood.com

Printed in the United States of America

The paper used in this book complies with the
Permanent Paper Standard issued by the National
Information Standards Organization (Z39.48–1984).

10 9 8 7 6 5 4 3 2 1

796.082
H 358s

Contents

Introduction

Most girls love to run and jump and climb and throw just as much as boys. But often, boys are encouraged to be active more and are taught organized sports earlier than girls. So, nearing the high school years, many boys are not only proficient in one or more sports but, for a lot of them, it's practically a given that they will continue to participate at the high school level.

In talking to adolescent girls, I found that while they were often eager to play high school sports, unless they were involved in athletics from a young age, they lacked information about the various sports available to them and the confidence to try out. I also discovered that many girls who had played sports early on dropped out when they reached puberty. This happens for a variety of reasons, some of which have to do with societal pressures and prejudice, but also because they lack the information about sports that would encourage them to get, or stay, involved.

In my research I noticed there weren't any books to let adolescent girls know about their opportunities to play sports at high school. I talked to girls who were unaware just how many sports existed and had no idea of how the sports were played or even what the game looked like. They often didn't know much about the most popular sports and knew even less about other sports. So how could they know whether they wanted to get involved or not? They were self-conscious about their lack of knowledge and wistfully said they would like to play if only they knew more about sports, how they could find a sport they liked, how to go about trying out for the team, and how they could get involved and have fun, rather than just sit on the side lines. I thought that writing a book giving them that information might make a difference and encourage them to continue participating in a favored sport or to take up a new sport entirely.

The result is *Sports for Her,* a book that offers girls a positive and knowledgeable look at sports available at high schools across the country: from the most popular to less well-known sports. *Sports for Her* gives girls a detailed look at the eight sports most participated in at the high school level—basketball, field hockey, soccer, softball, swimming and diving, tennis, track and field, and volleyball. Each one has its own chapter that includes: how to play the game, what to wear and what equipment is needed, a brief history of the sport, the most important rules, tips for pre-season training, the most common injuries and how to avoid them, and how to find places to learn and play. Additionally, each chapter is chock full of ideas and encouragement from high school coaches and athletes to help girls succeed.

Other high school sports for girls are also described, including badminton, rowing, golf, gymnastics, lacrosse, and skiing. Some sports, such as baseball, football, ice hockey, water polo, and wrestling have traditionally been boys-only sports—but not anymore. Today girls are breaking down the barriers in just about all sports. Knowing about all high school sports, and learning how to organize a girls team or how to join the boys team, encourages girls to expand their athletic experience. Particularly helpful in each chapter are the shared experiences and tips given by coaches and current, as well as former, high school athletes.

My research led me to believe that girls need to know about special issues that can cause problems, such as gender bias, nutrition, eating disorders, problems with coaches, teammate troubles, overtraining, drugs, and over-involved parents. While most girls report exceedingly positive sports experiences, some have run into situations that bother them or that have even hurt them. Discussing those issues helps girls deal with them if they come up.

Sports for Her concludes with the good news that girls don't have to hang up their cleats when they get their high school diplomas. There is a long future ahead for girls who want to continue with sports. College sports for women are huge now, and with the availability of athletic scholarships, student-athletes can help pay their educational expenses and play their sport at the same time. Many women can continue with a career in a sports-related field, having adopted sports as a lifetime of fitness and fun beginning in adolescence or even earlier.

Girls and others, such as parents, coaches, and teachers, can read this book from cover to cover or skip among chapters about sports that interest them the most. I hope girls will learn more about a sport they love or discover a new sport to play that will enhance their overall high school experience.

ACKNOWLEDGMENTS

Every successful team needs players, coaches, fans, and a support staff. From the book's starting kick-off to the game-ending whistle, I was blessed with a team of athletes, coaches, athletic directors, psychologists, nutritionists, librarians, sports historians, trainers, and athletic administrators from all over the country, who willingly gave of their time and expertise to ensure the accuracy and relevancy of *Sports for Her.*

I am especially grateful to the superstars: the girls and their parents who shared their experiences to make the book personal and lively. From Emily Birch, my editor at Greenwood Press, and Annette Gooch, my day-to-day editor, I received excellent coaching during what sometimes seemed like a marathon event. My family and friends were constant fans, always there to cheer me on. To all of you, my Dream Team, I am eternally grateful. Thanks, teammates.

Chapter 1

Girls Get a Kick Out of Sports

More than ever, girls are participating in sports and loving it! Photo reproduced by permission of the photographer, Arielle Kohn.

On an autumn weekend you can drive by just about any schoolyard or park and see girls running on a grassy field. Under sunny skies, with the pungent smell of burning leaves in the air, kids of different ages run and kick and shout—some of them so small that their shorts hang over the tops of their striped knee-high socks. There are others who are older, and each age group is divided into teams. Net-covered goals and orange side line cones mark off separate soccer fields. Brilliant blue shirts run alongside bright reds. Younger teams call themselves the Cardinals, Robins, Hawks, and Blue Jays, while the older players choose strong names like Strikers, Avalanches, and Speed Demons. As parents and grandparents watch, brothers and sisters play their own games on the sidelines. Spectators cheer and referees whistle and players call out to each other and laugh and whoop it up when someone gets off a good strong kick or a ball goes into the net for a goal. There is a celebratory feeling on the field, as if every girl is glad to be there—running and kicking and breathing hard.

As soccer balls are being booted in California, other sporting events are taking place across the country. In a high school gym in Kansas teenage girls run up and down the court in a fast game of basketball, while at a New Jersey park a game of field hockey is just starting. On tennis courts from San Diego to Miami Beach, girls serve, backhand, and volley a tennis ball. There is a revolution going on—a sports revolution, a collective movement by girls and women eager to run, jump, leap, throw and kick, and bat a ball—a revolution of gigantic proportions, and you are part of it, a major part. Today one in every three high school girls plays sports! While your mom didn't have it so well—in 1970 only one in every 27 girls participated—it was probably not because she didn't want to. It was because she didn't have the same opportunities you do.

As a young girl, she may have sat on the curb and watched the neighborhood boys playing baseball in the street. She may have asked if she could play too. If she was any good, she may have been included; if she was very good, she may have even been welcomed. But as she grew up, women of your mom's generation had very few chances to participate in sports, other than in physical education classes or in occasional after-school activities. Boys took sports for granted; girls took it for granted that they couldn't play. Young girls were called tomboys when they played ball with the boys rather than dolls with the girls. Many girls, therefore, subdued their own desire to compete, and as they got older, they became great spectators of boys' sports. They watched from the side lines as the boys they used to play with in the street scored a touchdown or charged down the basketball court. Some girls became cheerleaders, marched with the drill team, were part of the pep squad— their only chances to be part of the school sports scene.

Being a team mascot was the only way Tara VanDerveer could get on her high school basketball court. VanDerveer, the women's basketball coach at Stanford University and coach of the 1996 Olympic gold medal winning women's team, claims she wasn't very good at it. "I kept taking the mascot head off so I could watch the game."[1]

The only way some girls could make the team was to lie. So it was with Dot Richardson, the shortstop with the big bat who hit the winning home run when the U.S. women's softball team defeated China for the Olympic gold medal in 1996. She grew up tossing the ball with her father and two brothers. When she was ten, she tried to join a Little League team but was told she would have to cut her hair and call herself Bob. She was actually told to lie about her gender (which she refused to do) so she could be part of a game that only boys were allowed to play!

Luckily, girls today don't have to go to such extremes to participate in sports. They can now begin to play almost as soon as they can run, kick a ball, do a somersault, wield a hockey stick, hold a tennis racquet, climb on a horse, or swing a golf club.

WHAT ARE SPORTS?

There are many ways to describe sports. Dictionaries offer the following definitions: athletic pastime, physical activity, game, competition, contest, diversion, recreation, fun, distraction, entertainment, amusement, play, relaxation, hobby. These descriptions work for girls, but when asked why they play sports and how their sports participation benefits them, they go into far greater detail and share their thoughts enthusiastically. To most girls, sports are a way to get in shape and stay fit, to meet other girls and make friends, and to keep busy. They enjoy learning new skills, competing against others, and receiving attention and admiration from their family and friends. They say sports teach them to accomplish goals and to challenge themselves. Some even express their emotions through sports. Girls relate that participating in sports makes them feel better about themselves and more confident, not just in the sports arena but in other areas of their lives as well. There are more reasons girls give for participating in sports, maybe as many reasons as there are girls; but the main reason is: Sports are fun! Here's what girls who were surveyed said about sports and fun:

"I like to do active things and sports are a fun way to be active."

"I keep in shape and have *tons* of fun."

"[T]o push myself to extreme limits and have fun doing it."

"Sports are fun . . . challenging and competitive. I love that!"

"They're fun even when you're losing."

"[P]artly for fitness but mostly for fun."

"[F]un to be part of a team."

"[F]un and exciting and takes your mind off of everything else."

"I get a good workout while having fun."

"[T]o have fun and play the sport I love."

"I'm getting better at my sport and that makes it more fun."

"[B]eating the other team is fun."

"I get to play with my friends, and that's fun."

"Competing with all your heart . . . that's the fun of it."

Some of the same girls interviewed also believe that playing sports is advantageous for them. They say sports have taught them to think and act quickly; to set goals and work hard to achieve them; to get along with other girls and be a team player; to feel good about their bodies and what they can do, rather than how they look. They feel that staying busy with sports keeps them out of trouble, and many feel healthier, stronger, and more alive when they are playing a sport.

"One reason I play sports is so I can maintain my fitness and keep myself happy."

"I like to be athletic; it makes me feel good."

"[Sports] are a way to express your joys and angers."

"[There is] a lot of spirit. It gets you pumped up!"

"Sports are just games that help us along in our lives."

"They [sports] help me to overcome my shyness around people."

"Celebrating with my team when we've done something well makes me teary-eyed."

"[Through sports I] learn new things about myself."

"[Sports] give me confidence that I can do something well."

"Sports keep a lot of people off the streets and keep their heads in the right place."

"I am good at my sport and that makes me happy."

Being away from sports makes some girls miserable. One multisport athlete talked about an injury that kept her sidelined for months. She says, "When I wasn't playing soccer and running track, I was miserable. My weight increased and my self-confidence declined. I love sports! I can't imagine a sedentary life."

While many girls begin playing sports very early—some as young as three and four years old—others may not develop an interest or have the opportunity until they get to high school. Girls decide to play high school sports for many reasons. Some say they are following in the footsteps of an older brother or sister. Others want to do what their friends are doing. Some remark that they want to get exercise, be part of a team, try something new, or learn new skills.

HIGH SCHOOL SPORTS

High school sports are for experienced and inexperienced athletes alike. The number of sports offered to girls at the high school level is steadily increasing, so more girls have an opportunity to participate, not only in the sports that are most popular and have been around for awhile, like basketball, track, field hockey, and volleyball, but also in sports less familiar, like badminton, crew, golf, and water polo. High school is often the best place to learn and practice a new sport while enjoying the camaraderie and sense of belonging many girls experience when they join a team.

Coaches at most schools say they encourage all girls to try out for their sport, whether it's nordic skiing, soccer, tennis, or swimming. "Everyone is welcome," says high school lacrosse coach Beth Stone, "I rarely cut players." This isn't always the case, however. Some sports have smaller squads or are highly competitive. When more girls try out for the team than can be accommodated, the coaches have to be more selective. They generally keep the more experienced athletes, the ones with better skills and greater knowledge of the sport. Luckily, the increase in sports opportunities allows girls other choices: if they do not make one team, there may be another that welcomes them.

WHAT SPORTS ARE GIRLS PLAYING?

Information about the most popular sports (based on number of participants nationwide), as well as others available at many high schools, is presented in upcoming chapters. In each chapter, coaches and other experts, including high school and former high school athletes, offer advice on how girls can prepare themselves for the sport and maximize their chances of making the team. There is even a chapter about how some girls are breaking the barriers and getting involved in what traditionally have been male-dominated sports (see Chapter 11).

Girls now comprise about 37 percent of all high school athletes. (The term "girls" is commonly used at the high school level, while "women" is used for college sports.) Girls' sports programs were scarce in high schools until 1972, when federal legislation passed mandating equal opportunities for all in educational institutions. (See figure 1.1.) Today, much has changed. According to the National Federation of State High School Associations, 2,570,333 girls were involved in high school sports in the 1997–98 school year. That is an increase of more than 98,290 over the previous year.[2]

Not only are more girls participating at the high school level, but the number of sports offered has increased dramatically in the past decade (see table 1.1). At least 32 sports are played by girls in high schools throughout the country, with some girls playing on what are generally considered boys-only teams—such as football, wrestling, ice hockey, and baseball. Adaptive sports are offered for disabled athletes as well.

Women's sports at the college level also have grown. According to a National College Athletic Association (NCAA) study, 137,044 women played intercollegiate (competition between colleges) sports in the 1997–98 school year. These figures do not include the women at colleges that belong to other, smaller athletic associations or the numerous women who enjoy intramural (competition between clubs, residence halls, and other groups on campus) sports.

Girls haven't always had these opportunities. Looking back to the beginning of time—to cave drawings, ancient artifacts, and written accounts of earlier civilizations—there is scant evidence of women participating in sports. The reasons vary culture by culture, but most prevalent is the theory that historically sports have been thought of in

Figure 1.1
Title IX

Title IX is the portion of the Education Amendments of 1972 that prohibits sex discrimination in education institutions that receive federal funds. Title IX states:

No person in the United States shall, on the basis of sex, be excluded from participation in, be denied the benefits of, or be subjected to discrimination under any educational program or activity receiving Federal financial assistance.[3]

As a result of the enactment of Title IX, the number of girls participating in high school and college sports multiplied. In 1971, there were only 294,015 girls playing high school sports. By the 1972–73 school year, just after the passage of the landmark legislation, that number had more than doubled.

Similar, though not as spectacular, gains occurred in intercollegiate sports. In 1971, 31,852 women took part in college varsity sports. By 1977, the number had swelled to 64,375. Athletic scholarships, practically non-existent before Title IX, were added, and today there are more than 10,000 sports scholarships available to female athletes.

Although participation increased enormously at first, the momentum soon slowed and many female student-athletes found their opportunities limited by high schools and colleges who failed to adhere to the spirit of Title IX. Lack of enforcement further stalled the movement. It took the passage of the Civil Rights Restoration Act in March 1998, together with lawsuits brought by women who believed themselves discriminated against, for Title IX to be reaffirmed and the women's sports movement to move towards gender equity. Court decisions in virtually all cases since that time have upheld the provisions of Title IX.

much the same way as warfare, with only the men taking part. Women, whose traditional responsibility was giving birth and taking care of the home and family, were exempted from fighting and discouraged—in most cases forbidden—from taking part in sporting activities.

HISTORY OF WOMEN'S SPORTS

It is hard to believe now, but when the Olympic games were first held in ancient Greece in 776 B.C., women were not only kept from joining in the competition, they were condemned to death if they dared to watch!

Table 1.1
Numbers of Girls Participating in High School Sports

Sport	Number of Schools	Number of Participants
ADAPTED SPORTS		
bowling	4	61
floor hockey	59	155
soccer	58	160
softball	59	200
ARCHERY	3	3
BADMINTON	*369	9,084
BASEBALL	108	**1,262
BASKETBALL	16,428	454,000
BOWLING	729	7,932
CANOEING	15	435
COMPETITIVE SPIRIT SQUADS	3,154	58,737
CREW	34	1,008
CROSS COUNTRY	11,097	150,846
DECATHLON	1	1
EQUESTRIAN	36	351
FENCING	39	749
FIELD HOCKEY	1,491	56,589
FOOTBALL	**160	**779
GOLF	6,579	**49,690
GYMNASTICS	*1,592	21,347
HEPTATHLON	17	47
ICE HOCKEY	271	**3,016
JUDO	16	123
LACROSSE	509	**20,189
PENTATHLON	4	22
RIFLERY	156	900
SKIING		
alpine	387	4,268
cross-country	378	5,070
SOCCER	7,468	**246,687
SOFTBALL		
fastpitch	12,326	333,374
slowpitch	1,535	30,387
SWIMMING & DIVING	5,360	**126,062
TEAM TENNIS	659	
TENNIS	9,297	151,539
TRACK & FIELD		
indoor	1,862	41,591
outdoor	14,284	395,955
VOLLEYBALL	*13,019	373,219

Table 1.1 (Continued)

WATER POLO	466	**10,800
WEIGHT LIFTING	112	3,962
WRESTLING	619	**1,907
OTHER	252	7,813

*Includes some combined (coed) teams.
**Includes girls playing on boys' teams and boys playing on girls' teams.

Source: National Federation of State High School Associations 1998 Participation Survey.

Sports have long been associated with masculinity. Terminology used to describe men and boys includes *strong, courageous, daring,* and *bold.* Females, called "the weaker sex," have been characterized as *ladylike, soft, demure,* and *fragile,* even though a majority of women worked hard physically throughout their lifetimes in their homes, in the fields, and later, in factories. Girls today may have a hard time believing that women were ever considered too delicate to play sports. In the United States, as well in many other countries, sports-minded girls and women consider themselves feminine as well as athletic. This view is not universal, however. There are still parts of the world where females are discouraged or forbidden from participating in sports. Even in this country, society continues to have conflicting attitudes and concerns about female athletes.

From the time of those early Olympics, when women who dared to watch men playing sports were thrown off Mount Typaion in Olympia, athletic participation was limited to men, with few exceptions, until the late 19th century. What propelled women into the sporting life, among other factors, was the bicycle. The introduction of the bicycle in the late 1800s gave women a sense of freedom they had never before experienced. Before that time, women were mainly limited to walking, dancing, and horseback riding—sidesaddle only.

Prior to the 20th century, clothing, along with society's attitudes about what constituted femininity, limited the options for women. Floor-length skirts, corsets, and petticoats hindered movement. Yet women, determined to have a good time and be physically active, began taking up tennis, basketball, volleyball, and swimming—in spite of their restrictive clothing. Some women faced ridicule and even imprisonment for trying to break out of their corsets. In 1919, Ethelda Bleibtrey was arrested at a New York City beach for exposing her legs in public when she took off her stockings before going for a swim. A crusader for women's sports, Bleibtrey used this as a way to call attention to the ridiculous bathing costumes—bloomers (calf-length pants with full legs), heavy dresses and stockings—that women customarily wore. Gradually, as more women challenged convention, clothing styles began to change. Stiff corsets and long skirts gave way to shorter styles without petticoats and the even more controversial split-skirts.

The bicycling craze sweeping the country at the turn of the century coincided with social reform and the women's right-to-vote movement. Pioneer feminist Susan B. Anthony stated that "the bicycle did more to emancipate women than anything else in the world."[4] Along with more than one million other American women who owned and rode bicycles by 1890, Frances E. Willard, suffragette and president of the Women's Christian Temperance Union (WCTU), was a cycling advocate. In 1895, she wrote a book praising the virtues of cycling called *How I Learned to Ride the Bicycle—Reflections of an Influential 19th Century Woman*. Anthony and Willard, along with others who advocated for women's rights, promoted physical activity for women as a healthy, happy pursuit. This may not seem like a radical viewpoint now, but it was back then.

Many of the sports girls play today in American high schools had their beginnings in earlier centuries. Yet until the 1960s most physical educators, even though they believed that sports for girls were beneficial for health and social reasons, generally disapproved of females competing against each other. In the first half of the 20th century, individual rather than team sports achieved some acceptance because they were considered more playful than athletic and less competitive, because no physical contact was likely to occur.[5]

If it were not for early sportswomen who pushed against the societal boundaries that confined them to their homes and traditional roles, women might still be wearing corsets, carrying smelling salts, and believing that breaking a sweat is a bad thing. A salute to a few of these pioneers is surely in order:

• Eleanora Sears set Boston society on its blue-blooded heels in the early 1900s by playing multiple sports and wearing boyish clothes. Sears is credited with being the first woman in the country to publicly ride a horse astride rather than the traditional sidesaddle. She competed in national tennis and squash tournaments until she was 70 years old and remained a horsewoman well into her 80s.

- Helen Wills Moody helped the cause of women's sports in the 1920s by challenging the unflattering stereotype that sports were unfeminine. In addition to winning 11 U.S. tennis championships and a gold medal in the 1924 Olympic Games, she wore eyeshadow during her matches and was nicknamed "Queen Helen" for her refined behavior.[6]

- Gertrude Ederle was the first woman to swim the English Channel (20.6 miles) from France to England. Her record-breaking time in 1926 beat the men's record by two hours.

- Mildred "Babe" Didrickson (Zaharias) has been called the greatest female athlete in the first half of the 20th century. She played baseball, basketball, tennis, and volleyball; she also won two gold medals and a silver in the 1936 Olympics for track and field (she probably could have won more, but she was restricted to entering just three events). As if that weren't enough, she excelled in golf and went on to help organize the Ladies Professional Golf Association (LPGA).

- Althea Gibson was the first African American woman to compete in the prestigious U.S. Open and Wimbledon tournaments (in 1957 and 1958) at a time when the game of tennis was dominated by white athletes. She was the first African American, man or woman, to win a tennis title. Her perseverance and success in the face of tremendous opposition made her a role model for all women, especially women of color.

- Wilma Rudolph, another African American athlete, overcame polio and, with courage and determination, disproved doctors' predictions that she would be disabled for life. Rudolph made history at the 1960 Olympics in Rome by becoming the first American woman to win three gold medals in track and field competition. She later established a foundation to promote amateur athletics.

- Kathrine Switzer used her first initial to conceal her gender when she registered for the Boston Marathon in 1967. During the race, she was chased by an official of the all-male event, who attempted to pull her out of the race. At that time, international rules barred men and women from running in the same race and limited women's distance races to 1.5 miles. Switzer was instrumental in changing the rules, but it took five more years before women were finally allowed to race in marathon competitions.

- Billie Jean King challenged the male sports establishment and public perceptions about female athletes when she beat self-proclaimed male chauvinist and former Wimbledon champion Bobby Riggs in a 1973 tennis match at the Houston Astrodome. The event drew a crowd of over 30,000 and a television audience in the millions. The winner of 21 Wimbledon titles and numerous other competitions, King was the first female athlete to win $100,000 in prize money in a single year. She helped organize the first women's professional tennis tour, cofounded the Women's Sports Foundation, and continues to advocate for women's sports.

- Dorothy Hamill is still one of America's favorite ice skaters, even though her Olympic gold medal was won back in 1976. Among her other accomplishments are three consecutive national championships and a world championship. She turned professional after the Olympics and skated with the Ice Capades, later becoming an owner and saving the company from bankruptcy. She said she did it so that fans could continue to enjoy professional figure skating.

- Nancy Lopez led an otherwise all-male golf team to the high school state championships, was named All-American while at the University of Tulsa, and became a celebrity when, in 1978, she won eight tournaments—five in a row—as a rookie on the LPGA tour. Of Mexican descent, Lopez is a role model for Latinas, as well as for all women.

- Mary Lou Retton left an indelible mark on gymnastics. Her all-around gold medal performance at the 1984 Olympic Games when she was just 16 was a credit to her athleticism and competitive personality. *Sports Illustrated* named her 1984 Sportswoman of the Year, and hers was the first female face to grace the front of a Wheaties box. Although long-since retired (there are no professional gymnastics opportunities for females), Retton remains popular as a television commentator and a motivational speaker.

- Janet Guthrie astounded the racecar-driving world in 1978 by becoming the first woman to qualify for the Indianapolis 500 and finishing in the top 10 of all racers—in spite of competing with a broken wrist! Though forced to contend with negative attention from many of the other drivers (all male) and the press, Guthrie paved the way for other women to compete in motor-sport racing.

- Jackie Joyner-Kersee, after excelling in both basketball and track during high school and college, won six Olympic medals—two golds and one silver in the heptathlon, and one gold and two bronzes in the long jump—during her 20-year career, as well as numerous other awards. When she retired in 1998, she still held the world's record for the heptathlon, a mega-sport that combines seven running, jumping, and throwing events over a grueling two days. She now heads a sports foundation to benefit inner-city girls.

Many other athletes, by their enormous struggles and achievements in sports, have helped bring athletics for females to the point where girls participate in unprecedented numbers. Close to 55 million females now participate in sports in the United States, and that number appears to be increasing. Thanks to these sports pioneers as well as numerous others—male and female alike—who have lent their time, effort, and money to the cause, there is a women's sports revolution to celebrate.

BENEFITS OF SPORTS FOR GIRLS

Fortunately, what girls say they like about sports—having fun, making friends, keeping busy, and getting in shape—is also good for them. Research indicates that participation in sports has tremendous benefits for girls. Females who participate in sports are healthier, happier, less likely to participate in risk-taking behavior, and more likely to get an education.

Many of the things girls learn through their sports experiences are valuable in other parts of their lives. Girls gain self-confidence, physical strength and agility, self-discipline, and the ability to focus, as well as to work in a team setting. They learn to be assertive, competitive, persistent, and self-motivated. They have the opportunity to become leaders and problem solvers. Additionally, girls involved in sports say they experience higher levels of energy and greater feelings of well-being. (See figure 1.2.)

Figure 1.2
Sports Benefit All Females

Females of all ages who participate in sports

- have higher levels of self-esteem than nonathletes
- suffer less depression than nonathletes
- develop a more positive body image than nonathletes
- lower their risk of breast cancer
- lower their risk of osteoporosis and heart disease

Girls who participate in sports are

- 3 times more likely to graduate from high school
- 80 percent less likely to have an unwanted pregnancy
- 92 percent less likely to use drugs

College female athletes who participate in sports

- have access to athletic scholarships to help pay for their educations
- are more likely to graduate at a significantly higher rate than the overall female student population

Socialization

Sports provide an opportunity for socialization. "Sports give girls a ready-made group of friends," says Karen Stanley-Kehl, women's soccer coach and former college player. Even girls playing individual sports like golf, gymnastics, tennis, and track are part of a team that practices and competes together.

Self-Confidence

Girls grow in confidence as they learn about a sport, practice to increase their skills, and then see their level of play improve. They learn to contend with problems and work toward a common goal. Donna Wade, a middle school physical education instructor, says, "Girls who play sports hold their heads high when they walk around our school. They look proud."

Self-Discipline

Sports teach self-discipline. Girls learn about commitment—that they have to show up, on time, for practices and competitions. There will be times when that commitment is hard to keep, when something else comes up that they really want to do, or when they're just feeling tired or lazy. But, being committed to a sport means not letting teammates down.

Working with Others

Teamwork is a valuable skill learned in sports that girls can use throughout their lifetimes as they interact with others—in the classroom, on the job, within the family, in the neighborhood, and in other groups and organizations.

Time Management

Sports help with time management. Many athletes say they have learned to structure their time so they can get their homework done and take care of their other obligations in order to participate in their sports.

Body Awareness and Strength

Participating in sports increases a girl's body awareness. She gains strength, agility, and endurance and is more physically fit than less active girls. Feeling more confident about her body's ability to do what she wants it to do and to take her where she wants to go, she learns to respect her body for what it can do, as well as for its appearance.

Focus

Another lesson sports teach is the ability to focus, to keep the mind on whatever activity one is engaged in, rather than letting it wander. Whether serving a volleyball, getting ready to hit a softball, or thinking about game strategy, the more concentration, or focus, given to the task, the quicker the athlete learns and the better she does.

Self-Motivation

Athletes learn to motivate themselves. It takes a lot of inner motivation for a runner to take off by herself for an early morning run, or for a swimmer to swim laps, or for a gymnast to practice her floor exercises. Sports, especially individual sports, challenge participants to get out there and practice their skills, whether anyone is telling them to or not. In every aspect of life, self-motivation is extremely important.

Competition

Competition is everywhere—in school, in sports, and on the job. Yet, learning to be competitive can be a challenge for some girls. They may have been taught in their families, or by society at large, that competition is okay for boys but not for girls. Sports can provide girls with an understanding of and the ability to engage in healthy competition. Mostly, competition is viewed as a rivalry between opponents, but an athlete also competes against herself. In alpine skiing, for instance, skiers try to race faster and with better form to improve their own performance while at the same time attempting to beat someone else to the bottom of the hill. Competition is as much about improving one's self as it is about winning.

Leadership

Sports teach leadership skills. Kathryn Herrfeldt was the intramural sports director and a member of the ski team for her Colorado college, Regis University. "When your teammates look to you for guidance, you rise to the occasion," she says. "You know they are counting on you, so you force yourself to stay focused and project a positive attitude." Herrfeldt believes the leadership role she practiced on the field now serves her well in her career.

SPECIAL ISSUES FOR HIGH SCHOOL ATHLETES

For most girls, sports are a rich, fulfilling experience. Yet, certain issues and situations that female athletes may encounter can puzzle, confuse, or even hurt them. Chapter 12 introduces some of these special issues and offers suggestions on how to handle the challenges they present. Among the topics discussed are gender prejudice surrounding female sports; getting along with teammates; balancing school, sports, and social life; risks of overtraining, nutrition, and eating disorders; and problems with coaches, over-involved parents, and drugs. While it is important to understand that some girls have encountered these issues, for most girls sports experiences are happy, positive, and fulfilling. But, to be aware is to be able to recognize and deal with problems when they occur, rather than let them become discouraging, hurtful, un-healthy, or even dangerous.

SPORTS OFFER OPPORTUNITIES FOR THE FUTURE

A girl's sports career doesn't have to end with high school graduation. The desire to continue to participate at the next level, along with her athletic skills, can help her get into college. For the highly talented ath-lete, there are opportunities to obtain scholarships to help pay her ed-ucational expenses. Sports participation can also help women in their careers. Not only are there many jobs in sports fields, for which an athlete's knowledge and experience would make her uniquely qualified, but women with a sports background are often looked upon very fa-vorably by employers because of the valuable lessons learned through sports experience. Chapter 13 looks at opportunities after high school not only for the young woman but for women throughout their life-times.

The women's sports revolution is happening now, and every woman and girl can be involved, thanks to pioneering sportswomen who dared to break down barriers for women and Title IX, the federal legislation mandating equal opportunity for females in sports (see figure 1.1). Donna Lopiano, executive director of the Women's Sports Foundation says, "What we are seeing is the result of 25 years of girls and women being given the opportunity to play sports and the encouragement to pursue sports and fitness."[7] Experts see the women's sports revolution as part of a tremendous cultural change in the nature of the American female. Instead of seeing themselves as the weaker sex, women and girls today increasingly see themselves as strong, effective, and capable. In-creased opportunities and changing attitudes are propelling women and girls to involve themselves in all areas of life, including sports.

In subsequent chapters you will have a chance to learn about many of the sports available in high school. You will get an overview of each sport, along with tryout tips, and even suggestions on how to get a sport started at your high school. Hopefully, you will be inspired to try at least one, or maybe even all, of these sports.

NOTES

1. Quoted in "VanDerveer—Ideal Hero," by Penny Hastings, *The Press Dem-ocrat*, June 22, 1997, C4.

2. National Federation of State High School Associations 1998 Participation Survey.

3. Title IX of the Education Amendments Act, June 23, 1972.

4. Sue Macy, *Winning Ways: A Photohistory of American Women in Sports*, New York: Henry Holt and Co., 1996.

5. Carole A. Oglesby, *Encyclopedia of Women and Sports in America*, Phoenix, AZ: Oryx Press, 1998.

6. Anne Janette Johnson, *Great Women in Sports*, Detroit, MI: Visible Ink Press, 1996.

7. Donna Lopiano, from a presentation made at the Women Sports Foundation Summit, May 17, 1997.

Chapter 2
Basketball

A college player exhibits skill and determination as she shoots for a basket. Photo courtesy of Santa Rosa Junior College Athletic Department.

"I enjoy the strategy and quick transitions."
—Donna Wade, middle school basketball coach and former player

"Basketball is like a chess match; you move, then countermove—you have to focus on staying at least one mental step ahead of your opponent."
—Sue Keller, high school athletic director and former player

Basketball is a fast-paced game played by two teams. Simply put, it is a game of keep-away with the added challenge of each team trying to score points by throwing a ball through an elevated basket or hoop. Basketball can be played on an indoor or outdoor court. Teams consist of five players on the court at one time, with substitutions from the bench allowed. To play basketball, all that is needed is a ball slightly larger than a soccer ball and two baskets (nets attached to a hoop) with backboards. Clothing consists of a shirt, shorts, socks, and gym shoes. A very active game, basketball involves a lot of running back and forth on the court. Girls begin playing as early as four years old with lower baskets and a smaller ball, while women continue to play competitively as well as recreationally into their senior years. The high school game includes four 8-minute quarters with a 10-minute half-time break.

COURT OF PLAY

Basketball is played on a hard-surface court. The standard size court is rectangular, 94 feet long and 50 feet wide (see figure 2.1), although the length of the court can be shortened to 84 feet for high school. Boundary lines surrounding the court are not considered part of the play, so players or the ball are out of bounds if they touch the line. Each side has a free-throw line 15 feet from the backboard, set in the center of the free-throw circle. Another circle of the same size in the center of the court is used for the start of the game jump ball. At high schools and colleges the possession rule is used when "jumps" or held balls occur, other than to start a game and overtime period. A line divides the center circle and the court in half. A free-throw lane runs from the free-throw line to the end line on both sides of the court, defining the area behind which players of both teams line up during a free throw and the area in which an offensive player, whose team is in control of

Figure 2.1
Basketball Court

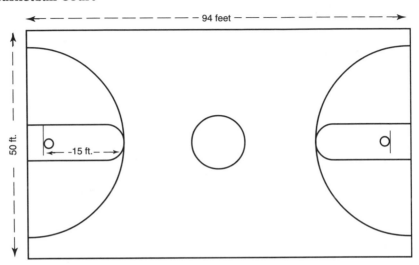

Source: Madrid Designs, Santa Rosa, CA

the ball, cannot remain for more than three seconds while at their team's offensive basket. The defense can stay in the lane with no time constraints with or without the ball.

EQUIPMENT

A basketball, backboard, and hoop are needed for a game of basketball. For regulation games, however, equipment must be specific. The ball is made of leather or composition material. Girls and women use a smaller basketball (8 inches in diameter and weighing 18–20 ounces) than the ball used by men (9 inches, 20–22 ounces). Backboards, to which baskets are attached, are rigidly affixed to support posts that are brightly colored and padded to prevent injury at each end of the court. Baskets are usually orange-painted iron rims mounted 10 feet above the floor, with white or colored cord nets.

DRESS

Basic basketball dress is simple and inexpensive, consisting of shorts, a short-sleeve or sleeveless jersey, knee socks, and rubber-soled, athletic shoes. For competitive play, uniforms in team colors are usually worn, with the team logo, player number, and sometimes the player name displayed on the shirt. Some players prefer to wear a short-sleeve shirt under a sleeveless jersey. Shorts have become increasingly longer and looser, mimicking the style of college and professional basketball players. Shoes, the most important part of a basketball player's uniform, should be selected carefully for comfort and fit. High-top tennis shoes, designed to support and protect the ankles, are preferred.

A BRIEF HISTORY

Basketball today is the world's most popular indoor sport—and it all began with a soccer ball and a couple of peach baskets. The man who created basketball was Dr. James Naismith, a college physical education instructor. He taught at Springfield College in Massachusetts where the long, cold winters kept his physical education classes inside. In searching for interesting games to keep his students motivated, he first tried modifying outdoor sports for indoor play. But games like football and soccer were too rough to play on a hard court and caused injuries. So, in 1891 Naismith invented a game that could be played in the gym: a combination of lacrosse, soccer, football, rugby, and hockey using a soccer ball and fruit baskets for goals. A drawback to the early version of the game was that each time a player scored, the game had to be stopped so the ball could be fished out of the basket. Finally, the wicker basket gave way to the net basket, and someone wisely decided to cut a hole in the bottom of the net so the ball could pass through, allowing the game to proceed at a decidedly faster pace.

Women were involved with the game almost from the beginning. When a couple of young female teachers passed by Naismith's Springfield College gym and saw a basketball game in progress, they asked to play, and in March 1892, the first women competed in an organized game. So much interest was generated that Vassar and Smith, two eastern women's colleges, added basketball to their list of intramural sports the following fall.

As the game evolved, not only did open-bottomed nets replace baskets, but basketballs became larger and backboards were added. Rules of the game changed from time to time, such as the introduction of dribbling as a way of moving the ball around the court. Women's basketball rules were different from the men's, however, mostly in response to fears that the physicality of the men's game was too vigorous for females. One such rule divided the court in half to "protect" women from running back and forth the full length of the court. It wasn't until the late 1960s that the rules changed and the half-court rule was deleted to allow women's basketball to more closely resemble the men's game.

Smith College held its first women's basketball game in 1893 between the freshmen and sophomore classes. Males were prohibited from viewing the competition because the young ladies were clad in bloomers. One of the first contests between two colleges took place in 1896 between the University of California at Berkeley and Stanford University. While women's basketball grew in popularity throughout the 20th century, it wasn't until the early 1980s that the NCAA held its first women's basketball tournament. Women's basketball was added to the Olympic Games in 1976, and in that year the U.S. team earned a silver medal. In 1984 the United States earned its first gold medal, which was followed by gold medals in 1984 and 1996.

In 1996 women's professional basketball got off the ground with the formation of the American Basketball League (ABL), followed the next year by the Women's National Basketball Association (WNBA). Although the ABL folded in late 1998, the WNBA has recently expanded. Today basketball is the most popular sport for girls and women to play and is increasingly popular as a spectator sport for both men and women. Expanded coverage by national television of college and professional women's games has increased attention and participation in the sport of basketball.

HOW THE GAME IS PLAYED

Each team consists of five players on the floor (court) at any one time, with five to ten substitutes on the bench. The object of the game is to score points by shooting the ball through the top of the opposing team's basket. Each successful shot (or "basket") counts as two points, with shots from 19 feet 9 inches and farther out counting three points, and free throws, from a penalty, counting as one point. Teams alternate possession following each basket.

The game begins with a jump ball between two players from the opposing teams in the center of the court. The visiting team gets to choose which end of court, or which basket, to defend; although in a neutral court, a coin toss is used to determine these factors. Always, the team in possession of the ball must move the ball from backcourt (the defensive end of the court) to frontcourt (the offensive end of the court), and once the ball enters the frontcourt, it cannot be returned to the backcourt unless it is touched by an opponent. The high school game includes four 8-minute quarters with a 10-minute half-time break. The team with the most points at the end of a regulation game is the winner, with a 3-minute overtime period required in the case of a tie. Additional overtime periods may be necessary to break the tie and finalize the game by declaring a winner.

KEY ELEMENTS OF THE SPORT

Passing

Passing is essential to the game of basketball. A successful pass allows one player to transfer the ball to a team member while keeping it away from an opposing player and is one technique used to move the ball from the defensive side of the court to the offensive side. Passing calls for vision, accuracy, and control. While there are a variety of passes, including the two-hand chest pass, two-hand overhead pass, baseball pass, and hook pass, the basic and most frequently used pass is the one-hand overarm or wrist pass. This pass can be modified for shorter or longer distances and used in many different game situations with varied speed. A good passer is able to affect a quick release of the ball and direct it with accuracy. The one-hand pass can be thrown directly to a teammate or bounced on the ground first.

Dribbling

Dribbling, or bouncing the ball on the floor, is another way to move the ball within the court. Primary uses include advancing the ball from the defensive end to the offensive end, repositioning to open up clear passing lanes and bypass opponents, and in driving to the basket. Dribbling, like passing, is essential to the game of basketball. It requires practice to learn the techniques and to be able to dribble with either hand. Controlling and protecting the dribble are the first skills to learn. After the player feels comfortable with these skills, she can begin working on more advanced techniques, like changes in speed and direction. To dribble, the ball should make contact with the pads of the fingers, the fingers spread wide. To maintain control, the dribbler must apply just the right amount of force as she bounces the ball, then cushion the rebound with hand and forearm as the ball comes up from the floor. To protect her dribble, a player must keep the ball close to her body and move her body to stay between the defender and the ball.

Shooting

The most important skill in basketball is shooting. Accurate shooting is required to put the ball up and into the basket. It is the only way to score points in basketball. Players can learn to pass and dribble, but if they cannot shoot accurately, the game will end 0–0. The accurate shot combines the coordination of trained muscle memories with correct hand position, elbow position, foot position, focus, and follow-through. Developing a consistent shooting style requires learning the fundamentals and many hours of practice.

Free throws, set shots, lay-ups, and jump shots are the most common types of shots. The *free throw*, which is usually a set shot, is the most simple (from an execution standpoint) and is awarded to a player who is fouled by an opponent. The shooter is allowed 10 seconds to take the free throw from behind the free-throw line and within the circle. It is the only instance in which a shot is taken from a stationary position and without help from one's own players or interference from opposing players. Because it is a solitary performance and often takes place at critical times in a game, the free throw can produce great anxiety in the shooter. The ability to concentrate on mechanics, rather than surrender to the emotional pressure, is vital for success in free-throw shooting.

The *lay-up* is used while running to put the ball into the basket. It is used by players driving to the basket or following a pass to a player cutting to the basket. The lay-up requires coordination and a delicate touch. The shooter must jump precisely at the time she releases the ball and the release must be done with the proper angle, spin, and touch, so that the ball banks off the backboard and into the basket.

The *jump shot* is an advanced shot usually combined with running or dribbling. In the jump shot the player must spring, momentarily hang in the air, and release the ball precisely at the height of her jump. The jump shot, perhaps more than any other, takes considerable coordination and strength to put the various skills together, along with plenty of practice.

Rebounding

Probably 50 percent of all shots taken miss the mark, allowing many opportunities for each team to gain possession of the ball following missed shots. Rebounding, the act of gaining possession after a missed shot, is therefore an extremely important part of the game, and many coaches believe it is 99 percent desire. Players who think rebound and establish good rebound position take possession of the ball more often than other players and are a valuable asset to their team. Getting a rebound allows the team that just shot another chance to score a basket. For the other team, it begins the transition from defense to offense.

Playing Defense

Each team constantly switches from offense to defense during a game. In fact, the team best able to make that transition is the stronger team and the one most likely to win the contest. When your team is on the defense, your mission is to keep the other team from shooting and scoring and to win back possession of the ball so your team can switch to offense. The basic rules of defense are:

1. Keep your body between the player and the basket so the opposing player does not get behind you (or closer to the basket than you are).
2. Guard the opposing player more closely the nearer she gets to the basket; give her more space when she is farther away from the basket.
3. Stop the pass from getting to the opposing player so she cannot get the ball and shoot. The closer a player with the ball is to the basket, the better chance she has to take a shot.

RULES OF BASKETBALL

1. Number of Players: Two teams of five players are on the court at any one time, with a minimum of three players necessary to continue game play. Substitutions are allowed only when the ball is dead. Substitutes may enter the game after checking in at the scorer's table and when beckoned on by an official. Unlimited substitutions are allowed.
2. Scoring: A point is scored when the ball passes through or lodges in the basket. Scoring from the field, a shot from within 19 feet 9 inches of the basket counts as two points, while a

basket made from outside that range nets three points. A free throw, taken as the result of a foul, counts for one point. After each basket, the opposing team takes possession of the ball.

3. Officials: A referee and umpire control the game on the floor, dividing the court between them, and change places after each foul and jump shot decision. They are assisted by an official scorer, timekeeper, and 30-second operator. (In the future, three officials—a referee and two umpires—may be the standard.)

4. Violations: Minor rule infractions cause the penalized team to lose possession of the ball. The opponents' team then receives a throw-in from the side or end line. The most common violations include traveling (running with the ball without dribbling it); kicking or hitting the ball with a fist; shooting up into the basket from below; double dribble (dribbling with more than one hand at a time or dribbling, catching the ball with two hands, then dribbling again); 5-seconds (a player at a standstill not passing the ball within 5 seconds while closely guarded by an opponent); 3-seconds (an offensive player remaining in the free-throw lane for more than 3 seconds).

5. Fouls and Penalties: These are more serious rule infractions than violations; there are two basic kinds of fouls—personal fouls and technical fouls.

   • Personal foul: An act committed by a player, involving illegal contact with an opponent, or unsportsmanlike conduct. The most common personal fouls are charging, blocking, pushing, holding, and illegal screens.

   • Technical foul: An infraction by a nonplayer (coach, substitute, or fan) or player that does not involve contact with an opponent (except flagrant contact when ball is not in play). The most common technical fouls are delay of game; unsportsmanlike conduct; illegal substitution; disrespectful behavior by a coach, player, or substitute; or a coach standing up and/or leaving the bench.

6. Each player is allowed four personal fouls before being disqualified for the remainder of the game.

7. Throw-ins from out of bounds are awarded to opponents until a team has committed six player fouls in a half. A free throw

is followed by a bonus shot for the seventh through the tenth foul; all subsequent fouls are then generally penalized by two free throws.

8. Out-of-bounds lines: The side and end lines define the court of play. When a player steps or a ball lands on or past the lines, which are not counted as part of the court, the ball is considered out of bounds.

9. Time-outs: These occur when the game is stopped by an official. Three full time-outs of one minute and two 20-second time-outs are allowed to each team per game, with an additional time-out allotted for each extra period of play.

10. After a point is scored, the ball is put into play by the opposing team.

TRYING OUT FOR THE SCHOOL TEAM

Naturally, if you have played basketball in the past, you have the advantage of already knowing some of the rules and mechanics of the sport. But, even so, the high school game is usually a challenge for even the most experienced youth player. Whether you have played before or are entirely new to the game, if you want to play high school ball, you need to prepare yourself. Basketball is such a popular sport for girls at the high school level that many schools have junior varsity teams. Some even support freshman and/or sophomore teams, which give less experienced, younger players the chance to learn and improve their game before competing at higher levels.

The best time to prepare to play high school basketball is several months before the season actually begins. Find out about the program by talking to the coach or assistant coach and asking how you can prepare yourself for team tryouts. They will be able to tell you what tryouts involve, what fitness and skill levels they are looking for, and even give you pointers on specific fitness and skill building exercises. Many high school coaches or their assistants make presentations to middle school or junior high physical education (P.E.) classes to introduce and explain their programs.

Older girls who are already playing on a high school team are another excellent source of information and assistance. They can tell you about their own experiences and give you tips about the program and what the coach expects. They might also allow you to play and workout with them to help you get ready. When you play with more experienced players, boys as well as girls, you learn and grow in your knowledge of the game and improve your skills.

If there is no program at your high school that teaches beginning-level basketball, you will need to find other places to learn and practice. Basketball is often offered through city park and recreation programs, YMCA, YWCA, Girl Scouts, and Boys and Girls Clubs. Church leagues and basketball clubs are other places where girls can learn the game and get playing experience. Club programs tend to focus more on competitive play, especially in the older age groups, than recreational programs, so they might not offer the novice an opportunity to learn about basketball from the beginning. They are, however, valuable for players desiring to improve their skills and compete at higher levels.

Basketball camps are an excellent way to get basic instruction, practice, and game experience in a short period of time. Camps are usually scheduled during school vacations. You can find out what is being offered through your local newspapers, P.E. teacher, or basketball coach. Local colleges, too, are a good source of information about where and when basketball camps are held. Colleges and high schools often host their own camps and sometimes offer basketball clinics for girls. You can also pick up a basketball magazine at your local newsstand. These publications often list college camps and even rate them. Talking to girls who have attended basketball camps is another way to discover programs that will benefit you the most.

Donna Wade, a middle school physical education instructor and basketball coach, advises girls to prepare for the basketball season by making sure they are physically fit. Basketball is a game requiring physical strength and endurance, yet, according to Wade, "too many kids don't do anything until the sport begins." That is too late, say coaches, and it puts the girl who is out of shape at a disadvantage. Most coaches report that they are impressed with the athlete who comes to tryouts mentally and physically prepared. Not only is she less likely to injure herself, she stands a better chance of making the school team. Preseason training should involve activities like running, sprinting, jumping, and weight training. Coaches or your P.E. teacher can advise you on what you need to do to get in shape for the upcoming season. Some might even provide written instructions involving fitness as well as skill-building activities that you could be working on long before the season begins.

Unique to the sport of basketball is the fact that you can practice on your own; you don't have to have a lot of—or even any—other people around to enjoy yourself and work on your skills. You can practice anywhere there is a basketball hoop: at a playground, in a gym, or in your own driveway. Shoot baskets from different places on the court; try different kinds of shots; take shots from the free-throw line. Practice dribbling and other ball handling. Coaches say the more players get used to the feel of the ball in their hands, the faster they gain confidence and improve their technique and skills. Pickup games at a local playground offer a good workout and the chance to increase your skills. Call a few friends, or go over to your neighborhood school to practice. While pickup games have long been a favorite pastime of boys who like basketball, it hasn't been as common to see girls out shooting hoops on the playground. One of the benefits, though, besides getting the practice, is meeting other players—boys and girls—who also enjoy pickup games.

How can you learn more about the game? Go to your school or public library and check out books and videos on basketball. Video and sporting goods stores also sell sports videos. You can decrease the expense by buying them with one or more of your friends, then sharing them or viewing them together. Watching basketball, especially women's basketball, on television is useful, too. Girls today are particularly fortunate because with the rise of basketball's popularity, networks are televising more college and professional women's basketball games than ever before. Seeing these high-caliber players helps younger girls by giving them female sports figures to look up to and to emulate, as well as by allowing them to see fine basketball being played. If you have a college nearby, you can go to their games. Attending local high school games is particularly advantageous. Besides learning as you watch, going to high school games gives you a good chance to check out the level of competition. It is especially valuable to watch the team you want to play on. You not only get a chance to observe the team's playing level, but you become more familiar with the coaching style.

The more you immerse yourself in the sport of basketball, the faster you will improve your game. Taking instruction, practicing by yourself and playing in pickup games, reading about and watching instructional videos, attending local high school or college games, and watching college and professional women's games are all ways of learning the game of basketball and improving your chances of making the high school team.

Training Tips for Basketball Players

1. Get fit first—run for endurance; do wind sprints; jump; weight train.
2. Play pickup games.
3. Play against more experienced players, boys as well as girls.
4. Attend vacation camps and sign up for local basketball programs.
5. Join a basketball club.
6. Practice on your own to increase skills.

OTHER SPORTS/CROSS-TRAINING

Soccer is a sport similar to basketball and is excellent for cross-training. The field of play is proportionate, and running in both sports enhances cardiovascular fitness. Also similar are the team play aspects of both games and the fact that players need to create triangles and mark players. "In high school and college programs, I know of no other sport that is better for cross-training," says Caren Franci, college women's basketball coach.

Team handball also is a compatible sport with basketball and uses similar skills; however, it is a sport seldom played in this country. Volleyball players need jumping skills, which are valuable for basketball players, too. In track, there are the high jump and running events, both complimentary skills to basketball. Additionally, throwing the shot put increases upper body strength and is similar in motion to shooting a basketball. Water polo, a sport you might not think of when you think of basketball, increases aerobic capacity, practices ball handling skills, and strengthens arms and shoulders. Almost any sport, particularly team sports, is beneficial for basketball players.

MOST COMMON INJURIES AND HOW TO AVOID THEM

Basketball is a game where ten bodies jostle for position and possession of the ball in a fairly confined area. This often leads to the most common basketball injuries: ankle sprains and trauma to the knees. Hand and finger injuries, while common, are usually fairly minor. Areas such as shoulders and backs can also be vulnerable.

- Ankle injuries—caused by constant running, jumping, and landing off balance. Also caused by landing on someone else's foot and twisting the ankle.

- Knee injuries—caused by twisting and cutting motions. Also caused by jamming stops and being bumped laterally.

- Finger and thumb injuries—caused by catching the ball on the end of a finger or thumb, bending the digit back.

- Shoulder separation—caused by player being contacted by another player or by contacting the floor with the arm in an extended position.

- Lower back injuries—caused by strain from inadequate conditioning to maintain a good stance.

While not all injuries are preventable, girls can minimize the chance of getting hurt by getting in the best physical shape possible. Caren Franci, college basketball coach and physical education instructor, says girls need to strengthen, build, and develop their muscles through weight training. "Oftentimes, females fail to recognize that lifting weights is important to conditioning for sports." Muscles are consistently recruited in basketball and can be overused, so they must be strengthened, not only in advance of but moderately during the season as well. "You don't have to bend a bar," says Franci. "Weight training should be done in moderation and only under the direction of a coach or fitness instructor." Weight training enhances flexibility and promotes endurance, as well as strengthens muscles. Stanford University women's basketball coach, Tara VanDerveer, who also coached the 1996 U.S. Olympic gold medal winning women's team, made weight lifting a big part of her team's daily workout. It paid off in fewer injuries than might have been expected at that level of fierce competition and in the level of fitness that allowed the U.S. players to outlast their opponents.

WHAT IF YOU DON'T MAKE THE HIGH SCHOOL TEAM?

What if you prepare yourself as much as you possibly can—by working out in the preceding months to increase your overall physical fitness and basketball skills and learning as much as you can about the game—and you still don't make the high school team? This can be a very disappointing experience. For some girls, it makes them feel rejected, discouraged, and even angry. Some question whether they even want to play anymore. After all, you have put in a great deal of time and effort in your quest to make the team. While it is only natural to feel badly for a few days, you need to pick yourself up as soon as possible and look at other options and possibilities. You enjoy basketball; that's why you wanted to play on the high school team in the first place, right? So get right back into it so you can still play and enjoy yourself while you continue to improve.

Let's look at your options. If there is a junior varsity team at your school, perhaps you can participate at that level. Junior varsity and freshman/sophomore teams are excellent training grounds for making the varsity sometime in the future. Coaches of these teams usually work closely with the varsity coaches. Often they will have the same philosophy and similar coaching styles. The varsity coach has a vested interest in watching players come up through the program and often will offer encouragement and advice.

What if your school does not have a junior varsity team, and making the varsity is the only way to play? That's too bad, because besides hurting the school's overall basketball program, it severely limits the number of girls who can participate. You still have options, however. You can either look for somewhere else to play or try to get a junior varsity team started. Earlier in the chapter other places you can play, such as recreational leagues, clubs, and camps, were discussed. You can also talk to your school's athletic director to indicate your interest in starting a junior varsity or freshman/sophomore team. Offer to help out and get your friends who are also interested involved.

Another thing you can do is to consider switching to another sport at your school or concentrating on a sport you are already involved in. Say you also run track. Take time you would have been spending practicing and playing basketball and devote it to your track workouts. Or check in your community for sports perhaps not available at the high school but ones you might like to learn about and participate in. How about martial arts, inline skating, ice or roller hockey, bowling, rock climbing, or fencing? It can be an adventure to branch out and try something new. Failing to make the basketball team could allow you to do that. Besides learning a new sport, you will have the opportunity to meet different people and make new friends.

HOW TO START A HIGH SCHOOL TEAM

What if there is no basketball program for girls at your school? That is unlikely with a sport as popular as basketball, but in case your high school does not offer girls' basketball as an interscholastic sport, how can you get a team organized? The best place to begin is with the athletic director or principal. Indicate your interest and ask for advice and support. Administrators want to know if enough other girls are interested in playing on a team. Probably 15–20 would show sufficient strength of numbers. They might also ask if you have someone willing to coach, perhaps a teacher on staff or another qualified adult in the community. Are there other girls' basketball teams in your geographical area or school district so you will have someone to play against? If you have the answers to these questions ready before you approach your administrator, you can save some time. Administrators might also be concerned about funding a new school team, but if there is already a boys' team at your school, then, according to the law, girls must be given the same opportunity as the boys to play the sport. (For more about Title IX, see Chapter 1.)

If you do not feel satisfied with the answers you receive from your athletic director or principal, you can take your case to the district superintendent and further, on to the school board. At this point, it would be best to enlist the assistance of parents and other interested adults. Usually, though, a strong show of support in organizing a girls' interscholastic sports team at the high school is sufficient to get a program started.

OTHER VERSIONS OF THE GAME

While other sports such as volleyball have several competitive versions of the game (hard court, grass, and sand), there is only one basketball. Not only is the game played the same universally, but high school and college rules are basically the same.

A LOOK INTO THE FUTURE OF BASKETBALL

Women's basketball has grown in popularity in recent years. Much of that is due to women's basketball going professional and the interest generated by the Olympic Games. There is a professional league, the Women's National Basketball Association (WNBA), whose games are often televised nationally. With the excitement of women's basketball at the Olympic Games (the U.S. team, led by Stanford University women's basketball coach Tara VanDerveer, won the gold medal in 1996), interest in the sport is soaring, and that trend is expected to continue.

Most watchers of the game predict that interest in elite basketball will trickle down to the grassroots level and increase participation in all age groups, both competitively and in recreational programs. High school athletic director Sue Keller says she sees "an explosion in female interest at the high school and college level." 454,000 girls currently play basketball at the high school level, making it the most popular high school sport for girls.[1]

Look for women's basketball to become faster and more physical and aggressive, more like the men's game. Some predict that girls may, in the not-too-distant future, play with protective elbow and knee pads similar to those worn by ice hockey players. Another prediction is that with the competition among professional teams to get the best women players, they will recruit directly from the college ranks rather than wait until graduation.

The opportunity to participate at the intercollegiate level is expected to increase as even more colleges add basketball to their list of interscholastic sports for women. In the latest National College Athletic Association (NCAA) participation study, over 13,700 women play interscholastic basketball at their member institutions.[2] The number of colleges offering athletic scholarships for women also continues to grow.

For the recreational player, basketball is most often offered through park and recreation departments, the YMCA, and through league play held at schools or churches. Basketball can be played by very young girls, especially if they are encouraged to start out with a smaller ball and lowered baskets, and throughout women's adult years. While basketball is a very active, often physical game, it can be played successfully and with pleasure by fit, energetic women into middle age.

TERMS TO KNOW

Backcourt: a team's defensive end of the court

Carrying the ball: illegal dribbling involving lifting from under the ball rather than pushing down on top of it

Defense: the team without the ball and defending its basket

Double dribble: illegal dribbling with both hands at the same time or dribbling, then catching the ball, and dribbling again

Dribble: a way to move the ball legally around the court other than passing

Foul: an infraction of the rules involving personal contact with an opponent or unsportsmanlike conduct

Free throw: a stationary and unimpeded shot for a basket from behind the free-throw line

Frontcourt: a team's offensive end of the court

Holding: using hands to grab an opponent

Offense: the team with the ball

Out of bounds: anytime the ball or a player lands on or goes over the side and end lines

Over and back: a violation occurring when a team goes into the backcourt after entering the frontcourt

Passing: a legal way to move the ball around the court other than dribbling

Personal foul: a player foul involving contact with an opponent

Pivot: stepping with the same foot in different directions while the other foot (the pivot foot) is stationary

Scorer: a person who records the score of a game and controls substitutions

Shooting: sending the ball up in the air to try to score a basket

Substitute: a player coming into the game and taking the place of another player

Technical foul: a misconduct foul by player, coach, or fan or intentional contact foul by a player usually when ball is not in play

Throw-in: a ball thrown in from out of bounds to begin play

Time-out: at an official's signal, play is suspended and the game clock stops

Traveling: anytime a player in possession of the ball takes more than one step without passing, shooting, or dribbling the ball

Violation: a minor rule infraction

NOTES

1. National Federation of State High School Associations 1998 Participation Survey.

2. National College Athletic Association 1997–98 Participation Study.

Chapter 3
Field Hockey

Kelly Darling caught in mid-swing during a field hockey game. Photo reproduced by permission of the photographer, Nancy McHale.

"Because the ball moves so quickly, you learn to make split-second strategic decisions."
—Marie Sugiyama, high school athletic director and former player

"Field hockey is complex enough to be interesting, [but] not so complex that you can't play even as a beginner."
—Shellie Onstead, NCAA Division I college coach and player

"I get to meet people from other schools [who] are really neat."
—Kelly Darling, youth player

"Wearing of the kilt is something special and traditional."
—Laura Darling, field hockey administrator and former player

Field hockey is a team sport somewhat similar to soccer. There are the same number of players to a side (11), the same basic tactics, and a similar-size outdoor field with a goal at each end. In field hockey, however, a hockey stick is used to propel a small, hard ball up and down the field and into the opponent's goal. The object of the game is to score the most goals. Each goal is worth one point. A fast-paced running game, field hockey is played by people of all ages. More girls play than boys at the high school level, and the game is most popular on the East Coast. The length of a high school field hockey game is 60 minutes (although junior varsity games may be shorter). Playing time is divided into two halves.

FIELD OF PLAY

Field hockey is played outdoors on a field of grass or a grasslike synthetic surface (see figure 3.1). The field is rectangular in shape, 100 yards long by 60 yards wide. Goals (cages) at each end of the field are 12 feet wide and 7 feet high. The field is divided into two halves of 50 yards each, with both teams defending their own goal and changing sides of the field at half-time. To score a goal, the attacking team must shoot the ball over the goal line from within 16 yards of the goal cage. This scoring zone (called the circle) is marked on the field by a giant half circle in front of the goal cage.

Figure 3.1
Field Hockey Playing Field

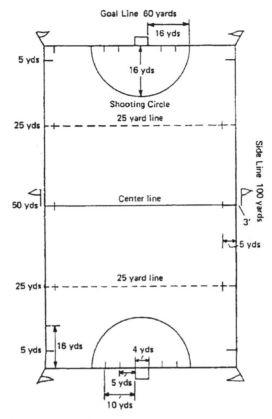

Source: Roxana Leiva, graphic designer

EQUIPMENT

A stick, ball, and goals (cages) are all that is basically needed to play a field hockey game. The length of a hockey stick varies according to size and experience of the player, but most sticks are about 3 feet long (the size of a yard stick). Most sticks are made of wood, although synthetic materials are sometimes used. The hockey stick is used to move a small, rubber-coated ball, 3.5 inches in diameter (about the size of a tennis ball but harder and much heavier), on the ground. One side of the hockey stick head is flat, while the other side is rounded, and the ball may only be played with the flat side. All players (whether they are left- or right-handed) play with their left hand at the top of the stick and their right hand below the left hand. The left hand remains on top, while the right hand slides down or up depending on the skill being performed. Field hockey cages are most often constructed of heavy-gauge aluminum framing, with a nylon net.

DRESS

A short-sleeve or sleeveless jersey, short skirt (kilt) or shorts, and knee socks is the official field hockey uniform for girls. Well-fitting athletic shoes designed for either natural grass or artificial turf, depending on the field of play, are advised. Other items worn for safety are shin/ankle guards and plastic mouth guards to protect the teeth. Players also may wear a left-handed glove to protect the knuckles against abrasion when playing the ball. Additionally, goalkeepers wear protective head and body gear, essentially protecting them head to toe.

A BRIEF HISTORY

While drawings found in ancient Egyptian tombs put the date for the origins of field hockey back at least 4,000 years, it wasn't until one hot August afternoon at the turn of the 20th century that the sport was introduced to American women. While the game undoubtedly went through many changes throughout the years, the concept of a two team stick-and-ball game has remained the same.

It was in the early 19th century that field hockey for men became popular in Europe, particularly England, where the first hockey club was formed. Women took up the game in the mid 1800s, but it wasn't until Constance M. K. Applebee, an English-born physical education (P.E.) teacher, presented a hockey exhibition at Harvard University in 1901 that American women became acquainted with the sport. When Applebee introduced field hockey to America, it created quite a sensation. At that time, only the games of croquet and lawn tennis were considered suitable athletic endeavors for young women. As interest grew in the United States, it was also growing around the world, and in 1927, the International Federation of Women's Hockey Associations was organized. Women played according to the same rules as men, but cumbersome clothing hindered their movement. Modesty dictated that the legs be fully covered, so players wore skirts nearly touching the ground, along with heavy petticoats, corsets, long sleeves, and high, stiff collars. Women who pioneered the sport played despite ridicule and discomfort. Finally, the short plaid skirt was adopted, patterned after the outfit of European men who traditionally donned their family kilts for competitive play.

While men's field hockey was introduced at the 1908 Olympic Games, it wasn't until 1980 that women's teams were invited to participate. The American teams did not actually play that year, though, due to the U.S. boycott of the Moscow Games, but at their 1984 debut, the women won the bronze medal. In the 1996 Centennial Olympic Games in Atlanta, the U.S. women's team finished fifth.

Today field hockey is a popular sport played at many high schools across the nation. According to the National Federation of State High School Associations, there are over 56,000 girls currently playing inter-scholastic high school field hockey,[1] with many more participating at the intramural level. Played primarily by women in the United States, field hockey is played by both men and women in other countries. In fact, field hockey is second only to soccer as the most participated in sport in the world, and it is one of the oldest team sports in this country.

HOW THE GAME IS PLAYED

Field hockey is a fast, exciting game of attacks and counterattacks. Each team is allowed 11 players on the field. The object of the game is to score more goals than the opponent by moving a small, rock-hard ball into the other team's cage using a hand-held hockey stick. A coin is tossed and the visiting captain calls heads or tails. The winner of the toss elects whether to start the game with possession of the ball or in which direction her team would like to attack in the first half of the game. Both teams start out on their own half of the field after the umpire blows the whistle to start the game, and the team with possession pushes or hits the ball from the center of the field in any direction to begin play.

There are a variety of strategies used to set up players on the field. However, common to each system are the positions of forward, mid-fielder, defender, and goalkeeper.

- Forwards: These are offensive players who move the ball forward and attack the goal.
- Midfielders: Players linking forwards and defenders, they must be equally skilled in both defense and offense.

- Defenders: Defensive players, who closely guard the other team's forwards, strive to protect the goal.
- Goalkeeper: She is the player charged with keeping the ball out of the goal. The goalkeeper (or goalie) can kick the ball, move the ball with her stick, and can also block the ball with her body. She cannot catch or throw the ball and must stay in the circle to maintain her goalkeeping privileges.

KEY ELEMENTS OF THE SPORT

Defensive skills, such as tackling and marking, are very important, but in order to be successful and play a game, all players must learn how to run with, pass, and receive the ball.

Ball possession skills

Ball possession skills include all the skills needed to run with the ball. In a game, players need to know how to run with the ball on their stick and how to dodge around opponents while moving the ball as quickly as possible. Possession skills include dribbling in all directions, being able to pull the ball sharply in one direction and then to move quickly in the other direction, and body and stick fakes. All possession skills need to be learned utilizing changes of speed while moving the ball.

Passing

Passing is the method of sending the ball from teammate to teammate. Using a combination of passes, teammates move the ball around opponents in an effort to set up scoring opportunities. During game action most passing is done on the move. Players must learn to keep the ball on their stick and see where their teammates are on the field. The ball must be played with the flat side of the stick. Different types of passing include a hit, a push pass, a flick, and a variation of all three. A backswing is needed to hit the ball with power; it is not used in push passing and flicking.

Receiving

Receiving is the other skill players must learn in order to move the ball and score goals. When the ball is passed to a teammate, she must learn to stop the ball on her stick while moving and looking at where she will now pass the ball. Although receiving is relatively easy to learn, to perfect the skill of receiving the ball quickly, on the move, takes practice.

RULES OF FIELD HOCKEY

1. Number of players: Two teams of 11 players are on the field at the same time.

2. Substitution: There is no limit to the number of players who may be substituted (only two players can be substituted at the same time) or to the number of times any player may substitute or be substituted.

3. Scoring: The game is won by the team scoring the greatest number of goals. A goal (worth one point) is scored when the ball goes completely over the goal line and under the crossbar. Goals can only be scored from within 16 yards of the goal cage. That area is called the circle or scoring zone.

4. Officials: Two umpires control the game; each is primarily responsible for the decisions in his or her half of the field.

5. Out of bounds: The side and end lines define the field of play. For the ball to be considered out of play (out of bounds), it must completely cross over the side or end lines. A ball on the line is in play.

6. Time-outs: Two are allowed per team in each game.

7. Penalties: These are rule infractions by a team causing the umpire to award a penalty to the other team. Penalties are awarded for conduct that affects the safety of players; this includes improper playing equipment; the improper use of body, hands, and feet; dangerously raising the ball; obstruction; and delay of game. Free hits are awarded from the place where the foul occurs, except in the following situations:

   • Long hits: If the ball last touched by a defender goes over the end line and is not intentionally sent out of bounds, the offense gets to take a free hit near the corner of the field.

   • Penalty corner: If the defense accidentally fouls within the circle or intentionally fouls within 25 yards of the end line, the offense is awarded a penalty corner.

- Penalty stroke: If the defense breaks the rules while preventing a sure goal, the offense is awarded a one-on-one opportunity with the goalkeeper. The ball is placed seven yards in front of the center of the goal cage. A lone attacker positions herself just behind the ball; the goalkeeper waits on the goal line. The umpire blows the whistle and the attacker may flick or push the ball at the goal. As soon as the attacker touches the ball, the goalkeeper is allowed to move.

8. Advantage rule: A penalty shall be awarded only when a player or team has been clearly disadvantaged by an opponent's foul.

9. Personal penalties include rough or dangerous play, misconduct, or any intentional foul. In addition to awarding the appropriate penalty, the umpire may warn the offending player (green card); remove the offending player to the bench area for a short period of time (yellow card); or expel the offending player for the remainder of the game and possibly for more games, depending on the extent of the foul (red card).

TRYING OUT FOR THE SCHOOL TEAM

Trying out for the high school team is a challenge for even the most experienced youth field hockey player, a step up from previous competition. But for the inexperienced or beginning player it can be a daunting task. Advance preparation can mean the difference between making the team or being cut and can increase the chances for success for girls just starting out.

The first thing to do is to find out when the high school season begins and when tryouts take place. Do this early, because you will want to allow at least a couple of months to prepare yourself. Talk to the high school coach and ask what you can do to maximize your chances. Just introducing yourself to the coach and letting her know you are interested is advantageous, but finding out what the coach is looking for and what she expects from prospective players is invaluable. Coaches will tell you what they expect; some even hand out written guidelines along with workout suggestions. Most stress fitness. Field hockey players probably run two to three miles a game, so the player who comes to tryouts fit and ready to run is seen by coaches as hardworking and eager to play. High school coach and former player Tracy Paul says she encourages girls to contact her before the season begins, both to indicate their interest in her high school program and to ask questions about the tryout process. Paul emphasizes fitness first: "Half the battle is won if girls come to tryouts well conditioned."

Training Tips for Field Hockey Players

1. Work on overall fitness: Stretching; jogging for endurance; sprinting for increased quickness and explosive speed; weight training to increase overall body strength.
2. Work on field hockey skills: Stick work; one- and two-handed pushes; dribble the ball; practice passing with a friend or by hitting the ball off a wall.
3. Play as often as possible: Attend park and recreation programs, sports camps, and clinics. Join a club or league.
4. Participate in other sports, particularly running-based sports like soccer, lacrosse, and basketball.
5. Be a field hockey fan: Watch games in person, on television, on video. Read about the game. Talk to players and learn from them.

INCREASING PHYSICAL FITNESS FOR FIELD HOCKEY

Conditioning should include stretching, jogging, sprinting, and light weight training. Running is the most obvious form of fitness training because field hockey is a game of almost constant running. It is estimated that field hockey players run 2–3 miles per game, so jogging for endurance should include a 2–3 mile run at least three times a week. Interval training, running a series of sprints of various lengths with brief rests in between, is advised by many high school coaches, as is a combination of jogging for endurance and sprinting for those short bursts of speed necessary during field hockey games. Coaches also advise girls to add an exercise during which they jog, sprint, stop, change direction, run backward, then jog again. This should be done in repetitions. Daily workouts should always begin with a light jog to warm up your muscles followed by stretching for flexibility and to prevent injury. Afterward, it is just as important to stretch again and cool off your muscles to keep from getting sore and stiff.

Weight training, done properly and safely, is imperative for strengthening your body. Overall body strength helps you to move quickly, improves your endurance and quickness, and enables you to move the ball quickly and decisively during play. A strong body helps you to keep going during games and offers protection against injury. Being able to run for miles, sprint with explosive speed, pass with strength, and hit with power are necessary skills for the successful field hockey player; all require strength. But before you begin weight training, you should talk with a trainer or P.E. specialist and let her help you set up the right program for you.

ACTIVITIES TO IMPROVE YOUR FIELD HOCKEY SKILLS

You can practice your field hockey skills with others or by yourself. Repetition of the skills needed during games is important. Dribbling can be done alone, as can hitting and receiving the ball. Run with your stick, keeping the ball close and under your control. Set up cones on the grass and dribble around them. Hit a ball against a wall, receive it back, and hit it again. Goalkeepers can practice kicking a ball against a wall or backboard, getting to the rebound and blocking the ball, and then kicking it again. With one or more other players you can practice controlling the ball on the dribble, passing from the left and right, and receiving from both sides. Going one-on-one with another player can sharpen possession skills for the attacker and help develop good defensive skills for the defender.

Many coaches advise girls to practice handling their sticks until they can do it correctly without even thinking about it. The "Yardstick" is a drill you can practice at home, at the park, or just about anywhere to get comfortable with and adept at handling your stick. According to the United States Field Hockey Association (USFHA) Coaching Manual, the Yardstick drill is described as follows:

Start with feet about one yard apart (stick length) and ball in front of right foot. Move ball in straight line to the left until you reach left foot. Use reverse stick to change direction of the ball back toward right foot. Move ball repeatedly from outside right foot to outside left foot and back. Increase speed but still keep control of ball. How many "drags" can you do in one minute? (Chapter 3, p. 7)

Watch field hockey being played. Go to games in person, or watch games on television. There are educational videos about the sport of field hockey as well as videos of game competition. Videos may be available through your public or school library or at your local video rental or sporting goods store.

Read articles and books about field hockey to learn the game rules. The more you understand field hockey, the better you will be able to develop and compete to your fullest potential. Join the USFHA. Membership fees for juniors are minimal, and you will receive their quarterly publication, *Hockey News*, which will keep you updated on the sport and provide you with playing tips, tournament schedules, and other news. You can contact USFHA at 719–578–4567 or write to them at One Olympic Plaza, Colorado Springs, Colorado 80909. Or check out their website: www.usfieldhockey.com.

OTHER SPORTS/CROSS-TRAINING

Soccer, lacrosse, basketball, cross-country running, and track are all sports that help keep you in condition for field hockey and increase your knowledge of sports. Soccer, in particular, is the game most like field hockey. Players can improve in one sport by participating in the other because not only are many of the physical skills similar, but the strategies and teamwork aspects of both games are alike. High school coach Tracy Paul encourages her players to learn how to juggle to develop eye-hand coordination. Many coaches concur that playing any other sport at all will help girls improve in their sport.

MOST COMMON INJURIES AND HOW TO AVOID THEM

Field hockey is one of the safest team sports. Injuries are relatively rare and happen mostly when field conditions are poor or players are not fit. Poor field conditions can set the stage for physical injuries, while a well-maintained, flat-surfaced field provides the safest conditions. At the high school level, most field hockey games are played on grass, although a few high schools have artificial turf. Knee injuries usually occur when the foot is planted and rotation occurs. Ankles can be sprained, and players can get hit with the stick. Although goalkeepers are well padded and field players wear the regulation protective equipment, the ball can injure the athlete if it is played dangerously. The game rules are written to eliminate dangerous play as much as possible.

To protect yourself against the possibility of injury, your best defense is to be as fit as possible and to have good overall body strength. You should also know and follow the rules of the game, many of which are designed to maximize safety and reduce the chance of injuries.

WHAT IF YOU DON'T MAKE THE HIGH SCHOOL TEAM?

What if, despite getting fit and practicing your skills and trying your best, you fail to make the team? You put a lot of time and energy into your preparation and looked forward to joining the team. Now you have been cut, and you are no doubt disappointed and discouraged. What do you do now? High school coach Tracy Paul says, "Try again! Never give up the effort. Michael Jordan did not make his high school basketball team the first time he tried out. Being cut made him more determined." That is good advice. But what do you do in the meantime? Jump right back into the sport by looking for another place to participate where you can practice and improve, all the while enjoying the fun of playing. If there is a junior varsity, perhaps you can play at that level. Some schools also have freshman/sophomore teams, which are excellent training grounds for future varsity players. There you can learn more about the game and increase your skills. Usually, the coaches of the various high school teams have common philosophies and training methods, so it is a natural progression from freshman/sophomore, to junior varsity, to the varsity team.

What if there is only a varsity team at your high school? In that case, you can either look for other opportunities off campus or try to start a junior varsity team. Off-campus options include recreational programs and field hockey clubs, camps, and clinics. To get a junior varsity team started at your high school, talk to your athletic director and indicate your interest. Offer to help out and get other girls who are interested involved. Your parents, too, might be able to help you make a case with the school administration. Certainly, if there is enough interest, it is unfair to allow only the most mature and advanced players to play on a team. It is also a disadvantage to the school's athletic program when younger players do not have the opportunity to hone their skills on junior varsity or freshman/sophomore teams.

HOW TO START A HIGH SCHOOL TEAM

What if your high school does not offer field hockey as an interscholastic sport? First, assess the interest of girls at the school. Find out how many girls would like to play on a team if one were formed. Next, go to your high school's athletic director and indicate your interest in starting a team. Your job will naturally be easier if you can demonstrate sufficient interest and if there is a program already established in local junior high schools or an active youth league. Are there teams at other high schools in your area or league? If there are, then your request should be viewed more positively. But if that is not the case, you wouldn't have anyone to play against interscholastically. The best solution might be to start an intramural league at your school while you drum up support for league-wide field hockey in the area. Other sports have begun this way. Badminton, for example, came up through the ranks. Interest was generated as girls learned how to play the game during their P.E. classes, then enough girls gathered together to organize teams, first at the intramural level and then for league (interscholastic) play. It also helps if you have a qualified adult willing to coach and support from other adults.

OTHER VERSIONS OF THE GAME

- Indoor field hockey: This is an indoor version of the outdoor game, using outdoor field hockey rules. Because of the smaller venue, there are fewer players on the floor at one time and smaller goals.
- Floor hockey: Players can use both sides of the stick and the game can be played off the walls in this version of the game which is more like ice or roller hockey. Like indoor soccer there are fewer players, a smaller court, and smaller goals.
- Seven-player field hockey: Another version of the game, this is exceptionally good for conditioning on regulation-size outdoor field.

A LOOK INTO THE FUTURE OF FIELD HOCKEY

Field hockey is a growing sport for females in the United States. Enjoying especially strong support on the East Coast, field hockey at both youth and collegiate levels is showing growing pockets of popularity in the rest of the country. Reasons for increased participation include overall awareness of the benefits of athletics for females, along with increasing sports opportunities made available because of Title IX (see Chapter 1), the federal legislation that mandates gender equity in sports and education. Additionally, increased media coverage of women's sports, most noticeably basketball, has drawn attention to team sports and encouraged female participation. "Field hockey provides the opportunity for girls and women to participate in a running, physically and mentally challenging game, while enjoying teamwork and camaraderie," according to Laura Darling, director of player and coach development for USFHA.

At the high school level more than 56,500 girls play on competitive teams. That number is expected to increase as more high schools add field hockey to their list of sports.

Field hockey is an intercollegiate sport at 233 NCAA institutions, according to the 1997–98 NCAA Participation Study.[2] Field hockey for women is a scholarship sport, so for girls who play the game at the high school and/or club level, opportunities exist to move up into college competition and enjoy scholarship assistance. For more information on college athletic scholarships, see Chapter 13.

While there are some professional men's teams in other parts of the world, there are currently no plans for either men's or women's field hockey to become a professional sport in the United States.

TERMS TO KNOW

Attack: the team in possession of ball

Bully: a method of putting ball back into play when possession is unable to be called by an umpire

Circle (striking circle): 16-foot half-circle in front of the goal area

Defense: the team without possession of ball

Dribbling: moving the ball down the field using short hits

Flick: a type of pass where the ball is lifted off the ground, controlled, and safely hit

Free hit: a method of putting the ball back into play after a foul is committed

Hit: a method of hitting the ball requiring a backswing

Indian dribble: moving the ball in all directions using reverse and open stick techniques

Jab: a defensive action to knock the ball off an opponent's stick

Long hit: a hit taken 5 yards up the side line from the end line, taken when the ball has been unintentionally hit over the end line by the defense

Marking: a defensive man-to-man system

Midfield: the middle area of the field

Obstruction: an illegal play using the body to prevent the opponent from playing the ball

Offense: the team with the ball

Passing: moving the ball from teammate to teammate

Penalty corner: a set play given to the attack when the defense fouls in the circle

Possession: having control of the ball

Push pass: a type of pass that does not use a backswing

Raised ball: a ball in the air

Receiving: getting the ball from a teammate's pass

Reverse stick: using the flat side of the stick on the left side of the body

Side in: putting the ball back into play after it has gone out of bounds over the side line

Tackle: the physical action of taking the ball from an opponent, but without physical contact with the other player

Tracking: going on immediate angle as the possession player, forcing defender to commit

NOTES

1. National Federation of State High School Associations 1998 Participation Survey.

2. National Collegiate Athletic Association 1997–98 Participation Study.

Chapter 4
Soccer

By working on kicking and passing skills during practice, soccer players can control the ball better at game time. Photo reproduced by permission of the photographer, Arielle Kohn.

"It's a players game; players make 95 percent of the decisions."
—Karen Stanley-Kehl, former Division I women's soccer coach and player

"It's such a wonderful game! There's no standing around; you're constantly moving."
—Nicole Nelson, youth player

"I love that it's a team sport and I get to play with my friends."
—Katie Freeman, high school player

"[W]hen I get a good save, I feel complete."
—Wendy Keppel, two-year college goalkeeper

Soccer is a fast-paced game played on a large grass field by two teams of 11 players each. The object of the game is to score points by getting the ball into your opponent's goal and to keep the ball out of your goal. The team that scores the most points, or goals, is the winner. Soccer is unique in that it is the only major sport where players may not use their hands or arms to touch the ball. They may, however, use any other part of their body, including feet, legs, chest, and even their head. Soccer, a game of constant action and motion, is fun for kids and adults alike. The high school game consists of two 40-minute halves, with a 10-minute half-time break.

FIELD OF PLAY

Soccer is an outdoor game played on a grassy (or synthetic-surface) field (see figure 4.1). The size of the playing field may vary; it is between 100 and 130 yards in length and 50 to 100 yards wide, although the shape of the field is always rectangular. Boundary lines surround the field and are considered part of the play area, so a ball must cross completely over the side lines (also called touch lines) or end lines to be considered out of bounds. At each end of the field is a goal 24 feet wide by 8 feet high. Other important areas on the field are defined by white lines. They are: the midfield line, which divides the field in half; the center circle, a circle with a 10-yard radius in the middle of the field; the penalty area, a rectangular box 44 yards wide by 18 yards deep in front of each goal; the goal area, a rectangular box 20 yards wide and 6

Figure 4.1
Soccer Field

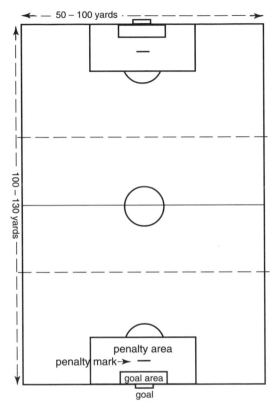

← — 50 – 100 yards · — — — — — — — →

100 – 130 yards

penalty area
penalty mark→ —
goal area
goal

Source: Madrid Designs, Santa Rosa, CA

yards deep inside the penalty area; the penalty spot, a small circle located 12 yards in front of the center of the goal line; and the corner arc,
a quarter-circle with a one-yard radius located in each of the four corners of the field.

EQUIPMENT

Soccer is a game that can be played just about anywhere, at any time,
which greatly contributes to its popularity. The only thing you really
need is a ball, although, for regulation play you also need a few other
things, such as a playing field and goals. The typical soccer ball is very
distinctive looking, with two-toned, usually black and white, checkered
markings. It is made of leather or a synthetic material. The standard

size ball for high school and adult play is the #5 ball, between 27 and 28 inches in circumference and weighing between 14 and 16 ounces. There are two goals, one on each end of the field, made of wood or metal and painted white. A soccer goal has two vertical goal posts and a horizontal cross bar that sits on top of the posts. The frame is covered by a woven net that drapes over the frame and extends behind the goal, creating a deep pocket. The net is needed so that a ball cannot pass through the opening without being recognized as a goal.

DRESS

Basic soccer dress is a knit shirt, shorts, knee-high socks, and soccer shoes. T-shirt styles or shirts with collars are most popular, with either long or short sleeves. Game shirts have the player's number on the back and front chest and are usually printed with the team name and logo. Shorts are loosely fitted for ease of movement. Knee-high socks are worn over shin guards, which are mandatory for high school play. Soccer shoes are made specifically for different playing surfaces, and selection of the proper shoes is extremely important. Rubber or plastic cleats help players with traction on the field for sudden stops and starts. Sometimes players wear wrist bands and head bands to absorb perspiration.

A BRIEF HISTORY

Sports historians claim that soccer is the oldest team sport in the world. While no one is quite sure exactly where it began, they know that a kicking game called *tsu chu* was played by the Chinese over 2,500 years ago, "where participants tried to kick a leather ball filled with hair between bamboo poles."[1] Almost all other cultures had their own games that combined kicking a ball with keeping it away from opposing players. According to folklore, the Pilgrim fathers, upon settling at Plymouth Rock, found American Indians along the Massachusetts coast playing a form of soccer they called *pasuckquakkohowog*, which means "they gather to play football."[2]

In Europe, the game we know as soccer is called football. In 1823, during a football match at England's Rugby College, a student named William Ellis, frustrated in his attempts to move the ball with his feet, picked it up and ran with it. Some people liked this pick-up version of the game, so they kept it, and the original game became two games: rugby and soccer. To keep them straight, the kicking-only game became

known as soccer football, which was later shortened in the United States
to soccer. In 1885 teams from the United States and Canada played each
other, representing the first international soccer games to take place
outside of the British Isles, where the game was wildly popular. Because
of the influence of the British Empire in the 19th century, soccer spread
quickly, first across Europe, and then to South America and Asia.

In 1904 the Federation Internationale de Football Association (FIFA)
was established to govern the sport around the world. The world championship of soccer, the World Cup, was organized and continues to be
governed by FIFA. In the same year, the Olympic Games in St. Louis
included soccer as an official sport. In 1932 soccer was eliminated due
to fighting between soccer organizations, and it wasn't until 1936 that
soccer again became an Olympic sport for men. Women's soccer did
not appear as an official Olympic sport until 1996, where the U.S.
women won the gold medal in Atlanta. The first FIFA Women's World
Cup competition (formerly called the Women's World Championships)
was in China in 1991 and the second was held in Sweden in 1995. At
the 1991 and 1999 World Cup competitions, the United States won the
gold medal. Beginning in 1999, all Women's World Cup competitions
will be held every four years in the year following the World Cup for
men.

HOW THE GAME IS PLAYED

Soccer is a team sport, with 11 players on the field at a time. Substitutes are allowed to come into the game upon permission of the referee.
Soccer players are on the run constantly, moving back and forth on the
field, either attacking the other team's goal and trying to score a point
(goal) or defending their own goal to keep the other team from scoring.
While a variety of formations are used in placing players on the field,
the positions in soccer are forwards (attackers), midfielders, defenders,
and goalies. Players are not allowed to touch the ball with their hands
or arms (except for throw-ins following the ball going out of bounds at
the side line), with the exception of the goalkeeper, who can use her
hands to catch and throw the ball.

To decide who kicks off, a coin is tossed. At kick-off, all players must
be on their own side of the field, and no opponent can enter the center
circle until the ball has been played. The object of the game is to score
goals (a goal is worth one point) by maneuvering the ball into the opponent's net (or goal). The attacking team is the team in possession of

the ball; the defensive team tries to keep the offense from scoring and to take the ball away. The high school game is divided into two 40-minute periods with a 10-minute half-time. The team that did not kick off the first half kicks off to start the second half. The teams switch sides following half-time.

Possession of the ball switches back and forth between the teams. Teams lose possession when they make a bad pass, send the ball out of bounds, are called for a foul, or score a goal. As soon as possession of the ball changes from one team to the other, the attacking team becomes the defense, and the defending team becomes the offense. Because this happens very frequently during a game, it is important for teams to make the transition quickly, both physically and mentally. When a game ends with an equal number of goals having been scored by each team, the game is tied and ends in a draw. Sometimes, over-time periods are used to determine a winner, followed by a tie-breaker—a series of penalty kicks (or penalty shots) taken by players from both teams. After five shots are taken by each team, the team with the most goals wins the game. If the teams are still tied, they continue to take shots, one at a time, until one team scores and the other does not.

KEY ELEMENTS OF THE SPORT

Dribbling

A player must be able to move with the ball until a shooting or passing opportunity occurs. This is called dribbling. Good dribblers keep the ball close to their feet using short, even strides and a soft touch. Dribbling should be done with the head—or at least the eyes—up, allowing the player with the ball to determine where other players are and utilize vision, an essential part of the game. Dribbling is used to maintain possession of the ball and to advance the ball toward the opposing team's goal. A player may use various surfaces of her feet in dribbling, the most common being the inside of the foot, but also the outside, the sole, and even the heel.

Passing

Passing is essential to soccer. It is almost impossible for even the best dribbler to penetrate the defense without passing. Passing is a matter of teamwork and involves communication, position, and good field vision. The best passes are simple and executed quickly. Passes can be short (less than 30 feet) or long, into open space or directly to a teammate's feet. As in dribbling, the player with the ball needs to have her head up so she can see where to pass the ball. Passing is usually done with the inside of the foot, but it can also be done with the outside or the heel and the laces (called the instep) for long passes of more than 40 feet or so.

Receiving

Receiving (or controlling) the ball is the way you bring the ball under control. In every game players will receive balls coming from different directions, at various heights, and at varied speeds. Players can use any part of the body to receive the ball except their hands and arms. Proper technique for controlling the ball and maintaining possession is to cushion the ball's impact by relaxing and slightly withdrawing the part of the body receiving the ball, with the most common parts being the foot, thigh, and chest.

Shooting

The only way to win a soccer game is to score more goals than your opponent. Yet, soccer is a low-scoring game because there are relatively few chances to make a goal. That makes shooting an important skill. Goals can be made from shots taken close in or farther out from the goal. The most important thing about shooting is accuracy. A ball should be shot so the goalkeeper is forced to defend the goal. Sometimes, because she knocks the ball away or doesn't catch it cleanly, this results in another scoring opportunity for the offense; but if a shot goes high or wide, the goalkeeper is not challenged and there is no chance for a goal. Successful shooting is not only a matter of technique but also focus, determination, and confidence. Shooting is usually done with the laces (instep), but at close distances a player may use the inside of her foot to simply pass it in.

Heading

Heading is moving the ball by striking it with the forehead. Heading the ball is used to pass, shoot, receive, or clear the ball. Proper heading

technique is keeping the eyes open and focused on the ball while striking the ball with the upper part of the forehead, near the hairline. It is
hard to learn to keep your eyes open when a ball is flying at your face,
but by closing the eyes, players can get hit on the top of the head or in
the face, which hurts. Heading the ball properly does not hurt. Learning
to head the ball takes practice, but because 30 percent of game is played
in the air, it is an important skill to master.

Tackling

Tackling is a technique used when a defender tries to steal the ball
away from an attacker who has the ball. It is a means of either dispos-
sessing the attacker of the ball or even better, of actually gaining possession yourself. Tackling is accomplished with the toe (called a poke
tackle), the inside of the foot (a block tackle), or, as a last resort effort
as the attacker is almost beyond the defender, with a sliding tackle,
where the defender slides feet first and on her side to try to contact the
ball and dispossess the attacker.

RULES OF SOCCER

1. Number of players: Two teams of 11 players are on the field
   at one time.
2. Substitution: A player may enter the game upon permission of
   the referee, during a stoppage of play anytime the ball crosses
   the goal line or side line, when an injury occurs, or following
   half-time. At the high school level, unlimited substitution is
   allowed.
3. Scoring: The team that scores the most goals wins the game.
   The ball must completely cross the goal line between the goal
   posts and under the cross bar to be considered a goal. The ball
   cannot be thrown, carried, or intentionally propelled by hand
   or arm over the goal line.
4. Officials: There are three, including one referee and two assistant referees.
5. Outside lines: These are counted as part of the field. The
   ball must wholly cross the end line, goal line, or touch line
   (side line) to be out of bounds. Play stops and ball is out of
   play.

6. Goal kick: This is awarded to the defending team when the ball crosses the end line and was last touched by an opposing player; the ball is kicked from within the goal area. It must leave the penalty area before it can be touched by another player.

7. Corner kick: When a member of the opposing team plays the ball over the end line this kick is awarded to the attacking team. The kick is taken from the quarter circle in the corner of the field nearest to where the ball went out of bounds. A goal can be scored from a corner kick. The kicker may not touch the ball a second time until it has been touched by another player.

8. Offside: A player is offside when she is in the opposing team's half of the field and nearer to the opponent's goal line than the ball, unless at least two opponents (including the goalkeeper) are between her and the goal or the ball is sent to her from a throw-in, corner kick, or goal kick. Offside is called at the moment the ball is passed forward, not when the player receives the ball, and an indirect free kick is awarded to the opposing team.

9. Fouls: There are nine major fouls that result in either a direct free kick or a penalty kick, depending on the location where the foul occurred. Five minor fouls give the opposing team an indirect free kick from the location where the infringement occurred.

   • Free kick: The two versions of a free kick are (1) direct free kick—a goal can be scored directly; (2) indirect free kick— the ball must be touched by a player other than the kicker before a goal can be scored.

   • Penalty kick: If any of the nine major fouls are committed by the defending team in its own penalty area, a penalty kick will be awarded to the opposing team. This is a one-on-one confrontation between the goalkeeper and an opposing player. Everyone else must stand outside the penalty area while the kicker shoots the ball at the goal from the penalty spot, 12 yards from the goal. The goalie cannot move off her line until the ball has been kicked. After the kick, the kicker cannot play the ball until another player has touched it.

10. Official cautions: There are two types of cautions. A yellow card is given for entering or leaving the game illegally, persistent infringement of rules, disrespect and/or unsportsmanlike conduct. If player gets two yellow cards in one game, she is given a red card and expelled from the game. A red card is reserved for violent conduct or serious foul play, foul or abusive language, and persistent misconduct following yellow card. A red-carded player must leave the field and her team must play short (only 10 players). Additionally, the carded player is usually barred from playing in the next game.

TRYING OUT FOR THE SCHOOL TEAM

Many girls begin playing soccer at a young age. On crisp fall days, parks and school yards across the nation are covered by girls as young as four running after a #3 ball. Maybe you started then and have played ever since. If so, you will have a lot of experience by the time you get to high school and will have an advantage when you try out for the team. Even then, soccer at this level is probably going to be a step up from your earlier experiences, so you need to prepare yourself. If you have not played before, or have not played for awhile, you may have trouble competing against others who have, though many schools have junior varsity and/or freshman/sophomore programs where you can practice and get game experience.

Soccer is played at different times of the year in high schools around the country. The first thing you need to do is find out when your school's season is and when tryouts will be held. No matter when the sport is played at your school, preparation for tryouts should begin months in advance. Your best bet is to talk to the high school coach, introduce yourself, indicate your interest in the team, and find out what the tryouts will consist of, so you can train accordingly. If, for whatever reason, you cannot contact the high school coach, try the athletic director or a physical education (P.E.) teacher at the school. Or call another coach in the area, such as a college coach or club team coach, to ask for advice on how to prepare yourself.

Some coaches have written guidelines with exercises and fitness regimens already spelled out. You might even find that there are programs in place in the community, such as classes at a local two-year or four-year college, leagues sponsored by your local park and recreation department, soccer clubs, or soccer camps. If any of these programs are available, consider getting involved. Most high school coaches say the best thing you can do to get ready is to play the game. The more you play, the better the skills you are likely to develop, and your fitness level will increase, too. Competition challenges you and helps you improve, so if you join a team or league, try to play up (playing against tougher players) whenever possible. It helps to play against players stronger and more experienced than you. You can also play coed, or in pickup games with older girls or boys who are generally bigger, stronger, and faster. Playing up challenges you and makes you try harder. Additionally, many communities offer indoor soccer, a fun, fast version of the game that is good for conditioning, as well as skill building.

Training Tips for Soccer Players

1. Increase your soccer fitness level, both aerobic and anaerobic.
2. Get into a total body weight-training program.
3. Play soccer as often as possible.
4. Practice on your own: dribble the ball, kick a ball against a wall, do wind sprints.
5. Build an aerobic base by running 3–4 times a week for 35–40 minutes.
6. Find good players and coaches and learn from them. Watch, ask questions, listen.
7. Play with players better, stronger, and faster than you.

INCREASING PHYSICAL FITNESS FOR SOCCER

Fitness is extremely important for the game of soccer. Estimates are that soccer players run between 7 and 9 miles in a regulation game! Soccer is a game of short bursts of speed and almost constant running back and forth on the field. Therefore, fitness training needs to include both sprinting and jogging. Interval training is an important component of an overall soccer fitness program. Interval training combines sprinting and jogging to strengthen muscles used in running and increase air capacity and overall fitness. An example of an interval training exercise is to sprint 100 feet, jog back, then do it again. This number of sprint-jog repetitions can be increased as your fitness level improves. Keeping track of the time it takes you to complete one set is valuable, both to watch your progress and to challenge yourself. Some coaches advocate interval training three or four days a week for two to three months in advance of the season. Interval training can be done alone or with others.

Jogging is important for warming up and building endurance. It is best to begin jogging at an easy pace for the first mile or so and then to pick up the tempo. But first, be sure to warm up and stretch. Karen Stanley-Kehl, former collegiate player and Division I women's soccer coach, finds that one good way to warm up is to jog halfway around the soccer field (or half a block or so), then do some stretches. Repeat this routine several times, doing different stretches each time for a total body stretch. A soccer coach, P.E. teacher, or fitness trainer can teach you the proper stretches to do before jogging, and there are books that describe and diagram soccer stretches. Stanley-Kehl recommends jogging three to four days a week for about 30–40 minutes to build a solid aerobic base.

Another component of soccer-preparedness is weight training. Becoming stronger all over helps you to be strong on the ball. When you and another player are going for a fifty-fifty ball (you both have an even chance of getting to the ball), it is most often the stronger player who gains possession. Your weight-training program should be set up by your coach or a fitness professional to give you the maximum benefits and minimize your chances of injury. A program for soccer should include strength training for the entire body, because the idea is to build up your overall strength to help you run for an entire game, beat your opponent to the ball, maintain possession and not get knocked off the ball, jump for headers, kick, and throw in the ball from the side lines.

ACTIVITIES TO IMPROVE YOUR SOCCER SKILLS

According to Stanley-Kehl, the most important way to prepare for the high school team is to practice your skills and play the game. To challenge yourself, play on a competitive team. Play in a summer league, take a class at your local college, attend clinics and soccer camps, and get your friends to practice soccer exercises and scrimmage. You can also practice by yourself. Kick a ball against a wall. Dribble the ball while varying your speed. Practice changing directions, and, says Stanley-Kehl, "Remember to use both feet." If you are training on your own, make yourself a schedule and adhere to it. Focus on overcoming your weaknesses as well as improving your strengths.

To get better at the game of soccer, it is imperative that you challenge yourself mentally as well as physically. You have to become mentally alert and tough. When you set goals for yourself, such as increasing your repetitions, improving your speed, and beating your previous times, you can measure your improvement. Watch soccer being played. Go to high school and college soccer games. Watch not only the overall play but also the players in your position. What are they doing well? What are their weaknesses? Watch critically, rather than casually, so you learn more. Talk the play over with a friend. Also, watch soccer, especially women's soccer, on television. There are an increasing number of soccer videos on the market. You can rent, buy, or check out a video at your local library.

OTHER SPORTS/CROSS-TRAINING

Whether you are preparing to try out for the high school team or working on year-round fitness, you can benefit by participating in other sports. Besides being fun and keeping you in shape, playing other sports helps prevent the burnout that sometimes occurs when a player gets too much of her primary sport. You learn new skills from different coaches and meet another group of athletes when you vary your training. Other sports that benefit soccer players are track, cross country, roller blading, mountain and road biking, swimming, basketball, lacrosse, and field hockey. But learning and playing any additional sport will be beneficial to you.

MOST COMMON INJURIES AND HOW TO AVOID THEM

Poor field conditions contribute to injuries, so it is important that playing fields be well maintained. Wearing well-designed and proper-fitting soccer shoes is crucial for stability and to maintain balance. Girls may need several types of shoes depending on the playing surface. Coaches recommend shoes with screw-in cleats for wet or long grass, molded cleats for medium or medium-dry grass, and turf shoes without cleats for short grass or hard field conditions.

Injuries to the lower extremities, mainly to ankles and knees, are most common to soccer players. These can range from minor strains to major injuries that require surgery and lengthy rehabilitation. Less long-lasting, but painful and temporarily disabling, are strains and pulled muscles to areas like the groin, hamstrings, and quadriceps. Getting hit in the head or face with the ball or bumping heads with another player sometimes occurs on the soccer field. Increasing your overall fitness level and improving your soccer technique are both important ways to reduce the risk of injury.

- Ankle injuries—caused by twisting, going in for a tackle, planting the foot, and turning. To avoid: If you know you have weak ankles, you can have them taped before practice sessions or games, or wear elastic ankle training wraps for support. Do exercises to increase strength in the legs, feet, and ankles.
- Knee injuries—caused by twisting, going in for a fifty-fifty ball, tackling, or being tackled. To avoid: Do weight training to strengthen quadriceps, hamstrings, and other muscles around the knee. Learn proper tackling and pivoting techniques.
- Head injuries—caused by going up with another player for the ball; going one-on-one with the goalkeeper; getting hit in the head with the ball. To avoid: Learn and practice better techniques for heading, including jumping correctly and using your arms and hands for protection; do neck strengthening exercises; weight train to strengthen those muscles that brace and support your head and neck.

WHAT IF YOU DON'T MAKE THE HIGH SCHOOL TEAM?

Because of soccer's popularity, the number of girls who want to play at the high school level is greater than can be accommodated on most rosters. For coaches, decisions about whom to keep and whom to let go are difficult. For the prospective player, being cut can be extremely painful. It is perfectly natural to feel disappointed. But, rather than just walk away and nurse your hurt feelings, talk to the coach. Ask to discuss your evaluation and find out what the coach perceives as your weaknesses, so you can work on improving those areas in preparation for the next season's tryouts. Also, maybe the coach can recommend other places for you to play, so you can continue to learn and improve.

If you have a junior varsity or freshman/sophomore program, you might be able to play there. If you don't, and there are many other girls who tried out for the varsity and didn't make it, talk to the athletic director about starting such a program. This would not only provide a place for you and other girls to play, it would provide a training program for varsity teams of the future. Other places you might play include soccer clubs, recreational indoor and outdoor leagues, camps, and clinics. Soccer is so popular that in many areas girls can play all year around if they really want to. Another way to stay involved with the varsity team and continue to learn is by volunteering to help out as team manager, equipment manager, or as a volunteer assistant coach. In this way you can be part of the team as they practice and play, and you can learn from what the coach is teaching the players.

HOW TO START A HIGH SCHOOL TEAM

What if your high school does not sponsor a girls' team? While more than 7,400 schools do offer interscholastic soccer,[3] your school might not be one of them. To form a team, first find out how many girls are interested in playing. You could put a notice in your school newspaper asking girls to contact you, or just ask around informally. Next, set up a meeting with your school's athletic director to indicate your interest in having girls' soccer become an interscholastic sport. You might find out that there is already an effort under way to form such a team, especially if other high schools in your area field a girls' team. If there are no other programs, though, there is probably little incentive for your school's athletic department to consider adding the sport. But, if there are other teams and if enough girls at your school are interested, your athletic director should be inclined to support a girls' soccer program.

Sometimes schools are hesitant to add a new sport, even at the suggestion of the athletic director. Reasons given, besides not enough interest by prospective players or no league to play in, might include insufficient funding and lack of facilities and/or coaching personnel. While these are real concerns, federal law mandates that girls and boys be given equal access to sports. This means that if there are facilities and funds available for boys' sports, they must also be available for girls'. If there is enough interest from girls in playing soccer, and boys' teams are being supported and funded, your school has an obligation to provide the same kinds of opportunities for girls. If you do not receive satisfaction when you talk with the athletic director, you can take your case to the principal, then on to the district superintendent and school board, if necessary.

Even if the school intends to start a program, it will take time. Another option for you is to try out for the boys' team. Legally, if your school does not offer a girls' team, you have the right to try out for, and play on, the boys' team. You could also organize an intramural program while you are waiting for an interscholastic team to be formed. Invite girls to practice and scrimmage together a few days a week after school. You might get enough for a couple of teams. Solicit the services of a volunteer coach—either a teacher at your school who is willing to donate the time or a knowledgeable parent or college player in the area. In this way, you get the fun of playing, along with the opportunity to learn and practice, so you will be ready to play when the school team forms. (See more about federal law—Title IX—in Chapter 1.)

OTHER VERSIONS OF THE GAME

- Indoor soccer/Off the wall: Soccer is played indoors, usually in a gym or an indoor arena, with a #5 ball. A fast game, the play is continuous as substitution is done on the run. The game is played off the walls, with fewer players on the field, and with smaller goals. Scoring is usually higher than for outdoor soccer.

- Fusbal: This indoor game is played with a #1 ball and played on a court similar to the one used for basketball. Quick, short, controlled passes, rather than long kicks or air balls, define this game.

- Small-side soccer: For this variation, games are played on smaller outdoor fields and with fewer players to a side. Teams can be six-on-six, seven-on-seven, or more. Especially used for practice and conditioning, there are sporadic attempts to develop this as a separate game.

A LOOK INTO THE FUTURE OF SOCCER

Soccer is the most popular sport in the entire world. In the United States it continues to grow as a participation sport, as well as a spectator sport. Girls begin playing as early as four years old and women continue to play into mid-life. Soccer is the fastest growing sport for girls at the high school and college level. Included in the benefits of playing the sport, soccer-playing girls and women have opportunities to travel and to meet people from other parts of the country and all over the world.

Over 15,000 women compete at the intercollegiate level,[4] and the number of soccer scholarships continues to increase allowing many young women to take advantage of their athletic skills to help pay their college expenses. The success of women's soccer as an Olympic sport in 1996, when the U.S. team won the gold medal, brought girls off the side lines and onto the soccer field in droves. Following the Women's World Cup of 1999, proponents hope that a women's professional soccer league, much like the professional women's basketball leagues, will be inaugurated. Expect soccer to continue to be one of the most popular sports for girls and women of just about all ages.

TERMS TO KNOW

Advantage: rule that lets play continue after a foul if stopping the play immediately would be disadvantageous to the team that was fouled

Back pass: a pass made to a player in a support position behind the player with the ball

Bicycle kick: an overhead kick, also called a scissors kick

Chip: a high, looping pass or shot, designed to go over defender's head

Corner kick: method to restart play after the defending team has cleared the ball over its own goal line, the ball is placed in quarter circle in corner of field, closest to where the ball went out

Dangerous play: an action that could, according to the referee, cause injury to a player

Defender: a player trying to keep the ball out of the goal and to dispossess the ball from the opposing team

Direct free kick: a free kick that can result directly in a goal

Dribble: to control and move the ball on the ground with the feet

End lines: boundary lines marking the ends of the field

Far post: goal post farthest from the ball

Field: regulation field of play for soccer

Formations: the system used to position players on the field; for example, 4-3-3 refers to four defenders, three midfielders, and three forwards

Forward: an offensive player trying to score, or set up, a goal

Give-and-go: a player making a short pass to a teammate and then receiving the return pass, also referred to as the wall pass or a 1-2

Header: the act of heading the ball

Heading: using one's head to score, pass, or control the ball

Indirect free kick: free kick that cannot result in a goal until it touches another player first

Injury time: time added by the referee to the end of each half to accommodate for lost time due to injury, scoring a goal, or time-wasting

Midfielder: a player who functions primarily in the middle of the field; a link between the attackers and defenders

Near post: goal post nearest to the ball

Obstruction: illegally preventing an opponent from playing the ball by blocking her path to the ball

Offside: an infraction in which an offensive player does not have at least two defensive players between herself and the goal line when the ball is played forward by a member of the attacking team

Penalty area: 44-yard by 18-yard area in front of the goal in which the goal-keeper may use her hands

Penalty kick: direct free kick from the penalty spot, 12 yards directly in front of the goal

Pitch: British term for playing field

Red card: card held up to a player following grievous or persistent rules in-fraction, signifying expulsion from game

Shielding: when the dribbler stays between the ball and opponent to protect and maintain possession of the ball

Slide tackle: taking the ball away from the dribbler by sliding on the turf and connecting with the ball

Striker: a forward-position player whose main responsibility is scoring

Sweeper: a roving defender who plays between the fullbacks and goalkeeper

Tackle: to take the ball away from an opponent by using the feet

Through-pass (or ball): a pass that splits a group of defenders

Throw-in: a method of returning the ball to play after it has gone over the side line performed by the team not responsible for sending it out

Touch line (or side line): a line marking a side of the field

Trap: to bring the ball under control with any part of the body, except the hands and arms

Volley: kicking the ball in mid-air

Wall: a group of defenders standing shoulder-to-shoulder, usually near the goal, to block a free kick

Yellow card: card held aloft by the referee to caution a player that further rules infraction or misconduct will result in a red card and game expulsion

NOTES

1. David Ominsky, and P. J. Harari, *Soccer Made Simple: A Spectator's Guide*, rev. ed., Los Angeles: First Base Sports, 1999.

2. 1998 United States Olympic Committee.

3. National Federation of State High School Associations 1998 Participation Survey.

4. National Collegiate Athletic Association 1997–98 Participation Study.

Chapter 5
Softball

Softball pitcher Gina McFarland winds up for what she hopes will be a strike. Photo courtesy of the McFarland Family Collection.

"In softball you experience immediate success . . . and failure. Luckily, you almost always get another chance; if you strike out, you get the chance to get a hit the next time you're up."
—Chris Elze, college coach and former college player

"I love the pressure of pitching and being involved in every play."
—Stacy Myers, former high school player

"I like the feeling that you're never alone. Your team is always with you. Together you win and together you lose."
—Gina McFarland, high school player

"It's the team spirit that keeps me in the game!"
—Stacey Sheehan, high school player

Some people call softball baseball's "cousin" because of its similarity to baseball. Like baseball, softball is a game played by two teams of nine players, where the object is to score points (runs) by advancing runners around the four bases. Players attempt to hit the ball with a bat in such a way that a member of the opposing team cannot catch or easily play the ball. Players in the field try to prevent the batter from running around the bases by means of tagging the base or the runner with the ball. Each team gets a chance to be the offensive (at bat) team until it makes three outs; then teams change places and the defensive (fielding) team is at bat and the team that was just up goes out to the field. An inning is finished when each team has had one turn at bat and one turn in the field. After seven innings, the team with the highest score wins the game.

At the high school level, softball is played by girls, while baseball is played mainly by boys. (See more about male-dominated sports in Chapter 11.) This book will talk primarily about fastpitch softball because it is played more at the high school level than is slowpitch softball. But for a bird's eye view of the slowpitch version, look at the end of this chapter.

FIELD OF PLAY

The playing area consists of an infield diamond and an outfield area that may or may not be enclosed by a fence (see figure 5.1). If the ball

Figure 5.1
Softball Field

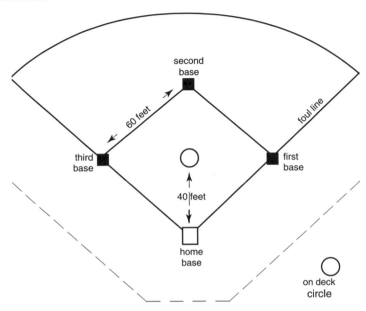

Source: Madrid Designs, Santa Rosa, CA

is played or lands within the playing area, including its landing on the foul (boundary) lines, it is considered fair territory. Any other area is foul territory. The infield is 60 feet square on a diagonal (the diamond), with bases at each of the four corners: home plate, first base, second base, third base. The pitching rubber (plate) is set in a line between home plate and second base, 40 feet from home plate. The infield is usually a flat, packed dirt surface. The outfield, usually a grassy surface, is shaped like a quarter-circle and is the area between the two foul lines.

EQUIPMENT

Players need a bat, ball, and a glove to play softball. Girls usually must purchase their own gloves, while bats and balls are supplied by the high school, along with uniforms and batting helmets. Catchers and umpires wear face masks and body protectors that cover the chest and shin areas.

Softballs, which are larger than baseballs, are made of an approved material such as a mixture of cork and rubber, covered with leather or a synthetic material. The regulation high school ball weighs between

6.25 and 7 ounces and has a circumference of 12 inches. Most balls are white, though some states use optic orange or optic yellow balls. Bats can be no more than 34 inches in length and must be made of wood, aluminum, magnesium, or a graphite-composite.

Softball gloves (sometimes called mitts) are made of leather. Except for the catcher's glove, players' gloves must be the same size. All defensive team players (fielders) must wear a glove.

DRESS

Teams wear pants with elastic on the leg bottoms or shorts, and a shirt or jersey. These should be all the same. Shirts have the name and logo of the team on the front, with the girl's number on the back. The length of the sleeve may vary. Softball shoes are made of leather or a synthetic material and have nonmetal cleats on the bottom for stability and to prevent slipping. Teams may choose to wear either caps or visors. Batting helmets are mandatory. Players often wear batting gloves to protect their hands and to give them a better grip on the bat. Catchers must wear approved equipment, including head and body protectors.

A SHORT HISTORY OF THE SPORT

Softball was the brainchild of a young man named George Hancock. One fall day in 1887 in Chicago, Illinois, Hancock and his friends were at a gym when one young man threw a boxing glove at his buddy, who hit it with a stick. Hancock tied the glove into a ball, using the laces, drew a baseball diamond on the floor, then said, "Play ball!" The word spread about this great new game of "indoor baseball," and within a short time it became popular both indoors and outdoors. Hancock wrote and published the first set of standard rules for what became known as indoor-outdoor ball.

It wasn't until 1933 that the name softball was adopted and the Amateur Softball Association drew up rules to standardize the game throughout the world. During that same year, the first national fastpitch softball championship tournament for both men and women was held at the Chicago World's Fair. While women's softball was growing in popularity in the 1930s, it wasn't until World War II, when many professional baseball players went into the service, that women were invited to fill the gap. In 1943 hundreds of women tried out for a spot on four teams in the newly created All-American Girls Softball League (later changed to All-American Girls Baseball League). The young women wore short, one-piece dresses with satin briefs underneath. After daily practices they were sent to charm school, where they learned the art of walking, selecting clothes, and applying makeup![1] After the war, attendance dwindled, and the league disappeared.

Softball, which today is the most popular participation sport in the United States, began to develop as an international sport in the late 1940s, and the International Softball Federation was formed in 1952. Despite the increase in participation and popularity of the game, softball did not become an Olympic medal sport until 1996 at the Atlanta Games, where the U.S. women's team won the gold medal. Today there are more than 333,000 girls participating in fastpitch softball, while 30,000 play slowpitch at high schools in the United States[2] and 13,750 playing intercollegiate softball.[3]

HOW THE GAME IS PLAYED

Softball is a team sport, with nine players from each team on the field at one time. It is a game of special skills, including throwing, catching, running, and hitting. It is also a game of strategy and decision making. The visiting team is the first to take its turn at bat, while the home team bats last. A game lasts seven innings unless the score is tied; then extra innings are added. The team with the highest score at the end of an extra inning is the winner.

Each team bats in its turn, with the objective of hitting the ball, advancing around the bases, and crossing home plate to score a run (point). The pitcher attempts to keep the batter from hitting the ball, and her teammates (the fielding team) try to catch a batted ball hit into fair territory and/or throw the batter out as she's running to a base. Each team spends half the inning at bat and half in the field. After both teams have made three outs in their turn at bat, that inning is over and the next inning begins.

The plate umpire watches to see that the pitched ball is thrown in an area called the strike zone—the space above home plate between the batter's knees and her armpits. If it does, he calls it a strike if the batter doesn't hit it. If the batter swings at a ball and misses, it is also a strike, even if it isn't in the strike zone. If the ball does not come over the plate in the strike zone, it is called a ball. A girl is called out if she gets three strikes. If four balls are called, the batter gets to advance to first base without risk. This is called a walk, or bases on balls.

KEY ELEMENTS OF THE SPORT

Batting

Hitting the ball with a bat takes quick reflexes and well-developed eye-hand coordination. Girls have to watch the ball, as it is thrown by a pitcher, and decide in seconds whether or not the ball is coming over the plate in the strike zone. If she thinks it is, she takes a swing. It takes practice to develop that quick and accurate eye and to see the ball well enough to hit it, especially when facing a fast pitcher.

Players must bat in the order listed on the scoresheet. If three outs are made before all nine players have taken their turn, the player who is next in the lineup is leadoff batter in the following inning. A player's turn at bat is over when she strikes out or advances safely to a base. She then becomes a baserunner.

Scoring

If a player hits a ball over the fence or the fielders are unable catch the ball and/or throw the baserunner out before she crosses home plate, the hit is considered a home run. She must tag each base in order (first, second, third, and home plate) with her foot as she passes. If there are runners on base, they precede her and score also. A hit that allows the batter to reach first base safely is called a single; if she reaches second base it is a double; a triple is when she reaches third base safely on her own hit ball.

Base Running

Generally, a batter becomes a runner when she hits the ball or after she leaves first base following a walk. She is then at risk of being tagged out or forced out at a base. Because the rules are fairly intricate, all of them will not be detailed here, but basically a runner may advance to the next base when (1) the batter following her hits a ball into fair territory or walks; (2) she "steals" a base; (3) the runner tags the base she is on after a fielder catches a fly ball and then runs to the next base. Runners are aided by a coach at first base and a coach at third base.

Baserunners cannot overrun a base (except first base), but must reach the base either standing up or sliding. Sliding gives the batter a better chance of being safe on a tag play, and additionally, a proper slide can prevent injury.

Pitching

The pitcher must throw from a pitching rubber, set within the pitching circle, 40 feet from home plate. The ball is pitched underhand, with a windup. Usually, a windmill motion is used. Pitchers can throw the ball very hard and fast using the windmill motion. A fastball is not the only pitch a good pitcher throws. Other pitches are used to confound the batters, such as the drop ball, changeup, and rise ball. A pitcher is in constant communication with her catcher, who uses hand signals to indicate which pitch she thinks the pitcher should use.

A good pitcher can practically control the game of high school softball. If she pitches strikes and the batter cannot hit what she throws, then almost single-handedly she can keep the other team from scoring. The pitcher is involved with every play when her team is in the field. She is allowed one minute or five warmup pitches at the beginning of each half inning. There are no limits to the number of innings a girl can pitch.

Fielding

Fielding positions are pitcher, catcher, first base, second base, third base, shortstop, left field, center field, and right field. The pitcher and catcher are involved with every play, so they get plenty of action. For the rest of the fielders, their job is to stay alert, even though they might not ever touch a ball the entire inning! Still, they must think in advance about possibilities. They must ask themselves questions like: If the ball were to be hit to me, how would I play it? What supporting position do I have to move into if the ball is hit elsewhere? This is particularly true of the outfielders, because the majority of hits stay in the infield.

To get the baserunner out, a fielder touches, or tags, a base (when the runner is being forced to run to that base) while she holds the ball in her hand or glove. Or, she tags the runner anytime the baserunner is between bases (except when she has been walked at bat). Outfielders have to develop a strong throwing arm to get the ball from the outfield to an infielder or, occasionally, to the pitcher or catcher. Outfielders have to be able to run fast to get the ball. Additionally, they have to be able to gauge where a fly ball will drop, so they can get under it.

RULES OF SOFTBALL

1. Number of players: Two teams of nine players are on the field at any one time.

2. Scoring: A point (run) is scored when a player completes a circuit of the bases, having touched each one in the proper sequence. The winning team is the one that finishes the game with the highest score.

3. Officials: The plate umpire stands behind the catcher and judges batting and pitching; he is the official that generally controls the game. One or two base umpires take different positions on the field to see the action of baserunners and defensive players. An official scorer records the process of the game.

4. Substitutions: All players may be substituted; only starting players may be returned to the game and only one time. A player must return to the same batting order as when she was taken out of the game.

5. Designated hitters: One "DH" is allowed per game; she must start the game and bat in the place of a designated defensive player.

6. Infractions: Softball has a fairly complex set of playing rules and penalties for infractions. For the most flagrant infractions, such as disruptive behavior, abusive language, and dangerous play, penalties can include ejection from the game.

7. Jewelry is prohibited.

8. The visiting team is the first to take its turn at bat. The game begins when the umpire calls, "Play ball!"

9. The game is finished when the team with fewer home runs has completed its turn at bat in the seventh inning or in any subsequent extra inning (extra innings are taken if the score is tied after seven innings), or if the game is called by the umpire due to weather conditions or darkness.

10. A game will be forfeited upon the decision of the umpire. This may happen when a team (1) is late in arriving or in beginning the game; (2) cannot provide nine players; (3) refuses to play after the game has started; (4) attempts to manipulate the length of the game; (5) willfully violates rules after being warned by the umpire.

TRYING OUT FOR THE HIGH SCHOOL TEAM

Softball is a game of multiple skills, both physical and mental. It takes time and experience to learn the game. Therefore, if you have played softball before you get to high school, you have an advantage over girls who have never played before.

Softball is a fall sport in some schools, a spring sport in others. Finding out when softball is played at your high school is your first step. Then, find out the name of the coach, either through the athletic department or the main office at your high school, and contact the coach directly, if possible. If that information isn't available, talk to the athletic director and ask some questions including when the season starts. He or she will also be able to tell you what you can do to prepare yourself for tryouts and when you should get started. In the meantime, however, if you have no or only limited experience with softball, you would benefit from getting involved in other programs to help you learn about the game. In addition to school programs, check with your city park and recreation department, and local youth recreation programs, such as YMCA, YWCA, Girl Scouts, and Boys and Girls Clubs, to see if they sponsor softball teams. Joining clubs, playing in softball leagues, and going to sports camps or clinics are other ways to learn.

Clubs

Softball clubs offer girls as young as five or six the opportunity to get basic instruction and to play the game. Clubs for older, more advanced players may practice and play almost year round. Your high school coach can usually tell you how to contact club coaches for information, or talk to girls who belong to a softball club and ask questions about participation.

Softball Leagues

Recreational programs often sponsor league play for girls, where they can get instruction and play games, too. Call your local park and recreation department and youth organizations to find out what they offer.

Camps and Clinics

Softball camps and clinics are often held during vacation breaks and are an excellent way to get intensive instruction in a short time. Camps may last for a week or more. They may be held at high schools or colleges in your community. Clinics are shorter, usually one or two days, and sometimes they specialize in a certain skill such as hitting or pitching. You can find out about camps and clinics by calling local colleges or high schools. Or you can call the sports desk of your local newspaper for a list of camps and clinics. Softball magazines, available at newsstands or by subscription, usually list camps around the country and even rate them. Most programs charge a participation fee. Generally, community programs are less expensive, while softball clubs and camps can be quite expensive. Ask if scholarships are available.

Most coaches advise girls to prepare in advance of tryouts. Softball coach Diane Jurgensmeyer encourages girls to work on conditioning and play summer league ball to get in shape for the fall high school season. Many other high schools play in the spring. Whenever the seasons, coaches agree that it isn't enough to just show up at tryouts. If playing in an organized league is not an option in your area prior to the high school season, get together with friends or family to practice throwing and hitting.

Pitchers need even more advance preparation. Dick McFarland, high school and club coach, believes pitchers benefit by practicing year round. Even a few times a week helps strengthen muscles and sharpens technique. For several months before the season begins, pitchers need to increase their practice time. Attending a pitching clinic or camp or working individually with a pitching coach can improve technique for increased performance and to avoid injury. McFarland says, "If girls haven't thrown a ball in advance, they are wasting their tryouts, using them as warmups. Players who have been practicing definitely have the advantage."

Learn as much as you can about the game by reading about the rules and by watching the game being played either at local high schools or colleges or on video tapes, available through libraries, sporting goods stores, and softball organizations. The Amateur Softball Association of America (ASA), the national governing body, has a comprehensive library of books and videos for sale. Contact ASA at 2801 NE 50th Street, Oklahoma City, OK 73111-7203. Call 405-424-5266 for information. You can check out the website at www.softball.org.

Training Tips for Softball Players

1. Increase your overall fitness.
2. Throw, hit, and field the ball often to increase and maintain your skills.
3. Always warm up by stretching to prevent injury.
4. Play on competitive teams year round or in summer leagues.
5. Play catch with friends; trade off pitching and hitting to one another.
6. Practice by yourself: throw and hit against a net, visit batting cages.
7. Learn about the game: watch it being played, read up on the rules.

ACTIVITIES TO IMPROVE YOUR SOFTBALL SKILLS

Increasing physical fitness and working on your softball skills will make you more competitive during tryouts and also lessen your chances of injury. According to high school coaches, the most effective training is to practice the skills you are going to use, such as hitting, throwing, and catching the ball. Gather a few friends or family members and play catch. Field ground balls and fly balls. Have someone pitch to you so you can hit. Or, practice hitting with a pitcher who is also trying out for the team. In that way, you will both get a workout. You don't always need a field to practice. You can play catch in your own backyard and even practice hitting. Using a wiffle ball allows you to work on timing and coordination without jeopardizing your neighbor's windows! Work off a tee and hit the ball into a net (these items may be purchased at sporting goods stores). Many communities also have facilities with batting cages and pitching machines for fun and practice. Or go to your local school and practice or play a game.

OTHER SPORTS/CROSS-TRAINING

Many coaches believe girls benefit from participating in other sports during the year. In addition to maintaining overall fitness, other sports can offer cross-training benefits and prevent burnout that sometimes occurs from constant participation in one sport. Running-based sports, such as cross country and track, soccer, basketball, field hockey, and lacrosse, all build and maintain endurance. So does swimming, which some coaches claim is the best all-around conditioning for every part of the body. Other sports such as the throwing events in track and field, volleyball, basketball, and rowing all build upper-body strength. Tennis and badminton are good for improving eye-hand coordination, which is very important for hitting the softball.

In addition to cross-training benefits, participating in other sports gives girls the opportunity to learn from different coaches and to play with other teammates. Some coaches argue that to maximize your performance in one sport, you should stick to that sport; most coaches agree, however, that at the high school level, girls are better served by participating in several different sports.

MOST COMMON INJURIES AND HOW TO AVOID THEM

Arms, shoulders, and ankles are most prone to injury in softball.

- Arm and shoulder injuries—caused by straining or pulling muscles from repeated throwing and pitching motions. To avoid, strengthen muscles by throwing, increasing the repetitions and speed slowly; warm up slowly and thoroughly, stretching in advance; pursue weight training. Avoid overthrowing, especially early in the season.
- Ankle injuries—caused by improper sliding, turning an ankle while running or rounding the bases. To avoid, strengthen muscles around the ankles through exercise and weight training; learn to slide correctly.
- Other muscle pulls—to avoid, stretch out before and after practices or games; participate in a total-body strength training program.

WHAT IF YOU DON'T MAKE THE HIGH SCHOOL TEAM?

If you have your heart set on making the high school team and don't make the cut, what can you do? It's very disappointing—especially when you work out and practice in advance—to not make the team. Often, if you don't make the varsity team, there will be a junior varsity team you can play on. If you are a freshman or sophomore, this can be particularly to your advantage, because you can learn and probably get more game time at this level. Also, the junior varsity coach usually works closely with the varsity coach, who keeps an eye on future varsity players. During the high school season, players on junior varsity are sometimes "brought up" to the varsity team when the need arises.

But what if a junior varsity team is not available? You can talk to other girls who did not make the cut to gauge their interest in forming such a team. If there is enough interest, talk to the athletic director about the possibility and offer to help out. The varsity coach may even assist you in getting a team started, because it certainly benefits the entire softball program to have a junior varsity team. Some schools even have freshman/sophomore teams in addition to a junior varsity team.

Another option is to join a club or recreational team to increase your basic knowledge of the game and practice your skills for the next year's tryouts. As mentioned earlier in the chapter, there are undoubtedly other programs in your area that you can join. High school coaches suggest individual instruction. More advanced players and area coaches are often available to coach aspiring softball players, usually for a fee. Ask your high school coach or call your local college softball staff for references.

You might also consider switching to another sport or concentrating on a sport in which you already participate. Check out other sports available at your school during the softball season. Or look in your community. There are other activities not offered at the high school level that might interest you, such as bowling, fencing, kick boxing, inline skating, horseback riding, mountain biking, and hiking to name just a few. All of these activities can be fun and offer camaraderie and the chance to learn something new and perhaps to excel.

HOW TO START A HIGH SCHOOL TEAM

What if there is no softball program at your school? This is probably not very likely, since softball is the fourth most popular sport at the high school level, with almost 12,000 schools participating.[4] Yet, if there is no program, you can find other places to play. If there are teams at other schools in your district or nearby, you might be able to play with them. Or you can try to start a high school team, in which case your first step is to see whether there are enough other girls interested in forming a team. If there are, then contact your athletic director or principal and indicate your interest in organizing a team.

Is there an established league in your area that a new team could join? If there isn't, then it will be harder to make a case for starting a softball team at just one school. But if there is, it should be relatively easy to get a team going. Administrators might ask if you know someone willing to coach, perhaps a teacher on staff or another qualified adult from the community. They might also express concern about funding a new school team, but according to federal law, girls must be given equal opportunity with boys to play sports, and the lack of funding is not an acceptable reason for not letting girls play. (See more about Title IX in Chapter 1.)

If you do not feel satisfied after talking with your athletic director or principal, you can take your request to the district superintendent and to the school board. If you do this, it is best to seek the support of your parents and other adults. Usually, a strong show of interest in organizing a girls' interscholastic sports team at the high school is sufficient to get a program started. While the process is taking place, you could enlist the aid of a physical education teacher to help you organize intramural softball as an after-school activity. This would allow you and other girls to play while demonstrating that there are enough interested players to form a competitive team. Or, you might consider trying out for the baseball team. Title IX says that if your school does not offer a separate girls' team in a sport, then girls can try out for, and play on, the boys' team.

OTHER VERSIONS OF THE GAME

Slowpitch Softball

Slowpitch softball is not played at the high school level but is played in recreational leagues that include women as well as men of all ages. This version is similar in most ways to fastpitch; the most obvious difference is in the style and speed of pitching. While good pitchers can pretty much control a fastpitch game, that isn't true in slowpitch, where no windmill action is allowed and the ball must travel through a loopy arc of between 6 and 12 feet to the plate. Additionally, a tenth player called a short fielder is used in slowpitch and the strike zone is a little larger.

Baseball

While baseball, affectionately referred to as "America's national game," is not a version of softball, it is similar enough to make the comparison. More girls today play baseball than ever before, in spite of the increase in softball participation. Liberally interpreted, the major differences are: (1) a baseball is smaller than a softball; (2) there are nine innings in a baseball game; (3) a baseball field is larger than a softball field; (4) the pitcher's plate is set farther back from home plate and the bases are farther apart; (5) the ball is pitched overhand.

Some girls prefer baseball and participate on youth and high school teams, especially if there are no softball teams in the area. There is little opportunity for women to play baseball at the recreational level and there are very few opportunities professionally for women at this time.

A LOOK INTO THE FUTURE OF SOFTBALL

The future of softball looks very bright, says Brian McCall, director of communications of the Amateur Softball Association (ASA), the sport's national governing body. Today, there are nearly 40 million men, women, and children playing softball, making it the number one team sport in the United States, while at the international level, there are 60 million participants.[5] Interest in women's fastpitch softball has increased since 1996, the inaugural year for women's softball as an Olympic sport. The U.S. women's team, winner of the gold medal in Atlanta, brought the excitement of the game to the attention of the entire world and has increased participation at all age levels.

Youth programs are strong. According to McCall, "the girls' program continues to break past records for participation, which will ultimately reflect on our adult programs." In high schools and colleges, more programs are being added, and that trend is expected to continue. Not only will more girls get the opportunity to play, but the availability of college scholarships continues to grow, enabling more student-athletes to take advantage of their athletic talent and skills to help pay their educational expenses.

Professional opportunities do exist, though they are limited. In the United States, the Women's Professional Fastpitch (WPF) sponsors eight teams and has plans to expand the league, while some American athletes play in other countries, including Japan and Italy. Recent rule changes allow female softball players to play professionally and still compete in the Olympic Games.

While most adults play slowpitch softball, there are fastpitch leagues, as well. Masters leagues and the World Games, held every four years, bring adults over 30 together to play at a highly competitive level. Girls can begin playing softball as early as five years old, while women can continue to play indefinitely. The ASA annually conducts play in over 60 divisions from youth to 70 and over.

TERMS TO KNOW

Ball: awarded to the batter when a pitch is not touched by the bat and is not a strike

Batter up: called by the umpire after the pitcher has taken her practice pitches in each inning to signal to the first batter that it is time for her to hit

Batting order: the order in which batters are listed on the scoresheet; they must stay in that order throughout the game

Bunt: a fair ball that is accomplished by a batter holding the bat and just tapping the ball rather than taking a full swing

Catch a fly: to catch a ball in the air before it touches the ground

Dead ball: when the ball is not in play

Designated hitter: a 10th player who substitutes at bat for another team member on the roster

Diamond: the infield part of the playing area

Double play: when two players of the batting team are put out by fielders in a continuous play

Error: a misplay by a fielder

Fair ball: a ball batted into fair territory or out of the playing field over fair territory (home run)

Fair territory: the playing area of the field surrounded by and including boundary lines

Fielder: any of the nine players on the team who is not up to bat (defensive team)

Fly ball: a ball hit into the air, not on the ground

Force-out: an out caused when a runner has no choice but to advance to an occupied base

Foul ball: a batted ball that falls outside the boundaries of the field

Foul territory: the areas outside the playing field boundary lines

Ground ball: a ball hit on the ground

Home run: a ball batted out of the playing field over fair territory

Illegal pitch: a ball pitched in violation of pitching rules

Infield: the diamond area on the playing field, bordered by the four bases; infielders are players who play catcher, pitcher, first base, second base, shortstop, and third base

Inning: the portion of the game that for each team includes a turn at bat and a turn in the field

On-deck circle: a circle 5 feet in diameter located a safe distance away from home plate where the next up (on-deck) batter waits to bat

Out: a call by the umpire indicating a batter or baserunner must return to the dugout or players bench; three outs retire the side and the fielding team becomes the batting team

Outfield: the area beyond the infield and within the foul lines; outfielders are players who play in left field, right field, and center field

Overthrow: an off-the-mark throw by one teammate to another

Passed ball: a pitched ball that the catcher fails to catch or control that she should have been able to do with ordinary effort

Pitcher's plate: the place, 40 feet from home base, where pitchers stand to start their pitch

Slide: a means for a baserunner to get to the base by sliding either feet- or headfirst in a legal manner

Stolen base: an advance by the runner to the next base on a nonbatted ball

Strike: a call by the umpire for each ball pitched into the strike zone that the batter misses or doesn't swing at, or if the ball is hit foul (exception: no limit of foul balls after second strike); three strikes and the batter is out

Strike zone: the space above home plate between the batter's armpit and the top of her knees when she assumes a natural batting stance

Time-out: the command given by the umpire to suspend play

Triple play: when three players of the batting team are put out by fielders in a continuous play

Walk: a base on balls awarded to the batter when the pitcher throws four "balls"

Wild pitch: a pitch that cannot be handled with ordinary effort by the catcher

NOTES

1. Sue Macy, *A Whole New Ball Game*, New York: Henry Holt, 1993.
2. National Federation of State High School Associations 1998 Participation Survey.

3. National Collegiate Athletic Association 1997–98 Participation Study.

4. National Federation of State High School Associations 1998 Participation Survey.

5. Amateur Softball Association of America statistics.

Chapter 6
Swimming and Diving

Jill McCormick waits in perfect form for the starter's signal to begin her race. Photo courtesy of the Lombardi McCormick Family Collection.

"I love getting ready to race, waiting to dive into the water, the sound of the gun going off."
—Trisha Bergman, former college swimmer

"It's a sport you can do wherever you go—to the beach, the river or lake, to a public pool or fancy resort."
—Jill McCormick, high school swimming coach

"I love reading the clock and seeing that my time is one of the fastest; it's a feeling like no other."
—Lauren Garrett, high school swimmer

"Diving gives you a rush; it's daring; it's fun!"
—Melissa Mitchell, former high school diver

Swimming and diving are both aquatic sports, yet they are very different. Swimming is moving through the water coordinating body movement and breathing without flotation or mechanical devices. While swimming is strictly a recreational activity for most people, it is a highly competitive sport for others. Swimming is both an individual and team sport, where participants compete in races and the first racer to swim a predetermined distance is the winner.

Diving—plunging into the water, with arms stretched above the head and in line with the body—is considered part of the swimming program in high schools, but it utilizes very different skills from swimming. Athletes will sometimes do both, although at the very competitive and/or elite levels, they almost always specialize in one or the other. Because swimming and diving are treated as one sport at the high school level, they are discussed here in a single chapter.

COURT OF PLAY

Competitions are held in rectangular pools of varying lengths, but in high schools the regulation pool is 25 yards long. High school pools are generally called short-course pools. Long-course pools are for international competition; they are Olympic-size, 50 meters long. The short-course competitive pool is usually divided into six or eight lanes, numbered one through six or eight from left to right. The lanes keep swimmers separate during races, so they don't run into each other. Each lane is between seven to nine feet wide, depending on the width of the pool. The ideal water temperature is in the 78 to 80 degree range.

Oftentimes, diving is done at the deep end of the same pool; at other times, depending on the availability of facilities, it is done in a separate pool or a diving well. Athletes dive off of a 1 meter regulation spring-board.

EQUIPMENT

Pull buoys, kickboards, paddles, mitts, and fins are training equipment for competitive swimmers. They are usually supplied by the high school. Divers train on dry land as well as in the pool, learning their dives and practicing leadup skills on a mat or in a spotting rig on a trampoline.

DRESS

To start out in swimming or diving, all you really need is a swimsuit and towel. Swimsuits for girls are usually form-fitting to streamline their bodies and cut down on the drag in the water. Most high schools have a team swimsuit. Other equipment—such as a cap, goggles, chamois cloth, warmup suit or sweatshirt and other warm clothing—are advisable and might be mandatory if you swim for a high school team. Divers are not required to use goggles.

A BRIEF HISTORY

Swimming only became popular as a sport in the 19th century, even though ancient carvings found in areas of the Middle East indicate that people have been swimming for over four thousand years! While most swimming was surely a survival skill in early days, there are reports that swimming races took place in Japan as early as 36 B.C.

In modern times, the English were the first to develop swimming as a sport. The National Swimming Society, founded in the 1830s, promoted and regulated racing competitions. The breaststroke and side-stroke were the only strokes used. In 1844, Native American swimmers competed in London, where team member Flying Gull reportedly won a medal. His stroke, described as a windmill-type thrashing, was an early form of the front crawl. The stroke was ridiculed by the swimming establishment, who preferred the more genteel breaststroke. Races at that time were held in indoor pools and in natural bodies of water, where long-distance swimming got its start.

Throughout the 1800s different swimming strokes evolved as competitors tried to swim faster, and in 1902, Australian Richard Cavill used a new stroke to set a world record (100 yards in 58.4 seconds) at the International Championships. This stroke soon was called the Australian crawl. The first recorded swimming competition in the United States took place in 1883 at the New York Athletic Club. Today, United States Swimming (USS) is the governing body for competitive swimming in this country.

Swimming became an Olympic sport for men in 1896; however, women were excluded because of the common assumption during the Victorian era that women were too frail to engage in vigorous, and especially competitive, sports. Women's swimming made its debut at the 1912 Olympic Games. While at that time there were only four events, today there are 32 swimming races: 16 for men and 16 for women.

New training methods have increased the skills and decreased the times of competitive swimmers. Record times continue to fall and the sport of swimming continues to be popular, despite lack of media attention. Few swimming meets, even on the national or international level, are televised, and newspaper coverage is meager, except during the Olympic Games. Only then does the public see the beauty and precision of competitive swimming and diving and get an idea of the elite swimmer's dedication and skill. Today there are more than 126,000 girls participating in swimming and diving in high school,[1] while 9,413 females compete at the college level.[2]

Although there is some evidence of diving as early as the 6th century B.C., it wasn't until the late 1800s that diving became a sport. Prior to that, diving was a gymnastics exercise: as early as the 1600s, gymnasts in Germany and Sweden practiced their moves and flips on the beach and over the water to keep from hurting themselves when they fell. Gradually, diving branched away from gymnastics, although as late as the 1920s, diving events were frequently held along with gymnastic meets. Plunging, a headfirst crouching dive, was one of the first popular dives, with part of the competition being that once the diver entered the water, he would glide, not swim, face downward, as far down the length of the pool as possible in one minute. (Fat men were particularly good at this!)

Diving became part of the Olympic Games for men in 1904, but it wasn't until 1912 that women were allowed to compete in platform diving. Women's springboard diving was introduced at the 1920 Olympics. (Bathing suits were knee-length with wide shoulder straps or partial sleeves. This was actually an improvement on earlier suits, which covered the ankle and were often worn with stockings.) In the 1920s two men, Ernst Bransten and Mike Peppe, came to the United States and shared the diving techniques they had learned in their native Sweden. They are credited with popularizing diving as a competitive sport in America. U.S. Diving is the national organization that governs the sport.

ABOUT COMPETITIVE SWIMMING

Swimming is a full-body exercise that affords you total conditioning. It's the perfect way to have fun and stay in shape, too. Competitive swimming involves racing. Swimmers race to improve their own times and to help their team to win. Therefore, you can say that swimming is a team, as well as an individual, sport. Boys and girls often practice together, though during team competitions, they swim separately: varsity girls, varsity boys, junior varsity girls, junior varsity boys. High school swimmers race in different events at swim competitions, called meets, with one or more schools. Swimmers amass points for their teams, and only team scores count in the competition. Individual times are kept, but only team scores count for meet competition.

Strokes

Races are held in four strokes: freestyle, backstroke, breaststroke, and butterfly. Freestyle means that swimmers can choose any stroke they wish; most use the crawl stroke because it is the fastest stroke. The backstroke is similar to the crawl, except that it is done by the swimmer on her back. The breaststroke is the smoothest looking and may even be the most relaxing of the strokes, while the butterfly is the most taxing and difficult because the swimmer has to propel herself out of the water with each stroke. A fifth stroke, the sidestroke, is not done competitively.

The *crawl* is the most efficient and fastest stroke, with the swimmer horizontal, face down in the water. The arms, used alternately, propel her through the water, while at the same time her legs kick up and down in a flutter kick. To breathe, the swimmer rolls her head to the side with the arm that has just pulled back and inhales, then exhales into the water. This stroke is most often used in freestyle events. Swimmers begin the freestyle by entering the water forward in a shallow dive.

The *backstroke* is begun in the water, with the swimmer pushing off backward from the side of the pool. The position is nearly horizontal, with the back of the head in a natural line with the spine. Ears are just about level with the water surface. The arms should alternate in an extending back and pulling forward motion. The legs kick up and down in a flutter kick.

In the *breaststroke*, the arms and legs stay under the surface of the water at all times; this creates water resistance, making the breaststroke the slowest of the competitive strokes. Some swimmers think it is also the most relaxing and smoothest stoke. The swimmer starts out on her stomach, with legs slightly bent. The arms stretch out forward, almost touching, and push outward from each other in a circular motion. At the same time the knees come up toward the chest, then the feet move outward in what is commonly called a frog kick. This is done repetitively, and the swimmer breathes in as her head and shoulders come out of the water.

The *butterfly* is the newest of all the strokes. Similar in some ways to the breaststroke (actually, it started out as a variation of the breaststroke), the butterfly creates far less water resistance and so is a faster stroke. It also requires great strength and energy because both arms go forward together, out of the water, then pull back under the water toward the legs. The dolphin kick, which is similar to the flutter kick except that the legs move together, is used in the butterfly. The dolphin kick, when done correctly, forces the hips to move up and down in a motion that mimics the way a dolphin swims.

Competitive Racing

In high school competition, mainly sprint and middle-distance races are held. The only distance event is the 500 yard freestyle. At high school meets the competitive events are held in the following order: 200 yard medley relay, 200 yard freestyle, 200 yard individual medley, 50 yard freestyle, 1 meter diving, 100 yard butterfly, 100 yard freestyle, 500 yard freestyle, 200 yard freestyle relay, 100 yard backstroke, 100 yard breaststroke, and the 400 yard freestyle relay. The 1 meter diving event is usually held in the middle of the meet; however, because of differing high school facilities, the diving events might be held at a different time and/or in a separate pool. There is currently a total of 12 events in a high school swim meet.

The 200 yard medley is the first event of the competition. In this race, four girls swim four different strokes. No swimmer may swim more than one leg of the relay (50 yards) and the strokes used are the backstroke, breaststroke, butterfly, and freestyle. In this, as in all relays, each swimmer must wait until the teammate swimming ahead of her touches the side of the pool before entering the water. The backstroker leads off the race, starting in the water; each swimmer to follow starts her leg of the race using a shallow dive. The other relay event is the 200 yard freestyle (or "free") relay, where four swimmers each race using the stroke of their choice. Because it is the fastest stroke, the crawl is used by most swimmers.

The 200 yard individual medley (IM) is similar to the 200 yard medley in that four strokes are used. This event, however, features one girl doing all four legs. The swimmer begins with the butterfly, changes to the backstroke, then to the breaststroke, and finishes with the freestyle.

In the 200 yard free, another individual race, swimmers can use any one stroke they want, usually the crawl. The 50 yard free is an all-out scramble from start to finish. The shortest of the races, it is to swimming what the 100 meter dash is to track. The 100 yard free is another sprint utilizing the swimmer's choice of stroke—as always, the crawl is a favorite. The 500 yard free is the longest race of the meet. It is an individual event where each competitor swims 20 lengths of the pool, and swimmers must learn to pace themselves. Some elect to swim at an even pace throughout the race, while others may "negatively split" the race, choosing to cover the second half faster than the first half.

Other individual events involve one swimmer competing in a particular stroke. The 100 yard butterfly is a sprint race of four pool lengths using the butterfly stroke for the entire race. Swimmers compete in the 100 yard backstroke and 100 yard breaststroke in a similar manner, using the respective stroke.

The meet ends with the exciting 400 yard free relay. Four swimmers utilizing their choice of strokes (usually the crawl), swim all out for four lengths of the pool. No swimmer may swim more than one leg of the race.

The 1 meter diving events, scheduled to follow the 50 yard free, can be rearranged by coaches' agreement. A dual meet event consists of a series of six dives performed by each diver, one voluntary and five optional dives. (See "About Competitive Diving.")

Starts and Turns

Many races are won by swimmers who have the best starts and turns. Starts and turns are practiced over and over again because they are so important. The beginning of a race is signaled by the starter, who uses either a gun or an electronic device. If a racer jumps early (a false start), the race is stopped and that swimmer is disqualified. The race is re-started with the remaining swimmers. A shallow diving start is used for all races, except backstroke. Many swimmers use a track start, whereby the swimmer puts one foot behind the other, with the weight on the back leg. This start helps gain better forward movement and hopefully decreases the chance of being disqualified.

Quick turns are essential to swimming a good race. In all events the swimmer must touch the wall with some part of the body. In the free-style and backstroke the swimmer may somersault as she reaches the wall, touching only with her feet. In the breaststroke and butterfly, the swimmer must touch the wall with both hands before executing her turn.

ABOUT COMPETITIVE DIVING

In high school competition, the diving event is held on a 1 meter springboard. There is no platform diving or 3 meter competition like you see during the Olympic Games. There are five different groups of dives that can be performed.

Athletes in regular league meets perform six dives: one voluntary (re-quired) and five optional dives. Divers and/or their coaches select the optional dives (one from each category—see below) that the athlete will do at each meet. A diving scoresheet is filled out before each meet and lists the dives they will be performing and the order in which they will be done. The groups of dives are forward, back, reverse, inward, and twisting.

- Forward dive, with the body facing the water, is performed with a forward approach
- Back dive, with the body facing the fulcrum or back of the board, is performed with a back standing takeoff
- Reverse dive, with the body facing the water, is performed with a forward approach with the body rotating back toward the board

- Inward dive, with the body facing the fulcrum or back of the board, is performed with a standing takeoff that is directed in toward the board
- Twisting dive, with the body rotating around the longitudinal axis can be performed with forward, back, reverse, or inward dives

Components of a dive include the starting position, takeoff, flight through the air, and entry into the water. All dives may be performed in one of three basic positions: straight, pike, tuck. Good body position needs to be maintained during a dive. In twisting dives a diver often uses what's called the free position.

During the high school season, the number of divers allowed to be entered in each event is limited, as it is for swimmers. It isn't until league or regional competitions when qualifying rounds are used that the winners (those with the highest scores) advance to the next level of competition. Five to seven judges are ideal for each competition, although at regular season meets three judges are commonly used. Judges award points from 0–10, at half-point increments, with 10 being the highest score. The judges evaluate the overall dive on the basis of technique and execution. In championship competition (league championships and/or regional competitions) 11 dives are performed to include a combination of five voluntary (required) and six optional dives.

Cory Reeder, high school diving coach, believes, "Diving, above all, is a mental sport. It's about focus and overcoming fear." Divers are often afraid of hitting the board or painfully slapping the water. Coaches help divers overcome their fears by teaching the different dives on dry land first. Learning leadup skills in order to perform the dives correctly on mats or in spotting rigs before doing them on the diving board builds confidence and allows girls to get over their fear of hurting themselves while diving.

RULES OF SWIMMING

1. Number of swimmers: There is no official limit to how many girls can be on the team; normally only three may be entered in each event at each meet for scoring.

2. Scoring: Each individual's race is timed in minutes, seconds, and tenths of a second; teammates' scores are added together for team score. The team that has the lowest overall score wins.

3. Officials: There are numerous officials including the referee, who is the official in charge; starter; place, stroke, and turn judges; timers, recorders, and marshals.

4. Lanes: Lane lines are used to keep swimmers from colliding or impeding another swimmer's progress.

5. The start: Races begin upon a signal from the starter. All races, except for the backstroke, begin with swimmers diving in from starting blocks; in the backstroke, swimmers line up in the water facing the edge of the pool and then push off backwards.

6. A false start occurs when a swimmer moves before the official signals the start of a race. The starter recalls the swimmers to restart the race and disqualifies the swimmer who false started.

7. Lane assignments: Team members swim in alternate lanes in high school meets.

8. Disqualification: A competitor can be disqualified from an event for reasons such as impeding or obstructing another swimmer's progress; appearing late to the starting blocks; misconduct, including abusive language or failing to follow directions; walking on the floor of the pool; finishing a race in a lane other than the one started in; using any equipment such as fins to aid performance.

9. No jewelry of any kind is allowed.

RULES OF DIVING

1. Number of divers: There is no official limit to how many girls can be on the team, but for scoring at meets, three divers is standard.

2. Scoring: Judges score each dive in points and half-points from 0–10, with 10 being the highest score.

3. Officials: A judging panel consists of at least three judges (five, seven, or nine for championship meets), diving referee, announcer, and scorekeepers.

4. The diving board must be horizontal and 1 meter above the water surface, the top surface covered by a nonskid material.

5. The preferred depth of the diving pool is 12 feet.

6. In advance of the competition, each diver must submit a diving scoresheet to the diving referee listing the description, position, and degree of difficulty of her dives and the order in which dives will be attempted.

7. Failed dive: A failed dive occurs for a variety of infractions and receives a 0 from the judges and/or referee.

8. Disqualification: A diver is disqualified from the diving competition for the following reasons: a diver does not attempt to perform the dive; the dives listed on the scoresheet are too difficult for that diver; the diver unnecessarily delays performing her dive; the diver exhibits unsportsmanlike behavior.

9. Mandatory deductions: The diving referee shall deduct two points from each judge's award for a violation of the forward approach or a balk.

TRYING OUT FOR THE HIGH SCHOOL TEAM

Many children learn to swim before they begin school. Some start even earlier. In fact, parent-child swim sessions are often held for toddlers and even infants! Swimming, or at least water play, is a favorite pastime for kids and adults. But most people only learn to swim the crawl or the sidestroke, and then just enough to keep themselves afloat and to cover short distances. It takes more lessons and practice to become skillful and ready for competition. If you have been swimming regularly through a local swim club or in a recreational program, like the YMCA, then trying out for the high school team will be easier for you. Swim teams can carry upward to 50 athletes in their varsity and junior varsity programs, so they need members. Depending on the high school program, you might be able to make the team just by showing up! In highly competitive programs, however, you need to be fairly accomplished and show up prepared for tryouts.

At the high school level, the swim team is made up of divers and swimmers. Often, team members will perform in both categories. But, if an athlete is really competitive, it's more likely she will concentrate on swimming or diving, not both. Swimmers and divers usually try out together.

The high school swim season varies. Most often it is held during the winter, but not always. So, the first things to do are to find out who your high school coach is and when the season begins. You can call or go to your high school office to find out the coach's name and leave a message that you are interested in trying out for the swim team. Be sure to leave your phone number. When the coach calls back, ask questions about the tryouts, what the coach expects, and the commitment you are expected to make as a team member. Find out when the season starts and when you should begin preparing for tryouts. Coaches will be able to give you pre-season training suggestions, and may even give you written instructions.

Fitness is extremely important in competitive swimming and diving. For that reason, experts say that in pre-season preparation you should work on increasing your overall physical conditioning. That includes cardiovascular, weight, and flexibility training. Because of the short season, it helps for athletes to come to tryouts in the best condition possible. Coaches say it takes valuable instructional time to get girls into condition if they are out of shape when they come out for the team. If there are too many girls at tryouts, girls who have not been swimming or doing other pre-season training are usually the ones cut.

INCREASING PHYSICAL FITNESS FOR SWIMMING AND DIVING

Running, or any sport that includes running, such as basketball, soccer, or field hockey, will build up your cardiovascular system for endurance. Bicycling is another excellent cross-training sport. Experts say any aerobic activity helps build cardiovascular strength and increases your aerobic baseline.

Weight training is also important to build up the muscles you need for swimming, especially in the legs, shoulders, back, and stomach. Divers should pay special attention to strengthening the legs, stomach, and back. You can take weight-training classes at a local college or recreational facility, or you can join a gym. Just make sure you get proper instruction in how to work out properly to get the most out of your training and to avoid injury.

Flexibility is also important. It is harder to swim or dive if your muscles are tight and your range of motion limited. Lack of flexibility can also cause injuries. Therefore, athletes must be limber.

ACTIVITIES TO IMPROVE YOUR SWIMMING SKILLS

Jill McCormick, high school swim coach and master swimmer, tells girls, "Swimming is the best way to get ready for the season." She advises them to take swimming classes at a local recreational facility or nearby college, join a year around swim club, swim laps at a public pool—anything that will get them working out in the water.

Try out different strokes. Practicing each stroke helps you improve that stroke and increases your overall familiarity with the sport. It also helps you learn which strokes you feel more comfortable with and the ones you might want to specialize in.

Individual instruction can help you improve by learning correct stroke technique. One thing that often keeps a girl's time up, no matter how hard she's practicing, is poor technique. Even a few individual lessons can help correct a problem you might be having or teach you the right way in the first place.

Activities to specifically improve diving skills are gymnastics and dance. Sign up for a gymnastics class through a local youth recreation program or a gymnastics club. Floor exercises help with flexibility and grace, both important for divers. Dance, especially ballet, is a good cross-training activity and one that strengthens the legs while it teaches graceful movements.

Watch competitive swimming and diving whenever possible. Unfortunately, swimming meets are seldom broadcast on television, except for rare and special occasions like the Olympic Games. But you can check with your local high school or college for their meet schedule. Go to local swim club meets; you can learn a lot by watching other athletes perform. Another way of learning is by watching video tapes. There are tapes about swimming and diving ranging from basic stroke instruction to interviews with elite swimmers to racing and diving events. You can borrow them at public or school libraries or purchase them at sporting goods or video stores. Another source is through the national governing bodies of the two sports: U.S. Swimming (719–578–4578) and U.S. Diving (317–237–5252). Both organizations have many video tapes, books, and other written publications available for sale.

MOST COMMON INJURIES AND HOW TO AVOID THEM

Compared with other sport participants, swimmers incur very few injuries. For one thing, swimming is not a contact sport. There is little jarring or impact to the body. Injuries, when they do occur, usually are to the shoulders and knees. Shoulder injuries are often rotation-related and can result in tendonitis and/or rotator cuff problems. Knees can also suffer from tendonitis and other repetitive-use-type injuries.

According to Karen Chequer-Pfeiffer, high school swim coach and master swimmer, poor technique is one of the major reasons for swimming injuries. She recommends that girls concentrate on improving their stroke technique by getting individual instruction. Talk to your swim coach about your problem, she advises. A majority of swim injuries result from lack of conditioning. Girls coming into the program who have not been swimming or working out sometimes put too much stress on underconditioned muscles and joints, and, as a result, injure themselves. Working on total-body conditioning before and continuing throughout the swim season helps to avoid strains and other injuries. One other area in which girls can get hurt is lifting too much weight or lifting incorrectly. Talk to a trainer about the correct weight-training program for you.

Cramping results from muscles not getting enough oxygen. The best way to avoid cramps is to improve your aerobic conditioning. Dehydration can also be a problem. Most coaches encourage girls to keep a water bottle at the side of the pool and to drink from it often.

For divers injuries most often occur to shoulders and ankles. Overuse and overtraining are the most common causes of injuries to the shoulders. The majority of ankle injuries are caused by landing incorrectly. As with swimming, overall conditioning and commonsense training can minimize the chances of these injuries. The chance of hitting the diving board—which many girls fear—is minimal, according to Brigid DeVries, executive assistant commissioner at Kentucky High School Association, and former university swimming and diving coach. "It seldom happens," she says. "There are very few injuries to divers under supervised circumstances."

WHAT IF YOU DON'T MAKE THE HIGH SCHOOL TEAM?

If your high school coach needs to cut swimmers or divers because the team is too large, and you are one of those she lets go, what can you do? You're probably unhappy and feel rejected. For the girl who has her heart set on swimming for her high school, not being able to can be a real disappointment. Make sure you talk to the coach and discuss your evaluation. Listen carefully, then ask how you can improve. One of the things the coach will surely suggest is that you get more instruction and practice your strokes before you try out again. Also, ask the coach for suggestions on other places you can swim, so you can continue to learn and improve.

Most swim teams have junior varsity programs, though the whole team usually practices together. So, if you do not make the varsity, you may be able to be on the junior varsity team. If there is no junior varsity program, you might find out how many other girls tried out for the varsity team and didn't make it. If there are quite a few, talk to the athletic director about starting such a program. Junior varsity teams not only offer more athletes the opportunity to participate in the sport, but also act as a training program for future varsity teams. Other opportunities to swim are through local youth programs, in public pools, and through health clubs and swim clubs. Volunteer to work at swim meets as a timer or other helper, or ask to be the team manager. Stay involved with the team and learn from watching. Another way of increasing your own skill is by teaching. You can teach children in swim classes, either privately or through a youth swim program.

Unfortunately, there are not as many opportunities outside the schools for diving instruction. Some YMCA facilities offer diving along with their swimming programs, and summer swim leagues may include diving events. Call U.S. Diving (USD), 317-237-5252, and ask if they sponsor a program in your area.

Training Tips for Swimmers and Divers

1. Work on increasing overall fitness through aerobic sports, weight training, and flexibility training.
2. Always do a serious warmup and warm down after you swim or dive.
3. Become aware of the clock; learn how to internalize time and pace yourself.
4. Commit to swimming and diving regularly.
5. Push yourself in practice, using good technique.
6. Swim competitively everytime you get in the water; dive as if in competition even in practice.

HOW TO START A HIGH SCHOOL TEAM

What if your school does not have a swim team for girls? If there is a boys' team, chances are there is a team for girls, too. But what if there is no team at all? How can you get one started? First of all, you need to survey girls at your school to find out if there is enough interest to start a team. If there is, let the athletic director know and ask how you can help get one started. Considerations for starting up any new sport are cost, finding a qualified coach, the availability of other teams in the area to compete against, and in swimming's and diving's cases, the need for a regulation-size pool. When high schools don't have their own pool, they usually rent a local public or club pool.

Because high school swim teams usually carry a large roster in order to be able to compete at the league level, it might be hard to convince the athletic director that there is enough interest. As with any new program, interest usually builds over time. Swimming and diving coaches, unlike many others, usually welcome novice swimmers and divers and are willing to instruct them in the sport.

If you do not get any satisfaction from the athletic director, you can take your case to the principal and even on to the district superintendent and school board. If you have to go to that level, it's best to enlist the help of your parents and other interested adults. Girls today have the same opportunity to participate in sports as boys and to share equally in funding, facilities, and coaching, according to Title IX, the federal legislation that prohibits sex discrimination in education programs. If there are enough girls to form a team, and especially if there is already a boys' team at your school, you should learn more about Title IX and make sure your school district is informed about it, too. If your school does not offer a girls' team, you have the right to participate on the boys' team. (See Chapter 1 for more about Title IX.) While you are pursuing getting a school team formed, you can swim at local pools or join a recreational league or a club swim team for year-round swimming.

OTHER VERSIONS OF THE SPORT

Synchronized Swimming

Synchronized swimming became a popular form of entertainment in the 1930s, but it did not develop into an organized competitive sport for women until the 1950s. While it is not a sanctioned high school sport, synchronized swimming is now part of the Olympics. In fact, in its Games debut in 1996, the U.S. women's team won the gold medal. In synchronized swimming, competitors are judged on their performance in a set of compulsory figures and for creative swimming routines performed to musical accompaniment.

Open Water Swimming

Open water swimming is a growing sport. It is any swimming done not in a pool, but rather in natural bodies of water. Originally all swimming was done in open water. In fact, the first Olympic swimming competition took place in the ocean, with swimmers battling nine-foot waves. Not a sanctioned sport at the high school or college level, open water swimming is mainly a recreational sport, though there are four national championships held through U.S. Swimming for serious competitors. Fans of open water swimming enjoy the natural environment of ocean, river, and lake swimming.

Platform Diving

While not done at the high school level, platform diving competition is held at the college level and has been an Olympic sport since 1908. In this version, a diver jumps from a rigid surface that offers no bounce. The most popular platform is 10 meters (about 33 feet) above the water. The water in a pool used for platform diving is usually 16–18 feet deep. Girls can learn this kind of diving on youth swim teams and in summer recreation programs or camps. In platform diving, athletes may take off from a forward, backward, or armstand position. While some divers prefer the springboard, others like the platform best because it is so high above the water and allows plenty of space and time to maneuver.

TERMS TO KNOW

Anchor: the final leg of a relay, or the athlete who swims that leg

Approach: in forward and reverse dives, the steps taken on the board before the dive

Back dive: a dive in which the diver starts at the end of the board with her back to the water

Cap: a latex or lycra swim cap to protect a swimmer's hair and cut down on water resistance from the swimmer's hair

Dolphin kick: a kick used with butterfly stroke where both legs kick up and down together

Drag: resistance in the water that slows the swimmer down, such as a loose bathing suit

Entry: the moment when the diver enters the water

Execution: combination of a diver's technique, timing, and form

Explosive breathing: a technique where air is blown out quickly and forcefully before the next breath is inhaled

False start: occurs when a swimmer jumps out before the starter gives the signal, giving her an unfair advantage

Flip turn: a tumbling turn, used by a competitor swimming the crawl

Forward dive: a dive in which the diver faces the water

Goggles: eyewear worn by swimmers to see clearly and protect their eyes from chlorine in the water

Heat: a race within an event

Hypoxic: a physical condition caused by an insufficient amount of oxygen taken in by a swimmer

Inward dive: a dive in which the diver starts in the same position as for a back dive, then rotates toward the board and enters the pool

Kickboard: a float swimmer holds onto while doing a leg workout

Lap: the length of the pool; 25 yards for high school competition

Leg: one-quarter section of a relay; a swimmer must touch the side of the pool before the next swimmer can enter the race

Long course: a pool configured for swimming with a 50 meter racing course

Medley: a multiple-leg race that requires a variety of strokes; may be an individual or relay event

Platform: a fixed diving surface that offers no bounce, high above the water and reached by a ladder or stairs

Propulsion: Moving through the water by leg or arm action

Recovery: when a swimmer's arms or legs have finished a propulsion stage in a stroke and are returning to starting position

Relay: a race with four teammates each swimming one quarter (one leg) of it

Reverse dive: a dive in which the diver takes off facing the water, then rotates backward toward the board

Short course: a pool configured in 25 yard lengths; the size of the pool used for high school competition

Split: a timed section of a race, for example, a 200 meter race might have four 50 meter splits

Split time: the amount of time it takes to swim a certain part of a race

Springboard: type of diving board used for high school competition

Starting blocks: blocks securely attached to the deck or end wall used for starts in all events except the backstroke

Stroke: a combination of arm and leg movements used by the swimmer to propel herself through the water

Stroke drills: various exercises done in training to improve technique

Takeoff: in diving, both feet must leave the board at the same time

Touch: the finish of a race

Touch turn: a racing turn used with breaststroke and butterfly

Track start: a method of starting a race with one foot behind the other

Transition: occurs when swimmer is under water during a start or turn

Twisting dive: a forward, back, inward, or reverse dive with a twist as part of the dive after the takeoff and prior to entry into the water

Warm down: performed by the swimmer to rid the body of excess lactic acid generated during a race

Warmup: performed by the swimmer before the race to get her muscles loose and ready to race

Windup start: a start used in relay takeoffs to build up momentum

NOTES

1. National Federation of State High School Associations 1998 Participation Survey.

2. National Collegiate Athletic Association 1997–98 Participation Study.

Chapter 7
Tennis

Lauren Clark knows the importance of a strong swing in the game of tennis. Photo courtesy of the Clark Family Collection.

"You're in the game all the time; it's not like baseball, where you hit the ball and then go sit down."

—Lauren Clark, high school player

"I love the individual pressure and the team enthusiasm."

—Ann Slocomb, tennis administrator and former player

"You can play and play, and get out all your stresses and frustrations."

—Laura Veazey, college player

"I can play tennis all my life. I don't have to be on a team to continue playing or to fulfill my need to be a competitive athlete."

—Becky Kliewer, player and college tennis coach

Tennis is an action-filled sport for two (singles) or four players (doubles). While usually played on an indoor or outdoor hard-surface court, tennis is also played on grass and clay courts. The object of the game is to hit the ball over a low net and within the court boundaries but to a place and in a way that the opponent cannot return it. To play the game you need an oval-headed, fiber-strung racquet, and a baseball-sized, inflated ball, plus a court on which to play. It takes a minimum of four points to win a game, with six games required to win a set; the player who wins the best two out of three sets wins the match.

Tennis is a sport in which you can participate your whole life. It is a vigorous, challenging game, and one that is fun to play. Girls as young as two or three can begin hitting a ball with a small, paddle-like racquet. Some women play into middle age and beyond, because this is a game that can be adapted to the age and skill level of its participants.

COURT OF PLAY

A regulation-size tennis court measures 78 feet long by 27 feet wide for singles play and 36 feet wide for doubles—a little larger than a volleyball court (see figure 7.1). Doubles and singles play take place on the same court, with two sets of lines defining the appropriate boundaries. Although the game was played only on grass originally, today the surface is more often asphalt or a synthetic surface, occasionally clay. A net 3 feet high in the middle divides the court laterally. Boundary lines

Figure 7.1
Tennis Court

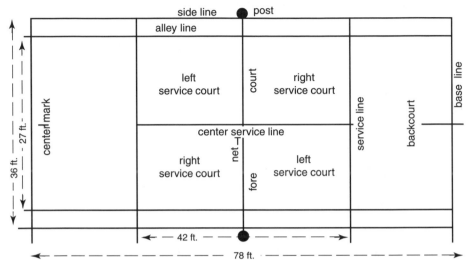

Source: Madrid Designs, Santa Rosa, CA

are considered part of the play. The ball is served from behind the end
line.

EQUIPMENT

A racquet, ball, and flat playing surface divided by a net are all that
are necessary for a game of tennis. For regulation competition, however,
the size of the court and equipment are specific.

Ball

A tennis ball is made of molded rubber, covered with a fuzzy fabric
(usually nylon-wool), and about the size of a baseball. The fuzz is there
to slow down the ball, making it easier to return the shot and to allow
the racquet strings to grip the ball, helping players to hit with topspin
or backspin. Tennis balls are usually optic yellow, which is thought to
be best for visibility. Balls in other bright colors, such as orange, green,
and fuschia, are also popular. Tennis balls are packed in pressurized
cans to ensure freshness and bounce.

Racquet

Before the 1960s, tennis racquets were made of wood and had a small face, or hitting area. Today's racquets are made of a variety of materials, including graphite, fiberglass, and a combination of these and other synthetics. Most are oval-headed and strung with gut, nylon, or other fibers. You can buy a prestrung racquet or have your racquet custom strung by a tennis professional with your choice of material. There are different size handle grips, and the racquet you choose should fit your hand correctly. Tennis racquets are traditionally 27 inches long.

Nets and Poles

The net is tautly strung, 3.5 feet high at the posts but only 3 feet high in the center. Suspended from a cord or metal cable held over two posts 3.5 feet tall and positioned 3 feet outside the center of the doubles side lines, tennis nets are made of a mesh weave tight enough to keep the ball from going through but wide enough to permit players to see the ball. The net is bound by white tape.

DRESS

Most popular attire for female players is the short tennis dress or a knit shirt and shorts or a skirt. In earlier times, tennis was a "stuffy" sport, with rigid, strictly adhered to dress codes, and everyone wore white only. Today, tennis clothing is often fashionably designed and brightly colored. While shorts and T-shirts are perfectly acceptable, for competitive matches there is still a standard for neatness and cleanliness that goes back to the earlier days of the sport. Athletic shoes, specifically designed for tennis, are essential and should be carefully selected. They should provide support, flexibility, durability, and a comfortable fit. They also need to have good tread on the bottom to prevent players from slipping and falling during play. Properly fitting socks are also important. They help prevent blisters and cushion the shock of the sudden starts and stops that are part of the game of tennis. Some players wear wristbands to keep perspiration from their hands and headbands to keep it from dripping into their eyes. Caps and visors are often worn to shield eyes from the sun.

A BRIEF HISTORY

The origins of tennis probably go back to prehistoric times, when people first used clubs to hit rocks back and forth. Lawn tennis became popular during Queen Victoria's reign, when it was played on the lawns of stately homes. The modern game was developed by Major Walter Clopfield Wingfield, an Englishman, in 1873. A year later, Mary Ewing Outerbridge brought the game to the United States, along with a borrowed net, racquet, and ball. So quickly did the sport gain enthusiastic acceptance that the U.S. Lawn Tennis Association was formed in 1881. The association later changed its name to the U.S. Tennis Association (USTA) and is still the sport's national governing body.

Smith College held its first collegiate women's tennis tournament in 1882. The school even charged admission: two hairpins (used to pin down the tape that outlined the court).[1] The national women's outdoor tennis tournament was established in 1887.

Tennis was an acceptable sport for women because it was not considered too strenuous, and costumes were appropriately modest: long, full skirts and long-sleeved, high-necked blouses. Also, because it was not a game of physical contact, it was allowed as a proper coed sport. Between 1923 and 1938, Helen Wills Moody won eight Wimbledon singles titles (the oldest and most famous of international tennis tournaments held in Wimbledon, England) along with numerous other honors, including the gold medal at the 1924 Olympic Games. Moody revolutionized not only the game but also tennis attire for women. Shocking the traditionalists, she played in sleeveless shirts and knee-length skirts. She is also credited with developing a more all-around physical game than had previously been in style.

Tennis was an Olympic sport from 1896–1924. After a long hiatus, tennis once again became part of the Olympic Games in Seoul, Korea, in 1988, where Steffi Graf of West Germany won the first women's Olympic tennis gold medal in 64 years.

Women initiated their own pro tour, as separate from the men's, in 1970. While the prize money was not as great as for male professionals, Billie Jean King, the world's number one female player, made more than $100,000 in 1971, the first woman in any sport to achieve that goal. Today, tennis is a way of life for female professionals. Their talent and hard work allow them to earn considerable prize money at tournaments held all over the world and to sign lucrative endorsement contracts with major companies. Once considered a sport for the elite, tennis today is played by women of all ages at parks, school yards, and other public and private recreational facilities.

HOW THE GAME IS PLAYED

The object of the game of tennis is to hit the ball over the net and inside your opponent's court. Quite simply, if you can do this more often than your opponent, you will win. Tennis can be played with two (singles) or four people (doubles). While the court used for playing both singles and doubles is the same, lines painted on the court distinguish the boundaries for each game. The lines count as "good," or fair territory, when a point is being played. Most high school tennis is played on a hard-surface, outdoor court. While there might be a few differences, rules are basically the same for high school competition as for college and professional tennis.

Before starting to play, the choice of ends and service is decided by tossing a coin or spinning a racquet. The winner may choose the right to serve first, the right to return service first, or the side of the court on which she wishes to start.

Play starts with one player serving the ball. The server delivers the ball from the right-hand side behind the base line and tries to serve it into the diagonal service box of the opponent. Two tries are permitted for each service. If the serve fails to clear the net and land within the opposing player's service box, a "fault" is called. A double fault (two failed serves) gives the opponent a point. Then the server begins to serve for the next point. After a successful serve the ball is hit back and forth until one player fails to return the ball, within bounds, to the opponent's side of the court.

Once the ball is served, players on both sides of the net hit the ball back and forth, or rally, trying to keep their shots in play and force an error on the part of the opponent. The ball can only bounce once before it is returned, or it can be hit before it bounces (except following the serve, when the ball must bounce before being returned). Play continues this way until one player fails to return the ball according to the rules of the game.

Scoring is the same for both singles and doubles. Each game begins at "Love" (0–0) and consists of at least four points, which are designated as 15, 30, 40, and Game. A tie at 40 is called "deuce." A game must be won by a margin of two points; games continue on if ties keep occurring. A player (or team) must win six games to win a set, but she must beat her opponent by at least two games. A tiebreaker is often used if a set is tied at 6–6. Tiebreakers are generally played to 7 points, and the victor must win the tiebreaker by at least two points. After the tiebreaker is completed, the set score is recorded as 7–6. High school tennis matches are two sets out of three.

Tennis is a physically and mentally challenging game. Like other sports, the more you practice and play, the better you get. Singles and doubles, while they are certainly similar, call for different styles of play and their own unique strategies. Teamwork and cooperation are essential in doubles play.

KEY ELEMENTS OF THE SPORT

Serving

Learning to serve the ball well and consistently is crucial, since service begins the play. The server gets two chances to serve each point, if necessary. If she double faults (fails to get the ball into the opponent's service box diagonally across the net), she loses the point before ever getting a rally started. So, consistency with your serve is more important in the beginning than speed or placement. The serve is tricky because it takes practice to coordinate your body stance, the toss of the ball, the correct positioning of the racquet, the point of contact (where the racquet hits the ball), the follow-through, and the recovery (getting ready for your opponent's return).

Ground Strokes

Ground strokes are shots you hit, or return, after the ball bounces on your side of the court. If you are right-handed, you hit the forehand stroke on your right side and the backhand stroke reaching across your body to the left side; left-handed players hit the forehand on their left side and the backhand reaching across their bodies to the right side. Ground strokes are hit with a low-to-high motion.

Forehand Stroke—You hit the forehand stroke with your whole body, turning sideways to the net as your racquet goes back, then shifting your weight to your front foot and contacting the ball at waist level in a position that is even with that foot. Your racquet face should be behind the ball and parallel to the net and your eyes should be focused on the ball. Another important part of the stroke is the follow-through, or finish, which completes the stroke and helps guide the ball to its destination.

Backhand Stroke—The backhand stroke can be hit with either one or two hands. The one-handed stroke is often used for a quicker shot and a longer reach, while some players prefer the two-handed backhand stroke for more power and better control. In either backhand stroke, you get ready by turning your body sideways to the net, pulling the racquet back low, then rotating your hips and bringing the racquet around until it is a few inches in front of your forward foot and at waist height as you make contact. As with the forehand, the backhand follow-through is important to guide the ball and finish the stroke.

Volley

A player using a ground stroke hits the ball after it touches the court once; the player opting for a volley hits the ball before it bounces. It can be hit from either the forehand or backhand side, with the player facing the net and hitting the ball with the racquet in a short, firm, punching motion. There is virtually no follow-through. A volley is most often used close to the net and is an attacking stroke, often used to finish a point.

RULES OF TENNIS

1. Number of players: Singles games consist of one player vs. one player; for doubles, a two-person team plays against another two-person team.

2. Scoring: Games are played to a minimum of four points, designated as 15, 30, 40, and Game. A tie at 40 is called deuce. A game must be won by two points. It takes six games to win a set, but sets must be won by at least two games. A match is the best two out of three sets.

3. Officials: Umpires are not used for high school matches. They are used in collegiate matches and tournament play.

4. Boundaries: For singles play, the court's inside lines are used and for doubles play, the outside lines are used. Lines are counted as part of the play. Therefore, a ball that lands on the line is in bounds.

5. Change of ends: Players change ends at the completion of the first and every odd-numbered game in a set. Players change ends at the completion of a set only if the score adds up to an odd number, for example, 6-1, 6-3, etc.

6. Serving order: *Singles*—a player serves for an entire game, after which service passes to the opponent, no matter who wins the game. The first point is served from behind her right-hand court and into the diagonal service court of her opponent. The second point is served from behind her left-hand court and into the diagonal service court of the opponent. Play continues in this manner, alternating with each serve. *Doubles*—partners decide between themselves who will begin their team's service. Each player serves an entire game, after which service passes on to the opposing team. Teammates rotate service; each player must serve in the same order for the entire set.

7. Service fault: If the ball hits the net, lands outside the correct service court, or is missed entirely when a player swings to hit the serve, it is called a fault. The player is given another chance to get the ball into play. If the second serve is also a fault (double fault), the server loses the point.

8. Let: If a serve is correctly delivered but touches the net before falling into the opponent's service court, it is called a let. A let serve is replayed. A ball that contacts the net and does not land in the service area is a fault, not a let.

9. Service return: The receiver must return the ball after it bounces and before it bounces twice.

10. Rally: A rally occurs when players hit the ball back and forth. If the ball touches the net and lands within the opponent's court, the return is good (not considered a let). A player can call a ball out as, or even right after, she hits it, though the call must be made before the ball is played by the opponent.

Tennis rules of etiquette are universal and are taken quite seriously. This chapter would not be complete without briefly addressing these "unwritten" rules. Because tennis is perhaps the only game which allows players to call the ball out or call a let ball, it is imperative that calls be made fairly and promptly. If you have any doubt as to whether a ball is out or good, you must give your opponent the benefit of the doubt and play the ball as good. While you are obligated to call the balls on your side of the net, you should also make a call against yourself if you can see the ball clearly on your opponent's side. It is also the responsibility of the players to keep track of the score. Therefore, to avoid confusion or controversy, the server should announce the set score before starting a game and the game score prior to serving each point.

Because there are usually several tennis courts in a row, when your ball goes into the next court or a ball comes into your court, you should wait until the players on the other court have completed a point before retrieving or returning a ball. Shouting, throwing your tennis racquet, disparaging your opponent, or any other disruptive behavior is considered poor sportsmanship and is not allowed. When a match is over, players advance to the net and shake hands before leaving the court.

TRYING OUT FOR THE SCHOOL TEAM

If you have played tennis before high school, you have a much better chance of making the team than if you are a novice. Unfortunately, many schools have only varsity teams, so younger, less experienced girls have to learn the sport outside of high school. Even if you are a player with some experience, the level of competition you will encounter in high school is probably going to be a step up from your earlier competition. If you make the team, only the top singles and doubles players actually participate in competitive matches, while the rest practice with the team and try to work their way up the ladder by practicing hard and improving their playing skills.

The best time to begin preparing for high school tennis is at least several months before tryouts. It takes that long to build up your physical conditioning and tennis skills. It is best, also, to do your homework in advance. If possible, talk to the high school coach. Introduce yourself and let her know that you are interested in trying out for the team. By doing that you will get a feel for what the coach is like, her personality and outlook. You can also get tips on what the coach expects from prospective tennis team members. Some coaches have written instructions about tryouts and ways in which you can prepare. Knowing these things in advance can give you a great advantage if you take what you know and apply it to getting ready for tryouts. Meeting girls already on the team is helpful. They can give you a good idea of what you need to work on and what the coach expects. They might also invite you to play and work out with them. In tennis, as in many sports, it is helpful to play against more experienced players, so playing with older girls or boys will increase your skills and boost your self-confidence.

If you cannot speak to the high school coach in advance (perhaps there is a new coach or he or she is a walk-on coach and is not available to meet with you), contact the athletic director at your high school. That person can give you information about tennis, as well as other sports you might want to participate in during the school year.

If you have not played tennis before or have very little experience, you need to put some time and effort into learning the game. City parks, schools, YMCA, and other youth organizations, as well as private clubs, have tennis courts. Usually while classes are in session, schools reserve their courts for students. But at other times, public-school courts are open to everyone. City parks, too, often have tennis courts. While the use of these courts is mostly free to community members, some levy a modest charge. You can use some courts on a first-come, first-served basis, while others rely on a reservation system. Rules (as well as your own common sense) limit the length of time you can use the court when others are waiting. Some youth organizations require membership before using their facilities. While private clubs generally limit use of their courts to members, they sometimes give clinics or put on camps that anyone can participate in, for a fee. Tournaments are often held in conjunction with recreation programs. These are a fun way to play, meet new people, and learn more about the game and how to compete. Also, contact the United States Tennis Association's national or local office for a list of tournaments, camps, or just for suggestions on how to get started.

Coaches say it is important for girls to focus on both fitness and skill training in preparation to try out for the high school team. Tennis is a strenuous game and requires conditioning to play with endurance for an entire match. Getting fit allows you not only to improve your performance but also to minimize the chance of injury. A complete fitness program for tennis includes exercises designed to develop stamina, agility, flexibility, strength, muscle coordination, and speed.

INCREASING PHYSICAL FITNESS FOR TENNIS

Tennis coaches recommend jogging to build cardiovascular fitness. A one-mile or longer jog, followed by wind sprints, is part of a typical tennis team's conditioning program. People rarely think of this, but moving backward on the court is a big part of the game, so it's helpful to practice running backwards. Paul Cash, high school tennis coach, has girls run a half mile forward and a half mile backward as part of his team tryouts, and he times them. Running and jumping rope are great for building endurance and strengthening your legs. A well-balanced fitness program that includes endurance work, flexibility (stretching), and basic strengthening exercises, especially for the upper body, will give a potential player a good foundation to be able to make it through an hour and a half to two hours at team practices and competitive matches.

"Play the game as often as possible," says Becky Kliewer, junior college tennis coach and player. "Play, play, and play some more! The more you play, the more you condition the muscles you use for tennis and build endurance." High school tennis coach Paul Cash says, "Be aggressive in trying to learn everything. Girls cannot be timid."

ACTIVITIES TO IMPROVE YOUR TENNIS SKILLS

Playing the game regularly and often is also the best way to improve your skills. Join programs and sign up for camps, junior tennis leagues, clinics, and tournaments whenever possible. Taking group lessons sponsored by your city's park and recreation department or other youth organization is often economical and a good way to learn or refine your game. The United States Tennis Association (USTA) runs camps and organizes summer leagues throughout the country and sponsors tournaments. The membership fee for juniors is minimal. In addition to playing in tournaments, members get event information and receive two monthly magazines that have articles and give tips about tennis. The USTA also has a library of videos and books. For membership information, write to USTA, 70 West Red Oak Lane, White Plains, NY 10602-5046, or call 914–696–7000. Their website is: www.usta.com.

Play with your friends, family members, anyone who will hit the ball with you. Have someone toss the ball to you; practice hitting forehands for awhile, then switch to backhands. Practice serving with a bucket of balls either with a friend or by yourself. A backboard or wall is a great partner. You can practice ball control by bouncing the ball on your racquet as many times as possible. Short sprints, running forward and backward, and doing slide steps on the court prepare and condition you for moving well in real-play situations.

Watch tennis being played, both amateur and professional, whenever possible. Professional tournaments are often shown on television. You can learn by observing these world-class athletes. Concentrate on their form and style, how they move, the way they position their body, and how they play the ball. You might turn the sound off sometimes so you can focus on the action and not be distracted by the announcers. Watch local high school or college matches. You will not only learn by observing but perhaps discover people you can play with. There are many books and periodicals about tennis. Look in your public library or book store. Watch tennis videos. They are often available to borrow from the library or to buy from sporting goods or video stores.

Taking lessons from experienced teachers or professionals can greatly benefit your game. While instruction can be costly, group lessons are usually less expensive than private lessons. You can find instructors through local tennis clubs, sporting goods stores, and through referrals from other tennis players. Play with as many different people as possible; try to play with people better than you are. It might increase your confidence to beat someone, but if you only play with people you can beat, you will not be challenged and your game will suffer.

Become an instructor. Sometimes the park and recreation department or a local tennis club seeks girls who know the game to give lessons to young, beginning players. This is an excellent way for you to work on your own skills, because as you teach someone else, you concentrate on doing things the right way.

The more you immerse yourself in the sport of tennis, the faster you will improve your game. Taking lessons, instructing others, practicing with others and by yourself, reading about tennis and watching instructional videos, attending local high school or college games, and watching professional women's games on television are all ways of preparing yourself for playing on the high school team.

Training Tips for Tennis

1. Build overall conditioning: jog, run wind sprints, roller blade, cycle, jump rope, train with weights.
2. Practice your strokes; rally with a partner and play the game regularly.
3. Play with more experienced players, boys and girls alike.
4. Attend clinics, camps, and local tournaments; take group or private lessons.
5. Watch and learn from the experts—both professional and amateur.

6. Eat healthy, nutritious food and drink plenty of water.
7. Keep it fun and filled with variety to maintain your interest and to avoid burnout.

OTHER SPORTS/CROSS-TRAINING

Sports that help you with tennis include softball and other throwing sports, such as the javelin throw in track and field. Becky Kliewer, college coach and tennis professional, says, "Tennis players need to be able to throw well. It's especially important to the serve." Other sports like soccer, basketball, field hockey, and track are helpful for endurance, speed, and quickness.

Participating in other sports is valuable for overall fitness and to prevent tennis burnout. While some coaches advise girls to concentrate on their major sport, most professionals agree that cross-training by playing different sports or participating in other physical activities is beneficial, both physically and mentally. Overtraining in one sport can cause injury and mental fatigue or burnout. So, try out other sports. You will improve your overall fitness, make new friends, and best of all, you'll have fun!

MOST COMMON INJURIES AND HOW TO AVOID THEM

Tennis is considered a low-injury sport. Mainly, when injuries occur, they are to the arms, ankles, and knees.

- Elbow injuries—tennis elbow, the inflammation of the tendon around the elbow joint, is fairly common. It is caused by repetitive movement, poor technique, and/or a tennis racquet that delivers too much shock when it connects with the ball. You can wear a pressure band on your forearm, which sometimes helps; but mainly, rest is recommended for healing tennis elbow. Once the pain subsides, you might want to have a professional look at your technique and racquet to help you prevent recurrence of the injury.
- Ankle and knee injuries—most common injuries while playing tennis. Running, sudden stops and starts, turning, pivoting, and

backing up all present the possibility of injury. General overall fitness is the best way to prevent injuries to the ankle and knee. Leg lifts can help strengthen quadricep muscles and muscles around the knee joints. Twisting an ankle by stepping on a ball can be minimized by clearing loose balls from the court.

- Injuries due to falling—during the fast pace of the game, players sometimes lunge for the ball, make quick stops, and turn suddenly, causing them to lose their balance. Increasing strength, flexibility, and balance helps to minimize falling.

WHAT IF YOU DON'T MAKE THE SCHOOL TEAM?

What if, despite all your advance training and preparation, you do not make the high school team? This happens, especially if you live in an area that has a strong youth tennis program. Some high schools may have a junior varsity team that you can play on, which is a tremendous advantage because you can improve your skills and get game experience, often with a coach who works closely with the varsity coach. But what if that is not the case? Undoubtedly, you are disappointed and maybe even angry. After all, you have worked hard and anticipated the fun of playing on the team. You may feel at loose ends. You may feel like not playing tennis anymore—or at least, not for awhile. Give yourself a few days, then look around for somewhere else to play and improve your skills. Be sure to ask the coach about your strengths and weaknesses, so you know what you need to work on. Ask also for suggestions about local instructors who can help you improve. Consider volunteering to be the team manager so you can watch and learn, and be part of the team at the same time.

You might also want to try a new sport or concentrate more on another sport you are already involved with. Perhaps another racquet sport would interest you. Racquetball is a vigorous sport similar in ways to tennis; it is played in some community recreation and health club facilities. Badminton is very popular and is a team sport played at the high school level. Investigate these sports and others. Maybe you will find another sport you can compete in, while keeping tennis as a recreational activity. Failing to make the tennis team could allow you to branch out and try something new, as well as give you the chance to meet different people and make new friends.

HOW TO START A HIGH SCHOOL TEAM

What if there is no tennis program for girls at your school? You can find other places to play, or you can try to start a high school tennis team. In that case, your first step is to contact your athletic director or principal and indicate your interest and desire to help organize a team. A question they probably will ask is: Are there enough girls interested to field a team? You might have to do your homework by asking around and making a list of girls who would play if there were a team. Another consideration: Is there already a league in your area that a new team could join? If there isn't, then it will be harder to make a case for starting a tennis team at just one school. But if there is, it should be relatively easy to get a team going. Administrators might ask you if you have someone willing to coach, perhaps a teacher on staff or another qualified adult from the community. They might also express concern about funding a new school team, but according to federal law, girls must be given equal opportunity with boys to play sports, and the lack of funding is not an acceptable reason for not letting girls play. (See more about Title IX in Chapter 1.)

If you do not feel satisfied with the results after you approach your athletic director or principal, you can take your request to the district superintendent and further, on to the school board. If you do this, it is best to seek the support of your parents and other adults. Usually, a strong show of interest in organizing a girls' interscholastic sports team at the high school is sufficient to get a program started. While the process is taking place, you could enlist the aid of a physical education teacher to help you organize intramural tennis after school. This would allow you and other girls to play while demonstrating that there are enough interested players to form a competitive team.

OTHER VERSIONS OF THE SPORT

Unlike some other sports, there are no real variations of this game. While tennis can be played on various court surfaces and the length of matches can differ depending on the type and level of competition, tennis is tennis. It is a universal game played the same way by elite athletes and recreational players, by young and old alike. Much of the popularity of tennis comes from the fact that anyone can play, wherever she goes, because the rules around the world are the same.

A LOOK INTO THE FUTURE OF TENNIS

Tennis will undoubtedly continue to be a very popular sport. At the high school level, it is the sixth most popular girls' sport, with over 151,000 participants.[2] More than 8,000 women play intercollegiate tennis on 852 teams.[3] Tennis participation among adolescent and adult women continues to grow. Part of the reason is the increased interest in women's sports overall and the expanded media coverage of women's sports, including tennis. The USTA is developing grassroots programs throughout the country to encourage new players of all ages to learn the game. A growing area of popularity is mixed (coed) doubles.

Opportunities for prize money at the professional level continues to attract ever greater numbers of players. Younger, developing players will continue to have the opportunity to gain necessary experience through future championships and Olympic Development programs. The increase in prize money (in less than 20 years the amount of prize money in women's professional tennis has grown from $5 million to a whopping $40 million[4]), the sponsorship endorsements, plus more and better tournaments encourage athletes to play the game of tennis.

So, whether you want to play for recreation, competitively at the high school and college level, or take it to the professional level, you can participate in the game of tennis from the time you are very young until well into your senior years.

TERMS TO KNOW

Ace: an exceptionally good serve that the opponent cannot reach

Backhand: a ground stroke hit by reaching across the body so the back of the hand swings out at the ball; can be one- or two-handed

Base line: the line on either end of the court marking the length of the court

Crosscourt: from one corner of the court to the corner diagonally opposite

Deuce: tie score at 40 points (40–40)

Double fault: both attempts at service fail to clear the net or ball does not land within the opponent's service area

Doubles: game played by four players, two players to a side

Doubles alleys: areas 4.5 feet wide on each side of the court used during doubles play

Doubles side lines: outermost lines on the court marking the doubles alleys

Down-the-line: a shot where the ball crosses the net close and parallel to a side line

Drop shot: a short, lightly hit shot that lands (or drops) just over the net

Fault: called if the ball is served into the net, or if it lands outside the opponent's service box

Foot fault: called if server's foot enters the court or touches the base line before ball is hit

Forehand: ground stroke hit on the same side of the body as the hand holding the racquet; palm of hand swings toward the ball

Game: four or more points, with one player scoring at least two more points than her opponent

Grip: the way a player holds the racquet in her hand

Ground stroke: forehand or backhand stroke used to return ball after it has landed in court

Half-volley: a low return of the ball just after it has bounced

Let: when the ball touches the net and then falls into the diagonally opposite service box; server is allowed to take serve over again

Lob: a high, soft return designed to land behind the opponent

Love: scoring term meaning zero points at the beginning of a game

Match: a term for a complete competition (best two out of three sets)

Match point: the point that, if won by the player who is ahead, wins the match

Overhead: aggressive overhead shot (often a return of a poorly hit lob) to put the ball away

Racquet: a lightweight frame with a long handle and string stretched across an open oval frame

Rally: when players hit the ball back and forth, keeping the ball in play

Ready position: the position of the body while waiting for a shot—knees bent, weight on the balls of the feet and ready to move in any direction, racquet held about waist high

Receiver: player who receives the ball from the server

Serve: stroke used to begin every point in a tennis match

Service box: the marked-off areas on the court into which a serve must land; a rectangle bordered by the net, the service lines, and the side line

Service break: when the receiver wins the service rather than the server

Service line: the line 21 feet from the net that defines the depth of the service box

Set: six or more games, with one player (or side) winning by at least two games

Singles: tennis played by two players, one against one

Singles side lines: the lines that define the sides of the court for singles

Sweet spot: an area of the strings in the middle of the racquet face; the best place to hit the ball

Tiebreaker: a play-off to determine the winner of a set tied at six games each; one player must win at least seven points and by at least two points to break the tie and win the set

Topspin: hitting low to high on the ball so that it spins forward as it travels

Umpire: the official who monitors a match, if applicable

Underspin: hitting high to low on the ball so that it spins backward as it travels (also called a "slice")

Volley: a shot that is used to strike the ball before it bounces

NOTES

1. Judith E. Greenberg, *Getting into the Game*. New York: Franklin Watts, 1997.

2. National Federation of State High School Associations 1998 Participation Survey.

3. National Collegiate Athletic Association 1997–98 Participation Study.

4. Women's Tennis Association Tour Publication, 1998.

Chapter 8
Track and Field

Runner Lindsy Johnson sets her pace for a strong finish. Photo courtesy of the Johnson Family Collection.

"You can always measure your results; you can't always do that in a team sport."

—Teresa Nelson, runner

"It's a no-fail sport."

—Heather Rosales, high school track and cross-country coach

"You can be last in a race but feel good because you made your own best time."

—Danny Aldridge, high school track coach and long-distance runner

"One of the very few sports that can accommodate just about everybody. It's a one-sport-fits all—all body types, sizes, and abilities."

—Ron Whitney, former collegiate runner and two-year college coach

"It's probably the closest I'll ever get to flying."

—Amy Bei, high school pole vaulter

"Half the fun is competing on different courses, in every kind of weather and terrain."

—Sara Bei, high school cross-country runner

Since the beginning of time, people were either fast, strong, and accurate with a rock or spear, or they fell prey to a hungry animal's appetite! Later, those basic survival skills turned into a collection of competitive sporting events, and today track and field athletes try to run faster, jump higher, and throw farther than anyone else. While track and field is itself a sport, many different events are involved, all of which are sports in themselves. In most cases, athletes compete in more than one event. Separating track events from field events makes the sport easier to understand.

Track events are running races: sprints, middle-distance, long-distance, relay, and hurdles. Field events are made up of the high jump, long jump, triple jump, shot put, and discus throw, and, in some states, the javelin, and the pole vault. While track and field is considered a group of individual sports, high school track teams practice and work out together, support each other, and travel together to competitions, creating a team-like atmosphere. Team scores are kept and team trophies are awarded. Relay races are definitely a team effort, with each

Figure 8.1
Track Field

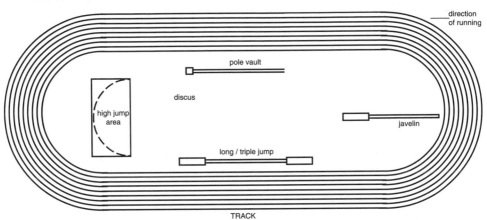

Source: Madrid Designs, Santa Rosa, CA

participant running a section, or leg, of the total distance. Relays, spectators report, are often the most exciting events at track meets.

In this chapter we will talk about outdoor track and field, although indoor track and field is also a sport at the high school level, particularly in some areas of the country. Approximately 394,000 high school girls compete in outdoor and 41,000 participate in indoor track and field.[1] Information about the indoor version of the sport will be included at the end of this chapter.

FIELD OF PLAY

Outdoor track and field events are held in football and/or soccer stadiums or outside facilities. The modern track is oval-shaped and has from six to eight evenly marked running lanes; most field events take place in the center of the track, although some are held outside the track area (see figure 8.1). Tracks have traditionally been composed of materials such as clay, sand, or dirt. But with the introduction of synthetic materials, many tracks are now made for all-weather conditions. Their springy texture allows athletes to run faster than on other surfaces and has revolutionized the sport.

EQUIPMENT

For most events, equipment is provided and maintained by the high school. Track and field athletes usually do not bring their own, except in rare cases. Equipment for each event varies according to the needs of that event.

DRESS

Clothing is made of lightweight materials and can be shorts and sleeveless jerseys. Warmup outfits, jackets and long pants, are important to keep participants warm before, after, and between events. Great care should be taken to purchase appropriate, well-fitting shoes for safety, comfort, and maximum performance. Athletes performing in more than one event sometimes require several pairs of shoes, depending on the events.

A BRIEF HISTORY

Considered the oldest form of organized sports, track and field was part of the first ancient Olympic Games in Athens, Greece, in 776 B.C. Thereafter, the games were held every four years to honor the god Zeus. Runners in the original Olympic Games, all men, wore helmets and carried shields, but competed naked. Women were barred not only from participating but from watching as well.

The ancient Olympic Games were abolished in A.D. 393, banned by Emperor Theodosius of Rome for political and religious reasons, yet people continued to compete in track and field–like events in Europe, sometimes in chivalrous or military tournaments. The birth of modern track and field took place in England in the 1800s. Eton College held a track meet between two of its classes in 1837, while Cambridge and Oxford universities sponsored the first intercollegiate track and field meet in 1864.

The Olympic Games were reinstated to promote international friendship through athletic competition, thanks to the dedication of Baron Pierre de Coubertin of France. Held in 1896 under the auspices of the International Olympic Committee (IOF), track and field was not the only sport at those Olympics. The games also included swimming and figure skating. The first race held in the modern games was the 100 meter, which was won by an American, Thomas Burke, in 12.0 seconds. Many years have passed since that day and many personal records and team triumphs have been recorded.

In the late 19th century, Vassar College started a track program for women, and in 1922 a group of high school and college women traveled to Europe to compete. It caused such an uproar that the American Physical Education Association decided to disband the sport in the schools as being too vigorous and "unhealthy" for females. It wasn't until Wilma Rudolph won three gold medals in the 1960 Olympics in Rome that track and field events made a comeback on the school athletic scene, allowing girls the opportunity to participate.

Today, as in ancient times, the Olympic Games officially begin when the Olympic flame is brought into the stadium by the last member of a team of relay runners who have carried it all the way from Greece. The summer Olympic Games, held every four years, and the World Championships (also held every four years, during the year before the Olympics) are the two biggest track and field competitions in the world.

HOW THE SPORT IS PLAYED

Track

High school track events are running races. They include sprints (shorter races, from 100 to 400 meters long) and middle-distance races (the 800 meter and the 1600 meter). The longest distance race in high school competition is the 3200 meter. Track events are held on an oval track. Races are run counterclockwise, with the athlete's left side facing the inside of the track. The winner is determined by the first torso (waist to shoulders) to cross the finish line.

Sprints

Sprint races (also called the "dash") and the relays are probably the most popular of the track and field events. The 100 meter, the 200 meter, and the 400 meter, while different in length and strategy, all have some similarities. Sprinting requires short, fast explosions of power, quickness combined with speed and stamina. While in earlier days, sprinters used to dig small holes in the ground to give them something to push off against at the start of a race, starting blocks are used today in just about all sprint races. When the official commands, "On your marks!" the sprinter places her feet in the blocks. On the command "Set!" the sprinter rises into a crouch, feet pressed hard against the blocks; then at the sound of the starter's gun, the sprinter uses that push and explodes from the blocks to propel herself forward and into the race. Runners are assigned lanes in which they must stay or be disqualified.

The *100 meter dash* is pure speed. The goal is to start out fast, try to reach full speed as quickly as possible, then hold the maximum speed to the finish line.

The *200 meter dash* is equal to one-half lap of the track. Runners have a staggered start, with runners in the outside lanes starting a little farther down the track to make up for having to run a longer distance around the turn. Since the race is not just a straight run, 200 meter runners have to keep up their speed as they make their turn and into the straightway.

The *400 meter dash* is perhaps the toughest of the sprints because it is four times longer than the 100 and twice as long as the 200, yet it is still a flat-out sprint requiring the runner to maintain top speed for one full lap of the track. This is also a staggered-start race.

There are two *relay* races, the 4 × 100, which starts the meet, and the 4 × 400, the very last event. Relays are often considered the highlight of a track meet for spectators. There are four members to a team and each girl runs one leg, or segment, of the race while carrying a baton—a smooth, hollow, lightweight tube. At the end of each runner's leg, she hands the baton off to the next runner. The two runners must exchange the baton within a specified area 20 meters long or be disqualified. The successful baton pass is executed smoothly while the receiver is running almost at full speed. Usually, the race will go to the team with the fastest speed plus best hand-offs.

The first *hurdles* used in a race were heavy wooden sheep barriers, nailed to a track and often dangerous for hurdlers. Modern hurdles are safer: a wooden bar supported by two adjustable metal stands. Like sprinters, hurdlers need to be fast and strong. However, hurdling also requires tremendous concentration, great flexibility, agility, and courage. There are ten hurdles to jump over in the 100 meter hurdles and eight hurdles in the 300 meter hurdles. While touching or even knocking over a hurdle during a race is not penalized, it does slow the runner down. So clearing each hurdle cleanly, and doing it as smoothly and with as much speed as possible, is the goal of each runner.

Middle-distance

After the sprints come the middle-distance races: the 800 meter and the 1600 meter. Athletes in these events must be able to run at a steady pace over longer distances, combining speed and endurance. Cardiovascular pulmonary strength and efficiency are the key to successful distance running.

The *800 meter run* is the shortest of the middle-distance races. It is close to a half mile. The 800 meter race is a two-lap fast-tempo run. It features a staggered start, and participants run in lanes through the first turn, then break for the pole (or try to run in the inside lane, because it's a shorter distance to the finish line).

The *1600 meter run* is approximately a mile long—four times around the track. It is the most famous middle-distance race, probably because of the "magical" 4-minute mile, which, incidentally, only three (all males) high school competitors have ever broken. It takes even more endurance and cardiovascular strength than the 800.

Long-Distance

The *3200 meter run* is about two miles and is a popular event among cross-country runners. Many cross-country athletes also compete in the 1600 meter run. Wholly aerobic, the race's greatest challenge for runners is to maintain cardiovascular strength and efficiency, to run with composure, and to finish fast and strong.

Field Events

Field events can be divided between throwing and jumping competitions. At the high school level throwing events include the shot put, discus throw and in some states, the javelin throw. Jumping events are the high jump, long jump, triple jump, and in some states, the pole vault.

Throwing Events

The *shot put* (putting the weight, as the shot, which originated at the Scottish Highland Games, was first called) requires great strength and agility. The shot is a metal ball that weighs almost nine pounds and is almost four inches in diameter. Shot putters must throw from inside a circle to a designated area, and only one hand may be used to put, or propel, the shot from the shoulder in a moving throw position. During the attempt, the shot cannot drop behind or below the shoulder.

The *discus* looks a little like a frisbee. It is about seven inches in diameter and weighs slightly more than 2 pounds. The thrower holds the discus flat, against her palm and forearm, then rotates her body in a circle to generate power before releasing the discus. The object is to throw the farthest within a prescribed area. Each competitor usually has six tries, or trials, and the best distance is the one counted.

The *javelin* looks like a spear and is usually made of wood or metal.

For high school girls, the javelin must weigh one pound, five ounces and be seven feet, 2.5 inches in length. The javelin competition takes place from a runway rather than from within a throwing circle for safety reasons. Essentially, the winner is the one who throws the longest distance. The throw is measured from the spot where first primary contact is made by the javelin.

Jumping Events

The *high jump* is made over a bar that rests on two upright supports. Jumpers run toward the bar, gaining momentum so they can lift themselves up and over the bar, landing on a foam material that cushions their fall. The popular style of jump is called the Fosbury Flop, started by the 1968 Olympic champion, Dick Fosbury, in which jumpers go over on their backs. The crossbar is raised after each round. Jumpers are given a maximum of three chances to clear the bar at a height. They may elect to pass a height and take a remaining trial at a subsequent height. If they fail to clear, they are eliminated from the competition, with their last successful clearing counting as their best height.

The *long jump* is sometimes said to be the easiest jump to learn because it is the most natural to perform. Jumpers start off behind a line, or mark, run as quickly as possible to build up momentum, and jump into a sand-filled pit. The long jump is measured from the takeoff board to the nearest mark the athlete makes in the sand upon landing nearest the scratch line. Sprinters often excel at this sport because the speed of the approach run directly affects the length of the jump.

The *triple jump* event takes place on the same runway as the long jump, but triple jumpers start from further back. It is a very complex and demanding jump because there are, like the name implies, three parts—a hop, step, and jump—to complete the action. The triple jump is measured, like the long jump, from the takeoff board to the closest mark made in the sand pit where the athlete lands nearest the scratch line. The emphasis is on speed of approach for this event as well as the long jump.

The *pole vault* is a very new sport for girls. In this event, the athlete uses a flexible pole to execute a leap, or vault, over a crossbar between two upright supports. Pole vaulters race down a runway carrying a lightweight, synthetic (carbon filament or fiberglass) pole that they plant in a box just in front of the bar. Their speed and body weight make the pole bend, and as the pole straightens, it carries the athlete over the bar. As in the high jump, the crossbar is raised after each round, and a vaulter remains in the competition until she fails three times to clear the bar, although she may elect to pass a height and take remaining trials at a subsequent height. The height she achieved in her last successful round is the one that counts.

Many officials are needed at every track and field event. Overseeing the event is meet director. In probably no other sport are so many volunteers needed to be starters, judges, timers, markers, recorders, and referees, as well as to help out with myriad other tasks that need doing for a track meet to run smoothly and efficiently. This is one of the few events where parents can really get involved by being a volunteer official.

TRYING OUT FOR THE SCHOOL TEAM

Most high school coaches say they welcome all students who want to participate in track and field. It is not so much a matter of trying out as coming out for the team. It seems to be the one sport where just about everyone can participate in some capacity. Still, it's a good idea to talk to the coach before the start of the track season. Many high school coaches go directly to the junior high or middle schools to let students know about their program. They tell the students about the different track and field events and invite students to show up and try any or all events that appeal to them. They also let interested students know what they can do to prepare themselves before the season starts.

If a coach doesn't come to your school, contact either the coach or the athletic director at the high school to indicate your interest and find out when the program begins. Track and field usually takes place in the spring, so you might even wait until the fall semester. In any case, it is best to start your pre-season training a few months in advance.

INCREASING PHYSICAL FITNESS FOR TRACK AND FIELD

If you plan on doing sprint or distance running, you want to start getting in condition and building your endurance. Many coaches recommend light running on a daily basis during pre-season. It is important to start out on soft surfaces, such as grass, dirt trails, or a good track and wear well-fitting shoes designed for running. According to Danny Aldridge, high school track coach and runner, athletes also need to work on weight training, flexibility, and body awareness. Girls can do this in a variety of ways. Aldridge says they should pick activities they enjoy. "You want to find something that's fun. If you enjoy it, you'll do it longer and more regularly."

Weight training should be started under the supervision of an expert: a physical education (P.E.) teacher, coach, or fitness instructor. It is important to get into an overall weight program that is designed especially for you so you can learn how to train safely and effectively. A program to increase total-body strength is best. For runners, exercises to build up the muscles around the joints are very important. Running during pre-season strengthens your legs, so make sure you work on strengthening your upper body in your weight-training program.

You can increase flexibility by stretching. Stretching is essential when working out; for track and field, it helps you in all events. Additionally, warming up and stretching minimizes the chances of injury. Many girls just want to jump right into practice and don't realize that stretching is part of a complete workout. Coaches that train track and field athletes recommend starting with an easy jog for the first ten minutes or so, then stretching. You can ask the coach for advice on which stretches are the most effective.

A body awareness program can be any activity that builds up your body and increases your sense of what it can do. Dancing is an excellent body awareness activity. Dancing builds muscle tone, teaches rhythm and balance, increases flexibility, and teaches concentration. Swimming is another activity that increases your confidence while it builds up your overall cardiovascular strength. Many coaches believe that just about all physical activity helps you in sports. "Do anything active," says Heather Rosales, high school coach, runner, and former professional cyclist, "Turn off the television!"

OTHER SPORTS/CROSS-TRAINING

Cross-training is not only good for overall conditioning and keeping active, but it also helps prevent burnout in your major sport. In addition to running to build up cardiovascular strength, experts recommend soccer, field hockey, lacrosse, swimming, basketball, and cycling as just a few sports that are beneficial cross-training activities for runners. In field events that require jumping, basketball and volleyball are particularly helpful. Gymnastics offers beneficial cross-training for pole vaulters. For throwers, other helpful sports are softball and basketball. Besides the cross-training benefits, you can have fun doing different sports. Not only will you stay in shape but you will meet and get the chance to interact with different athletes and coaches as well.

MOST COMMON INJURIES AND HOW TO AVOID THEM

Probably the most common track injuries are shin splints, pulled hamstring and quadricep muscles, and hip flexor and foot injuries. Besides these, participants most often suffer injuries particular to their specific events. Pulled muscles, injuries to shoulders, ankles, and hips are all more prevalent with field athletes.

Injuries can be reduced by warming up properly and thoroughly before you train. Experts emphasize the importance of warming up and stretching tight muscles before sprinting, throwing, or jumping. Taking the time to warm up adequately can make the difference between staying healthy and pulling muscles that can keep you out of the competition for weeks or even months. Cooling down after training is just as important. Sometimes you might be in a hurry and not want to take the time to do cooling down exercises and stretches. That is a big mistake. Most coaches build in time for warming up and cooling down during each practice or training session. When you are training on your own, you must do the same thing. If you wonder what exercises you should be doing and/or how long you should be warming up and cooling down, ask your coach.

Other injuries are caused by improper foot wear. Shoes are exceptionally important for track and field athletes. Because events are different, the shoes are often different. It is best to get advice from a salesperson who is knowledgeable about track and field shoes. Explain the activities you are interested in doing and let her suggest the right shoes for you. Another reason to seek expert help is to be fitted properly. Ill-fitting shoes can cause blisters and more serious injuries.

Poor technique can also cause injuries. It is important that you learn the right way to do a sport. That's another reason to talk to the high school coach in advance of the season. He or she can give you some tips on proper technique or suggest community programs or camps you can sign up for to learn how to do specific track or field events. It's easier to learn the right way from the beginning than to learn the wrong way, get injured, and then have to rehabilitate plus relearn proper technique.

OTHER PLACES TO LEARN AND PRACTICE

In many communities there are track clubs where youngsters can learn and practice with others. Track clubs often compete against other clubs, so you get the chance to experience running, throwing, or jumping against others in your age group. Most clubs charge a membership fee, and there could be additional costs, especially if you travel to meets in other areas. Check with your local park and recreation department and community youth groups, such as YMCA or Boys and Girls clubs, to find out whether they sponsor track and field programs. If they do, they are usually less expensive than clubs.

Private instruction is usually available for beginners and athletes seeking to learn more about particular events or increase their skills. Local coaches often provide private instruction for a fee. Ask your high school coach to recommend a good instructor for the events that interest you. For example, some coaches specialize in throwing events, while others are known to be experts in sprinting or long-distance racing. You can also ask at a nearby college or check with other athletes about private coaches with whom they have worked and can recommend.

Another valuable place to learn about track and field events, or to increase your skills, is at camps, usually held during school vacations. Check with local community youth organizations, colleges, high schools, and your local track club for information about track and field camps. Other helpful sources are track and field publications. There are dozens of magazines and newsletters that specialize in track and field in general or in specific events, and some advertise or list sports camps. *Track and Field News*, one of the most well-known magazines, publishes an annual nationwide listing of camps.

HOW TO START A HIGH SCHOOL TEAM

Because track and field can handle so many participants in the various events, most high schools have their own programs, or sometimes smaller schools combine to form teams. Therefore, how to start a high school team will not be discussed in this chapter. If somehow your school does not have its own team, you will have to look elsewhere to participate in the sport.

Training Tips for Track and Field

1. Strengthen your cardiovascular system with aerobic activities.
2. Build total-body strength with weight training.
3. Increase flexibility through stretching and other activities like gymnastics and dancing.
4. Avoid injury by increasing overall fitness.
5. Wear well-constructed, properly fitting shoes.
6. Drink plenty of fluids.
7. Warm up before and cool down after workouts.
8. Visualize your event and rehearse it in your mind for positive results.

OTHER VERSIONS OF THE SPORT

Cross-country Running

It may be misleading to refer to cross-country running as another version of track and field, because cross country is clearly a popular sport with more than 150,000 female high school participants.[2] Usually, it is considered a separate sport. Yet, for the purposes of this book, cross-country running is treated as part of track and field and is only discussed briefly.

Cross country is a fall sport, run not on a track, but on various terrains. Many courses wind through the countryside, along park trails, through fields and woods, and golf courses, while city streets may be the course, especially for training, in more urban areas. Maps are usually provided to runners, and before a race at an unfamiliar location, girls customarily walk or run the course. While routes are supposed to be marked clearly, some are not, so the map and an advance course walk help to minimize the chances of runners taking the wrong fork in the road and either losing time, or in some cases, getting lost altogether. In some races, course umpires are stationed along the trail to make sure runners stay on track. Most races are between 2,500 and 5,000 meters (1.5 to 3 miles) in length. The variance in courses—flat or hills—temperature, and wind factor, all make a difference in the way the race is run and in a runner's times.

The individual winner of a cross-country meet is the first runner to complete the course. Runners compete individually and as part of a team. Teams usually consist of seven, or even more, members, with the top five allowed to score for the team. Teams are judged by adding the points of each team member together. The team with the lowest combined score is the winner. In case of a tie, the sixth and seventh runners' points are counted. There is no limit to how many girls can train with a team. Often there are varsity, junior varsity, and even freshman/sophomore teams.

The loud pop of a starter gun signals the start of a cross-country race. When the race official calls out, "On your marks," athletes get in position and then take off from a starting line at the sound of the gun. Team members must wear team-issued matching uniforms: boxer-type or closed-leg shorts, sleeveless knit shirt (numbers on the chest are usually worn in invitational meets), and lightweight running shoes (sometimes called racing flats). No special equipment is needed for cross-country running. Warmup suits are not required, but many coaches believe warmups are important for keeping the muscles warm and for team unity.

As in track and field, both boys and girls usually train together, even if they compete separately. Many coaches place athletes in training groups according to their ability, not their gender. According to athletes that participate in both track and field and cross country, a sense of teamwork and camaraderie is more pronounced in cross country, and it is one of the things they like about it.

Indoor Track and Field

There are many differences between indoor and outdoor track and field. For one thing, there are fewer participants in the indoor version; only about 10 percent of girls taking part in track and field at the high school level do so indoors. It is the availability of a big enough building, like a multi-use facility or field house, that determines whether track and field is held indoors or outdoors at the high school level. Weather is a factor, and so there are more indoor facilities on the east coast.

While an indoor facility is larger than a gymnasium, there are still certain events that cannot be held inside for safety reasons, such as the discus and javelin throw. Other differences include fewer running lanes for indoor track, usually four compared to six or eight for outdoor; shorter tracks, less than one-third as long as the 300 meter outdoor tracks; and shorter races. The smaller indoor track affects racers because there are shorter straightways with many more turns to navigate than outdoors. So, runners' times are generally slower inside because they have to decrease their speed more often for the curves. Running on the narrower indoor track is more crowded; this sometimes results in injury, either from runners colliding or getting stepped on when racers are bunched together.

A LOOK INTO THE FUTURE OF TRACK AND FIELD

Track and field has a bright future, according to United States of America Track and Field (USATF) media information director, Pete Cava. "Track and field is a sport that women can compete in practically their entire lifetimes." USATF supports youth programs and competitions that anyone can enter at the local level. For serious competitors, they sponsor junior Olympic training programs and competitions for youngsters up to 18 years old. Call USATF at 317–261–0500 to locate the association office nearest you.

At the high school level, more girls compete in indoor and outdoor track and field and cross-country running than in any other sport, nearly 435,000.[3] Athletes who want to continue running, throwing, and jumping at the college level can do so at four-year and two-year schools, either through intercollegiate or intramural sports programs. For the talented and dedicated track and field and cross-country athlete, many colleges and universities offer sports scholarships. Over 28,600 women compete in indoor and outdoor track at the collegiate level, while more than 10,100 participate in cross-country.[4]

There are opportunities for the adult woman to participate in track and field events almost indefinitely, both recreationally and competitively. Masters competitions for women over 35 are held around the country, and many women who start running in high school continue to run for recreation, fitness, and competition throughout their lifetimes.

For the elite athlete, there are opportunities to compete professionally. Media coverage of track and field at the Olympic Games, the Goodwill Games, and the World Games have exposed more spectators to the many facets and excitement of track and field. Champions like heptathlon gold-medal winner Jackie Joyner-Kersee, who has been called the best female athlete in the world, are role models for the sport and encourage more girls to get involved.

All in all, track and field has something for just about everyone. It's pretty much a come-on-out-and-try-it sport at most high schools, and girls can find at least one, and usually more, events in which to participate and have fun.

TERMS TO KNOW

Athletics: another term for track and field; more popularly used in Europe

Baton: a smooth, hollow tube passed from the first runner on a relay team to the second, from the second to the third, and from the third to the fourth

Changeover zone: a specific 20 meter area in which the relay baton can be passed

Discus: a smooth, metal- or plastic-rimmed disc used in throwing event; distance wins

Disqualification: competitors can be disallowed from competition if they breach rules of their event

False start: when any part of the body is in contact with the starting line or running surface beyond the line when pistol is fired

Fun run: noncompetitive race; good for practicing, improving technique and stamina

Heat: a preliminary race to eliminate slower competitors so the final race includes the fastest runners

High jump: a field event; participant runs up, then jumps over a crossbar between rigid uprights; highest cleared jump wins

Hurdles: metal standards topped by a wooden crossbar, over which hurdlers jump

Hurdles races: runners must clear barriers, called hurdles, by jumping over them, then sprint to the finish line

Javelin: a spear-like instrument thrown for distance in competition

Lanes: the track is divided lengthwise into lanes; in some races, runners must run in the lane assigned to her

Lap: one complete counterclockwise circuit of the track

Leg: a portion of the race; in relay races, each team member runs one leg

Long-distance: the longest running races; the 3200 meter is the only long-distance race at the high school level

Long jump: competitors leap from a takeoff board into a soft landing area; longest jump wins

Middle-distance: running races; the 800 meter, 1600 meter, and 3200 meter

Photo finish: when a camera is used to differentiate runners who appear to cross the finish line at the same time

Pole vault: competitors use a flexible pole to vault or fling themselves over a crossbar between two uprights; winner clears highest raised crossbar

Relay: a team event in which four athletes each run a section, or leg, of the total distance

Shot put: a field event in which a heavy, cannon-like ball is propelled; distance wins

Sprints: short-distance races; the 100 meter, 200 meter, and 400 meter

Staggered start: each runner starts from set place on track to guarantee that the distance from start to finish shall be the same for each competitor

Starting blocks: rigid supports used to push against for a faster start; used by runners in the sprints, up to and including 300 meters

Starting gun: a pistol, fired into the air (with a blank, not a bullet), which starts a race

Triple jump: a field event; using a hop, step, and jump sequence competitors must leap into a sand landing area; distance wins

NOTES

1. National Federation of State High School Associations 1998 Participation Survey.

2. National Federation of State High School Associations 1998 Participation Survey.

3. National Federation of State High School Associations 1998 Participation Survey.

4. National College Athletic Association 1997–98 Participation Study.

Chapter 9
Volleyball

Teamwork is key to winning a volleyball game. Photo courtesy of Coronado High School Athletic Department.

"The mental challenge: it's sort of like a puzzle or board game."
—Jan Von Bueller, NCAA Division II college assistant volleyball coach

"I love the way the game is played. I love the strategy. I love the way that six individual people develop into a team. I love the camaraderie."
—Diane Campagna, two-year college head volleyball coach

"Volleyball requires exceptional cooperation in a confined space. The smaller court makes everything you do more magnified."
—Debbie Hunter, sports administrator and former player

"I love the camaraderie, the closeness of working together as a team."
—Julie Allen, college player

"The team concept allows players to contribute in the most minuscule or profound way—but everyone contributes."
—Kelly VanWindem, NCAA Division II coach and former player

Volleyball is a team sport offering great variety. It can be played indoors or outdoors on a regulation-sized court or in just about any open place: in a gym, at a park, or on the beach. The number of players varies depending on the game, with anywhere from two to four to six or even more players to a side. The only equipment you really need is a net and a ball. Just about everyone can play volleyball, from elementary schoolers to senior citizens, from first-time players to volleyball fanatics. Best of all, volleyball is an activity that can be participated in throughout a person's lifetime, and it is truly a sport for all seasons.

In this book, we will talk primarily about the indoor game because it is played in interscholastic competition at the high school level. For a bird's eye view of other versions of volleyball, look at the end of this chapter.

COURT OF PLAY

Indoor volleyball (simply called volleyball from here on) is played on a hard-surface court by two teams (see figure 9.1). A regulation volleyball court is rectangular, approximately 30 by 60 feet, and is enclosed

Figure 9.1
Volleyball Court

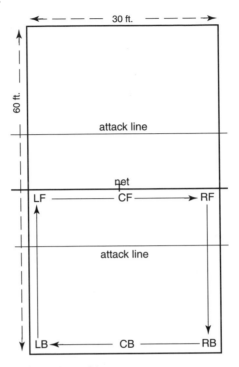

Source: Madrid Designs, Santa Rosa, CA

by boundary lines that are considered part of the play (if the ball lands on a line, it is in bounds). Each side of the court is a square (30 by 30 feet). A net divides the court in half directly over a center line and is stretched taut between two poles. The net height for women is a little lower (7 feet, 4⅛ inches) than for men (8 feet). The ball is served from anywhere behind the end line. Four volleyball courts could fit side by side on the average soccer field.

EQUIPMENT

A ball, poles, and a net are all that are necessary for a game of volleyball. For regulation competition, however, the equipment has strict specifications. A volleyball is like a heavy beach ball. Round and without laces, a regulation volleyball is between 25 to 27 inches in circumference and weighs nine to ten ounces. Most have a leather cover. The net is made of square mesh, with white bands on the top edge and along the side edges. Poles should be sunk directly into built-in receptacles on the floor a foot or two beyond the side lines. A multicolored antenna is fastened on the net directly over the side line to match the side line up through and above the net.

DRESS

Basic volleyball dress is simple and fairly economical, consisting of shorts, shirt, socks, and rubber-soled shoes. For competitive play, shorts and jerseys in team colors with numbers on the fronts and backs of the jerseys are usually worn. While long-sleeve shirts offer cushion for hitting and protection while sliding, some teams prefer short sleeves or even sleeveless jerseys. Shorts should be flexible and comfortable. The most popular shorts today for women are briefs with elastic legs. Volleyball shoes, probably the most important part of the uniform, should be selected carefully. Flexibility and strong ankle support for jumping, landing, twisting, and diving are important features to look for in a shoe. It is up to individual preference whether shoes have low, medium, or high tops. Mid-calf athletic socks are usually worn. Knee pads are worn to protect the knees when trying to play a low ball.

A BRIEF HISTORY

Volleyball is over a century old and an all-American sport! William G. Morgan, a Young Men's Christian Association (YMCA) fitness instructor in Holyoke, Massachusetts, gets credit for creating the game. In 1895, another relatively new sport—basketball—was popular. But it required too much exertion, too much physical contact, and too much time for the businessmen who came to the YMCA during their lunch hour for exercise. So, Morgan invented a game combining elements of basketball, baseball, tennis, and handball that has since become such a favorite. It is now played by over 800 million people worldwide, 46 million in the United States alone. Volleyball ranks second among participation sports. (The number one sport? Soccer.)

At first only men played the game, which was originally called mintonette. Soon women and girls began playing. The name changed to reflect the nature of the game and the way the ball was propelled, or "volleyed," back and forth over the net. Volleyball was originally designed as a hard-court sport, though it was quickly taken outside to be played on grass and sand.

Volleyball was introduced as an Olympic sport for both men and women (and the very first team sport for women) at the 1964 Tokyo Games; in the 1984 Olympic Games in Los Angeles the U.S. women's team captured the silver medal. The United States Volleyball Association, organized in 1928, is the national governing body.

It was not until 1970 that the National Collegiate Athletic Association (NCAA) held its first national collegiate volleyball championships for women. Two years later, when landmark federal legislation called Title IX passed mandating equal opportunities for women and girls in federally funded institutions, volleyball started to come into its own as a major sport for high school and college women.

Volleyball is the third most popular girls' sport at the high school level, with 373,000 participants.[1] Close to 13,000 high schools participate in interscholastic play, while many others feature the sport in their physical education programs.

HOW THE GAME IS PLAYED

Each team is composed of six players to a side: three in the front row (right front, left front, and middle front) and three in the back row (right back, left back, and middle back), with up to 12 substitutions allowed per game. The object of the game is to hit the ball over the net strategically so that the opposing team cannot return it. A point is scored when the serving team wins a play, either because the ball touches the floor on the opposing side or because the other team fails to return the ball.

Serve begins the play, and only the serving team can score. If the serving team fails to score, or win a point, the opposing team earns a side out and the right to serve. Players change position on the court, rotating in a clockwise manner when they begin their turn to serve. The first team to score 15 points wins the game, but they must be ahead by at least two points. For example, if the score is 15–14, play continues until one team wins by two points (17–15, 18–16, etc.). Teams switch sides at the end of each game. A match is concluded when a team wins the best two out of three or three out of five games. Volleyball matches last anywhere from one to three hours.

KEY ELEMENTS OF THE SPORT

Serving

Because every player rotates into every position on the court, all players end up serving the ball. The goal of the server is to get the ball across the net, hitting it or placing it so well that members of the opposing team cannot return it. Failing that, the server hopes the ball comes back over to her side weakly or poorly placed so that her teammates can return it decisively for a point. There are two main serves: the underhand and the overhand serve. The underhand serve is the easiest to learn and execute and is used mostly by beginning, recreational, or youth players. The overhand serve is more complicated and has many variations, taking practice and experience to learn and perfect. It is the most popular serve in competitive play. The different overhand serves offer power and speed and can be deceptive. Depending on the technique, the ball can be made to do unusual things, such as dropping quickly once it crosses the net (top spin serve), floating and bobbing erratically (floater serve), and the round house, a jump serve. The jump serve is the most dynamic serve. It requires a one- or two-handed toss, a jump, and a spike.

Passing

Passing is key to the transition from defense to offense. When the ball comes over the net, the first person to touch it (except when there is a block) is the passer. It is the passer's job to keep the ball in play and to get it to the setter, starting the offensive thrust. More points are lost on that first ball over the net than any other, so passing is extremely important. The most common and effective pass is the forearm pass. There are three hand positions used for the forearm pass, also known as the bump pass. Basically, however, it consists of joining the hands together and allowing the ball to hit the fleshy part of the forearms at the same time while using the thrust and position of the legs to direct the ball toward the target.

Setting

The setter is like the quarterback on a football team. She runs the offense, sets up plays, and determines who to set. She is usually a player with great coordination and physical skill and the ability to make split-second decisions. Teams either have one or sometimes two setters. Directing the height and speed of the ball consistently is what the setter tries to do. Her job is to take the pass from her teammate (the passer) and set it up in such a way that another of her players (the hitter) can effectively hit it into the opponents' court.

Hitting

The hit, or attack, is the final offensive skill in a play, when the player hits (or spikes) the ball over the net. It is used to place the ball out of reach of the opponents or to spike the ball with such power and speed that opponents cannot return it. It is perhaps the most dramatic part of the play and the one that most spectators notice, though a winning hit is usually proceeded by a good pass and consistent set, allowing the hitter to do her job. Hitters have options as to where they place the ball. They can hit with force and speed or use an off-speed shot. They can dink the ball over the outstretched hands of blockers or hit it around or directly at the opposing blockers, hoping that the ball will deflect off the blocker's hands and go out of bounds.

Before a game begins, captains toss a coin to determine first serve or choice of side. Play begins with the serve. For a serve to be legal, the ball must cross into the opponent's court after clearing the net. Players on the opposing team may contact the ball a maximum of three times before sending it back across the net. Play continues back and forth until one team wins a rally. An error by the receiving team earns the serving team a point, while an error by the serving team gives the opposing team a side out and earns them the serve. A point can only be scored by the serving team.

RULES OF VOLLEYBALL

1. Number of players: Two teams of six players are on the court at one time.

2. Substitution: A player may enter the game three times only, and she must substitute for the same player each time. Only 12 substitutions can be made in a game.

3. Scoring: A game is won by the first team to win 15 points, with a two-point lead. If the score is 15–14, play continues

until one team goes ahead by two points. A match is best two out of three, or three out of five games. Rally scoring is used in a deciding game: a team scores on both serve or side out.

4. Officials: There are five, including a first referee, second referee (umpire), scorer, and two linesmen.

5. Rotation: When a team gets the serve, team members rotate one position clockwise before serving and must be in position when the serve is contacted. Positions are numbered 1 through 6 with the position in the right back being number 1. Players cannot overlap teammates' positions.

6. Service: The server may stand anywhere along the end line to serve; she can jump forward into court after contacting the ball. If a player serves out of turn (or rotation), the team loses service and any points won during that service. Serving motion can begin when the referee blows the whistle. The server then has five seconds to contact the ball.

7. Contacts: A team can contact the ball no more than three times before sending the ball back over the net. Exception: when a player blocks an opponent's attack, that block is not counted as a contact.

8. Outside lines: These are counted as part of the court. Therefore, a ball that lands on the line is in bounds.

9. Switching sides: Teams switch sides after each game. Teams may choose to switch sides during the last (fifth) game after the eighth point; they must make that decision before the match begins.

10. Penalties: Certain actions can result in sanctions to a team (players or coaches), such as shouting at an opponent, addressing officials (except for the captain or coach), trying to distract the opponents, or other unsporting-like behavior. A yellow card is issued as a warning; a red card is more serious, causing the serving team to lose the serve or the receiving team to lose a point. Expulsion is given for extremely offensive behavior and the player is out for the rest of the game. A player must be substituted. Disqualification is the most extreme penalty, and the player is ordered from the playing area for the rest of the match.

TRYING OUT FOR THE SCHOOL TEAM

If you have played volleyball in elementary or junior high school, you have an advantage when you try out for the school team. Even then, the high school experience will be a step up. If you have not played the game before, you may have a difficult time competing against others who have. However, if your school has a junior varsity or freshman/sophomore team, you can often learn while you play.

The best time to begin training for the high school team is during the preceding summer or even earlier. Then you have at least three months to work on your physical conditioning and volleyball skills. Do some advance homework. If possible, talk to the high school coach in late spring or early summer. In that way, you can introduce yourself and let the coach know you want to play on the team, and you can also learn what to do to get ready for tryouts. Some coaches will give you a written list of what they expect players to be able to do, along with suggestions on how to maximize your chances of making the team. Also, ask girls already on the team for their advice. They can give you a good idea of what you need to work on and what the coach expects. They might also allow you to play and workout with them during the summer.

If you have not played volleyball before or have little experience yet want to play at the high school level, you need to learn, or increase your knowledge of, the game. In addition to schools, city park and recreation programs, YMCA, YWCA, Girl Scouts, and Boys and Girls Clubs often sponsor volleyball programs. Clubs and camps are other places where you can learn and practice.

Volleyball clubs offer girls as young as seven years old the opportunity to get basic instruction and game experience. With a focus on competitive play, clubs usually provide coaching, regular practices, and scheduled games. Find out if girls who are on the high school team also belong to a club team, and ask them for their opinion about the pros and cons of joining a club in your area.

Volleyball camps are a good way to learn a lot about the game in a short period of time. Camps are usually held during school vacations. As with clubs, sometimes camps for older girls focus on higher levels of competition. Call nearby high schools and colleges for their vacation camp schedules. You can also pick up a volleyball magazine at your local newsstand. These publications often list college camps and even rate them. If you know someone who has attended a volleyball camp, that person is your best source for finding out how good the camp is.

Most programs charge participation fees, which may vary widely. In your investigation you will want to look for the program best suited to you and the one that gives you the most for your money. In general, community programs charge a modest fee, while club volleyball and camps can be quite expensive.

Sometimes just jumping in and playing is the most important thing of all. According to Diane Campagna, head volleyball coach at Santa Rosa Junior College in California and former player, the best way to learn and get better at the game of volleyball is to play, play, and play some more. No matter where you play—at the park and recreation center, on the beach, in a pickup game at your local park, or in the backyard—you will learn something and build your skills and understanding of the game. While it might not be apparent to the casual spectator, volleyball is not just about hitting the ball over the net. Campagna says, "Volleyball is a game of strategy and teamwork, and the more you play, the more you increase your knowledge of the game and build up your skills." The more you immerse yourself in volleyball the faster your game will improve. Combined with playing frequently, taking instruction is important to learn the proper way to do things and to avoid bad habits. Other ways of learning are watching good teams play, either on television or by attending games in your area, and watching training films or videos of competitive teams. These films are sometimes available at your library or at local video or sporting goods stores.

Training Tips for Volleyball Players

1. Increase your overall fitness.
2. Get into a whole-body weight-lifting program.
3. Do drills and practice jumping to increase your strength and ability to jump higher.
4. Always warm up by stretching to prevent injury.
5. Find good players and coaches and learn from them. Watch, ask questions, listen.
6. Play with players better than you.
7. Play volleyball as often as possible.
8. Practice on your own; hand set, serve, and bump the ball against a wall.

INCREASING PHYSICAL FITNESS FOR VOLLEYBALL

Increasing overall physical fitness and working on your volleyball skills will give you an edge when high school tryouts come around, as well as minimize your chances of injury. Increasing your overall physical fitness makes you healthier and stronger. Aerobic training, while not a specific part of volleyball training, is important for strength and endurance. Jogging, hiking, cycling, and rowing are a few aerobic activities that you can mix and match to increase your fitness level, as are participating in other sports such as basketball, track, soccer, and swimming.

ACTIVITIES TO IMPROVE YOUR VOLLEYBALL SKILLS

Probably the best and most effective training is to practice playing volleyball. While sprint and weight training are valuable to increase overall fitness, defining the skills players need for volleyball and working on them are considered the most important part of training. At the high school level, the season is only about three months long. In this environment, skill and fitness training specific to what the players will be doing in games is the most successful. Volleyball is a game of quick stops and starts with lots of jumping and quick motions.

OTHER SPORTS/CROSS-TRAINING

Whether getting ready to try out for the high school volleyball team or working toward all-year-round fitness, you can benefit by participating in other sports. Karen Ricketts, high school coach and former three-sport college athlete, encourages her high school team members to play sports other than volleyball during the off-season. She thinks participation in multiple sports provides athletes with a chance to develop a broader scope of movement skills. "I believe high school athletes benefit from a variety of activities, rather than focusing solely on one sport," says Ricketts. Not all coaches agree. Some believe their players should focus on volleyball and urge them to participate in the game throughout the year. Other coaches side with Ricketts and cite taking time away from volleyball as preventive medicine for burnout.

Sports that tend to complement volleyball are softball, soccer, and track: softball for the throwing motion, soccer for foot movement, and track for throwing (javelin) and running. Since getting and then staying in good aerobic shape are important, keeping active and involved with other sports can help. Additionally, many coaches believe cross-training by playing several different sports helps prevent injuries.

MOST COMMON INJURIES AND HOW TO AVOID THEM

Soft-tissue injuries are most apt to occur among players who participate in this physically demanding sport. Ankles, knees, arms, shoulders, and backs are particularly vulnerable.

- Ankle injuries—Caused by landing on someone else's foot, landing off balance. To avoid: Strengthen muscles around the ankles; do side steps; frontward/backward hops; run lines as in basketball. Some experts believe high-top tennis sport shoes offer the most support; also ankle braces or supports can be worn.
- Shoulder injuries—Caused by repeated throwing, hitting motion. To avoid: Strengthen upper-body muscles. The triceps are especially important. Strengthen shoulder muscles.
- Knee injuries—Caused by constant cutting motion; patellar tendonitis; strained/sprained knees caused by landing more on one leg than the other. To avoid: Strengthen quadricep muscles. Strengthen muscles around the joints.

WHAT IF YOU DON'T MAKE THE HIGH SCHOOL TEAM?

What if you train all summer by working out and increasing your physical fitness as well as practicing your volleyball skills and still don't make the high school team? You are undoubtedly disappointed. You probably feel dejected and downhearted, especially if your best friend was chosen. You might even picture yourself going home alone after school while the girls who made the team are having a great time practicing volleyball and competing for the school.

First of all, understand that it is perfectly natural to feel this way. So, allow yourself to be disappointed, feel rejected, and, yes, even angry. Take a day or so to feel badly. Then it's time to find another place where you can enjoy playing volleyball, because isn't that the point of all this anyway? Work on your skills and techniques so that next year you can try out for the school team again.

What are your options? If there is a junior varsity team at your school, perhaps you can participate at that level. That gives you the opportunity to have the fun of playing for your school while you practice your game. Junior varsity or freshman/sophomore teams are also excellent training grounds for making the varsity team sometime in the future. Not only do the coaches of each team usually work together and have a common training philosophy, but the varsity coach will have an opportunity to follow you as you learn and grow.

If your school does not have a junior varsity team and the varsity team is the only place to play, you still have options. It severely limits the number of girls who can participate, but if that is the way it is, you can either look for somewhere else to play or try to form a junior varsity team at your school. As discussed earlier, there are probably recreational leagues, clubs, and camps in your area where you can play. Talk to your school's athletic director to indicate your interest in starting a junior varsity team, and offer to help out.

Another alternative when you have not made the school team is to consider switching to another sport or concentrating on another sport in which you already participate. Check out other sports available at your school; look around the community and maybe you will find a new sport that really interests you. Perhaps it is not a school sport at all but one offered through a local club or organization. How about taking up martial arts, inline skating, ice hockey, fencing, or bowling? What about horseback riding or any one of a number of sports that may not be part of your high school athletic program but one you could learn and might even excel in? In addition to experiencing a sport for enjoyment and exercise, you might well benefit in other ways by your participation. For instance, both fencing and bowling are scholarship sports at some colleges. So is equestrian. That means that you could participate in one of these sports and take it to the college level, even qualifying for scholarship assistance.

HOW TO START A HIGH SCHOOL TEAM

What if your high school does not have a volleyball team for girls at all? How can you get one started? The best place to begin is with the athletic director. Indicate your interest in having volleyball become an interscholastic sport and ask about the procedures for forming a team.

Reasons given for why some sports are not offered at all high schools are lack of facilities and/or coaching personnel, insufficient funding, no other teams in the area to play, and not enough interest by prospective players.

Usually, the argument of there not being enough interest is misleading. Obviously, if there is no volleyball team on which to play at your high school, it is difficult to gauge how many girls are interested. One way to find out about, as well as to increase interest in the sport, is to gather together enough girls to form a couple of teams for after-school, intramural play. You can solicit the services of a volunteer coach: either a teacher at your school who is willing to donate the time or a knowledgeable parent or college player in the area. Your format could be to practice several times a week, followed by games. By doing this you not only enjoy the fun of the game, but, by practicing and playing together, you build skills and enthusiasm and show that there is enough interest among prospective volleyball players to form a school team.

If despite your efforts to start a school team you are rebuffed by the athletic director, your next step is to talk to your school principal. If you are not satisfied by the principal's response, you can take your case to the district superintendent and further, on to the school board. If you have to go this far, you might want to enlist the support of your parents and others who are interested in your cause. You should also know about—and make sure your school district is informed about—Title IX, the federal legislation that prohibits sex discrimination in educational programs that receive federal funds. Title IX requires that girls receive the same opportunity to participate in sports as boys and to share equally in funding, facilities, coaching, and other athletic support. (See Chapter 1 for more about Title IX.)

OTHER VERSIONS OF THE GAME

Beach Volleyball

In 1930 the first two-man beach game was played in Santa Monica, California. Today, beach volleyball is played both for pleasure and profit. Recreational volleyball is popular at beaches and on man-made sand courts, while professional tournaments are held all over the world for both men and women. Beach volleyball was a first-time Olympic sport in 1996 at the Atlanta Games. According to some experts, beach volleyball requires its players to be in better shape than other games of volleyball because moving through the sand is difficult and increases the need for more endurance and power.

Grass-Court Volleyball

Grass volleyball began as a recreational sport and can be played anywhere there is a large, open, grassy area that is flat. Generally, the game—like the beach variety—is a two-to-a-side game. Four-player teams are also popular, with other variations possible. Six- or even more to-a-side teams are considered recreational. It is common to see families and other groups playing in public parks on warm summer evenings or on weekends. For more competitive players, grass tournaments are held throughout the country with considerable prize money awarded to winning teams.

A LOOK INTO THE FUTURE OF VOLLEYBALL

Volleyball has quite a healthy future, according to USA Volleyball's Director of Beach Volleyball and Grassroots Programs John Kessel, who says the sport continues to grow in participation and as a spectator sport. Kessel reports, "At USA Volleyball, we are seeing the strongest growth of the game at the junior and youth levels. For girls there are open and club divisions for each age—under-12 up through 18." Following that, there are national indoor championships held for women in open divisions and in all age groups from age 30 to 70 and over. In the outdoors, over-30s competitions for women are increasingly popular.

The excitement and success of both women's beach volleyball and indoor volleyball as Olympic sports are expected to generate more interest in the game overall. Prize money for men and women in the beach game is close to being equal, encouraging more girls to look at the possibility of playing professional volleyball. Meanwhile, the success of the indoor sport encourages the hope that a professional volleyball league, like women's professional basketball, will soon become a reality.

The opportunity to participate at the intercollegiate level is expected to increase as even more colleges add volleyball to their lists of interscholastic sports for women. In the latest NCAA participation study, over 12,000 women play interscholastic volleyball at their member institutions.[2] The number of scholarships continues to grow, as well, and increasingly high school athletes as well as players from two-year colleges are able to take advantage of their athletic talent and skills to help pay their educational expenses.

For the recreational player, volleyball can be a lifetime sport. Girls who begin playing around with a ball in early childhood can begin to really learn and play the game as early as seven years old. At the other end of the age spectrum there is an increasing number of senior women playing volleyball recreationally. In between, girls and women just about everywhere can play the game of volleyball in a gym, on the grass, or at the beach. Today, volleyball is played around the world, indoors and outdoors, recreationally and competitively. While skill, spirit, and strategy define the sport, volleyball is also a game for all ages and ability levels. Best of all, volleyball is fun!

TERMS TO KNOW

Ace: a serve that is not returned by the opposing team

Attack: the offensive action of hitting the ball

Attack line: a line 10 feet from the net that separates the front row players from the back row players

Blocking: preventing the ball from coming over the net by blocking the shot; slowing down the spike from the attacking team so that it can be set up and played

Bump: a pass used to receive the serve

Defense: resisting the attack

Digging: retrieving a hard-hit ball and getting it to the setter

Dink: a legal push of the ball around or over blockers

Fault: when the serving team loses service or opponents lose a point

Foot fault: when the server steps on the end line before hitting the ball

Foul: a violation of the rules

Goofy-footed: taking off from the wrong foot when attacking the ball

Hitting: sending the ball over the net, hopefully to uncovered spaces

Kill: any ball that hits the floor resulting in a point or side out

Offense: the attack

Out of bounds: a ball landing outside the court boundary lines

Passing: passers receive the ball from the server and pass it to the setter

Red card: a penalty calling for the ejection of a player from the game

Roof: a stuff block resulting in a point or side out

Rotation: clockwise changing of players through the serving position following a side out

Serving: getting the ball into play by hitting it over the net to the opposing team

Setting: placing the ball up in the right spot for the hitter

Side out: when the serving team loses possession of the ball and the opposing team gets the serve

Six-pack: hitting a ball into the face of the opponent

Spike: forcefully hitting down on the ball into the opposing court

Yellow card: a warning given to player by referee

NOTES

1. National Federation of State High School Associations 1998 Participation Survey.

2. National Collegiate Athletic Association 1997–98 Participation Study.

Chapter 10
Other Sports to Try

The thrill of racing downhill attracts many girls to the sport of skiing.
Photo courtesy of St. Lawrence University.

Table 10.1
High School Participation

Sport	Number of Schools	Number of Participants
Badminton	*396	9,084
Crew	34	1,008
Golf	6,579	**49,690
Gymnastics	*1,592	21,347
Lacrosse	509	**20,189
Skiing		
alpine	387	4,268
cross-country	378	5,070

*Includes some combined teams.
**Includes girls playing on boys' teams and boys playing on girls' teams.

Source: National Federation State High School Associations 1998 Participation Survey

Many other sports are played at the high school level. Some of the them—like badminton, crew, golf, gymnastics, lacrosse, and skiing—often receive less recognition than the sports highlighted in earlier chapters. On a national level, fewer girls are involved in these other sports and not as many high school programs exist. Sometimes, as in skiing and crew, geography is a factor in whether schools offer the sport. Or, as is the case of golf, the facility needed is very specialized, so a golf course must be nearby and available for use by the local high schools. In some areas, there may not be sufficient support for a particular sport to get a team or league started. Tradition is sometimes another factor. Lacrosse, for example, a popular high school sport on the East Coast for many years, has only recently taken hold in other areas of the country. Due to the overall growth of women's athletics, the interest in these other sports and the number of schools offering them has increased (see table 10.1). Gymnastics is the only sport mentioned in this chapter that has experienced a decrease in high school participation, although the sport is very popular and many girls participate in club and youth recreational programs.

Each of these sports will be briefly discussed here with pre-season and tryout training tips and suggestions on how you can get involved in your school sports program and those within your community. If the sport you want to participate in is not offered to girls at your school, you might want to try to get a team started. If there is only a boys' team, you are entitled under the law to try out for that team. (See Title IX information in Chapter 1.)

BADMINTON

Badminton is an immensely popular sport around the world, especially in Europe and Asia. Many people in the United States think of badminton strictly as a recreational game, yet it is also a highly competitive game of skill. In fact, some would say that comparing the sport of badminton to the relaxing backyard game is like comparing swimming the English Channel to splashing in the bathtub. At its competitive level, the sport is a physically demanding contest of both strategy and stamina. Badminton is the world's fastest racquet sport. The speed of the shuttlecock being hit off the racquet in top international competition has been measured as high as 200 miles per hour!

Badminton is played by two players (singles) or four players (doubles). Like tennis, badminton is a racquet sport. Rather than a ball, though, a projectile-shaped "shuttlecock" is hit back and forth across a net. Each player, or team, tries to place the shuttlecock in the other team's court so that it cannot be returned across the net. The game is played on an indoor rectangular court (similar to a tennis court but a third smaller) 44 feet by 17 feet for singles, 44 feet by 20 feet for doubles. A 5 foot high net divides the court in half.

Players wear shorts and knit shirts, usually in team colors, with badminton or volleyball-type athletic shoes. Badminton racquets are made of light-weight materials for flexibility and speed. They weigh a little over 3 ounces and are no longer than 27 inches. The shuttlecock (also called the shuttle, never the birdie, by serious players) is very unique, with 14 to 16 natural or artificial feathers affixed to a cork base, covered with a thin layer of leather or similar material.

Badminton originated in Asia as early as the 5th century B.C. Designs on ancient pottery indicate an early version of the sport used the feet instead of a racquet. The modern game was developed in India in the 1800s. It wasn't called by its present name until 1873, when England's Duke of Beaufort introduced the game during a party at Badminton, his country estate.

The first U.S. championships were held in 1937 and included women.

Badminton became an Olympic sport in 1992 with singles and doubles events for both men and women, and in 1996 mixed doubles was added, making badminton the only Olympic sport with a coed event. Today more than 9,000 girls participate at the high school level,[1] while in colleges badminton is being added and is considered an emerging sport, that is, a sport given special support to help it become established. (See more about emerging sports in Chapter 11.)

Before the game begins, a coin is tossed, and the winner selects to serve first, receive first, or choose ends (of the court). The game starts with a serve, and the shuttle is hit back and forth across the net until one side is unable to return it before it hits the floor or until there is a foul. Points are scored by the serving side only. Unlike tennis, only one attempt to serve is allowed, and the serve must be underhanded. The singles game for women is played to 11 points, while women's doubles is played to 15 points. A match is the best two out of three games.

Badminton is fun. You may be surprised to learn that it is a very strenuous game, demanding both agility and quick reflexes. To prepare for the high school season, a player needs to increase her overall fitness. Jogging, biking, and jumping rope are a few ways to build cardiovascular strength and endurance. Begin your training several months before tryouts.

Increasing agility and becoming quicker to respond are very important because players need to be able to stop, turn, change direction, and then take off again quickly. An exercise to help build this quickness is to have a coach or team leader shout out directions, like "forward," then after a few seconds, blow a whistle and have you change course. Directions should include forward, backward, and diagonal. Or sit or lie on the ground, then upon hearing the whistle, jump up and run in one direction until the whistle blows again and you change directions. Exercises where you practice sliding from side to side and playing games like basketball or tennis, where you use motions similar to those you use in badminton, are good ways to increase quickness and agility.

To improve your badminton skills, set up a net in your backyard, then invite a friend or family member to play with you. Call your local park and recreation department and find out if there any camps or leagues where you can gain experience. Seek the advice of coaches or other players in the sport. The more you can learn about the game, the better off you will be at tryout time.

The national governing body for badminton is the United States Badminton Association (USBA), One Olympic Plaza, Colorado Springs, CO 80909. Call 317–237–5646 for information about badminton in your area. The website is www.usa.badminton.org.

CREW

Rowing a boat has been a popular pastime for people all over the world for centuries. Recreationally, it allows people to be out on the water, surrounded by nature. In movies we see couples leisurely drifting on a river or lake, with one person (usually male) rowing the boat, while the passenger (usually female) lies back and trails her fingers in the water. But rowing is not only recreational; rowing, also known as crew, has been a competitive sport for over 3,000 years. Inscriptions on the tombs of Egyptian kings suggest that rowing existed as a men's sport as well as a means of transportation as far back as 1430 B.C. It wasn't until 1877, however, that a few women began rowing for sport at Wellesley College in 1877 and in a limited number of clubs and colleges soon after; it was strictly a recreational activity, intended to be healthful, rather than competitive. Women's rowing gained status as a serious sport with the formation of the National Women's Rowing Association in 1962, and in 1976, women's rowing became an Olympic event. Increased interest in crew coincided with the passage of Title IX in 1972, and colleges and some high schools and clubs began providing programs for girls at about that time.

Women's crew at the college level has grown steadily, though there are still not many high school programs. Figures show that just over 1,000 girls participate in high school rowing competitions.[2] More than five times that many women are involved in collegiate programs, according to the NCAA,[3] and scholarships are now awarded to young women rowers.

Sponsoring a high school crew program depends on a number of factors. One is geographical. Rowing takes place on a flat body of water: a river, lake, or reasonably protected bay. Not all schools have such access. Another factor is cost. Boats, oars, rowing machines, and other necessary equipment are expensive. Tradition is another factor: rowing has typically been an east coast sport, and while interest in women's crew is growing nationally, it is still more prevalent in the eastern part of the country. Sometimes girls can learn and compete at a rowing club or through a community recreation program, even when there is no team at their high school.

Rowing is a rigorous workout, utilizing the entire body. High school races may vary in length from 1,500 to 2,000 meters. To start up from a dead stop and row hard the entire distance takes enormous strength and precision teamwork. "Crew lets you push your body to the ultimate limit. Just when you can't imagine the burn getting any worse, your body finds more power. It's just you, the boat, and the water," says Monica Hilcu, high school girls' crew coach and rower.

There are two major types of rowing called sweep races and sculling. In sweep races, rowers use both hands on one oar. In scull races, rowers use one oar in each hand. Boats of different lengths are used, depending on the size of the crew. A crew can be a single rower, two-person (doubles), four-person, and eight-person. The four-person and eight-person crew consists of four and eight rowers, respectively, and a coxswain (pronounced cox'in), a nonrowing team member, who steers the boat and acts as race coach. The coxswain sits in the back of the boat and faces her teammates, who row facing backward. The coxswain is the only one who looks ahead. She guides her team both with a rudder and string system and a megaphone, keeping them informed about the location of other boats, how they are doing, and when to speed up their strokes.

Racing events, called regattas, are exciting for spectators as well as competitors. In each race, six boats line up at the starting line and take off when the official signals with a red flag. The first boat to cross the finish line is the winner. If there are more boats entered than available lanes, a series of elimination races is held. The fastest boats then compete in a final race.

To get ready for the season—spring or fall depending on the area—girls need to build up their cardiovascular systems and increase endurance. Coaches advise long-distance running, roller blading, bicycling, and swimming, along with other running-based sports like basketball, soccer, and field hockey. While upper-body strength is necessary for rowing, it is also important to have strong leg, back, and abdominal muscles. Before you start a weight-training program, ask a trainer or coach how to exercise effectively and safely. Many coaches advise using rowing machines, available at schools, recreation centers, or health clubs.

Rowers enjoy the sport for many reasons. "I love being out in the water," says Coach Hilcu, "especially in the early mornings. I like getting away from everything." There's a sense of camaraderie, as teammates synchronize their movements and oars to reach their goal.

If you like rowing in high school, you will be happy to know you can continue on after graduation. Rowing is a sport for life. According to the United States Rowing Association (USRowing), the sport's national governing body, there are age group, skill-level, and even weight-class competitions for just about everyone. Look into clubs and park and recreation facilities in your community for rowing opportunities or contact USRowing at Pan American Plaza, Suite 400, 201 South Capitol Avenue, Indianapolis, IN 46225, or call 1–800–314–4769 for information about programs sponsored in your area. The website is www.usrowing.org.

GOLF

The idea of hitting a small, dimpled ball with a knob on the end of a thin stick toward a tiny hole in the ground several hundred yards away sounds pretty ludicrous to most nongolfers, yet more than 26.5 million people of all ages in the United States play golf today.[4] Golf is played outside usually on lush, exquisitely landscaped courses, affording golfers the opportunity to commune with nature and get plenty of exercise (although carts are sometimes used) as they play nine or 18 holes of golf.

While golf probably had its beginnings as early as A.D. 400 when the Romans played a game with a bent stick and a feather-filled leather ball, it wasn't until the mid-1800s that the modern game was developed in Scotland. Women began playing early on; in fact, some claim that the world's earliest female golfer was Mary, Queen of Scots.[5] By the 1880s golf had crossed the Atlantic Ocean, and by the end of the century, the United States held championship competitions for both men and women. The first Women's Professional Golf Association, organized in 1944, became known as the Ladies Professional Golf Association (LPGA) five years later.

The number of girls participating in golf at the high school level has increased dramatically over the past few years. While there are also increasing numbers of girls' teams, many of the 49,690 girls currently competing do so on boys', or student, teams.[6] In intercollegiate competition, there are over 2,300 female golfers.[7]

Long pants (sometimes shorts) and knit shirts in school colors are worn by most high school golf teams. Shoes specially designed for golf are made of leather or a leather-like material with metal, rubber, or plastic spikes on the soles to prevent slipping. Many golfers wear a golf glove to protect against blisters.

Golf is a relatively expensive sport; there are fees for using the golf course (although golf courses sometimes waive fees for high school teams) and golfers must either purchase or rent their own clubs, as well as buy their own balls and tees (small pegs on which the ball is placed to begin play at each hole), unless the school provides them.

A golf course consists of 18 "holes," the playing areas from the teeing ground to (and including) the putting green. Courses are carefully designed with mainly grassy areas surrounded or intersected by obstacles such as sand bunkers or traps, water hazards, rough ground, and high grass to make them more challenging. Every hole is different, but each includes the teeing ground, a smooth, level area from which the first stroke is taken; the fairway, the mowed area between the tee and the green; and the putting green, the closely cut grass area surrounding the hole. A removable flag is placed in each hole to help the golfer locate it from a distance.

The object of golf is to get the ball into each hole (4.5 inches in diameter by 4 inches deep) using as few hits, or strokes, as possible. Golf is an individual sport, and each golfer's score is kept. The high school team score is made up of the top five out of six players' scores. Different clubs are used, depending how far the golfer is from the hole and the type of shot she is attempting. A "wood," a club with a head of wood, plastic, or light metal, is used for long shots. An "iron," with a steel head, is used for medium- to short-range shots; while a putter, a metal or wood-headed club, is used to play the ball on the putting green.

Golfers are expected to observe certain rules of etiquette and safety. Among them are:

- Play without delay
- Invite faster groups to play through (move ahead of you)
- Don't move, talk, or stand close to a player making a stroke
- Don't play until the group in front is out of the way
- Replace divots (clumps of grass you have dislodged during a shot) and repair ball marks on the green

Coaches recommend that athletes prepare for team tryouts in advance of the season. Kathleen Klawitter, professional golf coach, says walking briskly at least 30 minutes each day helps build the endurance necessary to walk an entire 18-hole course. She also recommends strength training concentrating on arms and legs, and abdominal and back muscles. A golf instructor or trainer can advise you about an overall conditioning program to help build up the strength in these areas, as well as the entire body. Pre-season training should include stretching exercises for flexibility and agility, important for golfers.

A novice to the game would be well-advised to take a series of lessons, focusing on grip, stance, alignment, posture, ball position, and club face. Experts recommend that girls take lessons from certified instructors. "The only connection you have with the club is through your hands," says Klawitter. "Therefore, it's important that you learn how to grip your club correctly." Other ways in which girls can learn about the game is though recreational programs or by watching golf on television. Instructional videos are also helpful.

The United States Golf Association is the national governing body for golf. You can contact USGA at P.O. Box 708, Far Hills, NJ 07931. Call 908–234–2300, or visit their website at www.usga.org.

GYMNASTICS

Gymnastics combines the thrill of tumbling and acrobatics with the grace of dancing. Artistic gymnastics, the form of the sport most familiar to fans, is performed at the junior and senior high school levels. While many sports require participants to concentrate on doing one or two things really well, in gymnastics there are a series of events, using distinctly different skills. So, in a sense, the gymnast has to be good at everything.

Gymnastics competition takes place in a gymnasium, that is, an indoor activity center. As in track, several events might be taking place at once. Gymnastics competitions, called "meets," feature four events: the side horse vault, uneven parallel bars, balance beam, and floor exercise.

In the vault event girls perform acrobatic moves while jumping, or vaulting, over a padded piece of equipment called a vaulting horse. The gymnast starts by sprinting down a runway, then jumping or hurdling onto a springboard that launches her into the air and onto the top of the horse. She momentarily places her hands on the horse and pushes off before vaulting over it to land on the other side.

The uneven bars, two wooden/fiberglass bars connected by adjustable supports (one bar is 7 feet 9 inches high; the other is 5 feet 2 inches high) calls for strength, concentration, and split-second timing as the athlete swings back and forth, over, around, and between the bars in a routine that usually lasts less than 30 seconds.

The balance beam is 15 feet long, 4 feet high, and only 4 inches wide. On it, athletes perform many difficult moves, including running steps, jumps and leaps, turns, and tumbling. The most experienced gymnasts use their advanced skills to perform front and back handsprings and aerial moves.

The floor exercise event is tumbling combined with dance, and it is performed to music. Gymnasts use strength, flexibility, and balance, along with artistic expression for their floor exercise routine, performed on a 40 foot square mat. Each routine lasts between 60 and 90 seconds.

Gymnasts wear one-piece leotards in a variety of colors. They perform either barefooted or wearing specialized gymnastics footwear. Special grips are worn on their hands when performing on the uneven bars to protect hands from blisters and to help keep a firm grip.

Gymnastics is not a new sport. In fact, it has been in existence for more than 2,000 years, as discovered on ancient pottery and paintings that depict athletes running, jumping, and tumbling. During the 17th century, gymnastics was more entertainment than sport, however, and wandering acrobats often jumped through hoops, leaped over obstacles, did flips and somersaults, and even juggled to amuse audiences. It wasn't until the late 1800s that gymnastics developed into a popular competitive event, with men's gymnastics being one of the original sports in the first modern Olympic Games, held in Athens, Greece, in 1896.

While the first women's gymnastics class was held in Mt. Holyoke, Massachusetts, in 1862, it wasn't until 1928 that women first competed in the Olympics at Amsterdam, and then only in the all-around team competition and not on current-day equipment. They did not compete in individual events until the 1952 Games. Women's gymnastics since then has evolved into a sport combining physical strength, grace, and precise form.

High school gymnastics came into existence mostly due to public demand and by the passage of Title IX in 1972. Schools looking for ways to provide sports for girls added gymnastics, because many young girls, after watching the Olympics on television, wanted to be gymnasts. For a decade, gymnastics flourished in the schools, with almost 65,000 girls involved at the high school level during the 1981–82 school year, making it one of the top ten high school sports for girls. Since then, participation has decreased, and today there are fewer than 22,000 girls participating in high schools nationwide. According to Susan True, assistant director of the National Federation of State High School Associations (NFHS), cost of equipment, lack of qualified coaching, cost of insurance, and competition from other sports all play a part in the declining participation. "Artistic gymnastics [the events of uneven parallel bars, balance beam, vault, and floor exercise] is a sport demanding complex motor skills. Coaches must have a knowledge of highly technical skills, and safety considerations require a small athlete-to-coach ratio. Therefore, teams are small, yet the space requirements are large and the equipment expensive. Still, the combination of dance, artistic expression, and athleticism attracts a certain group of young women to the sport," says True. At the college level, there are more than 1,300 female gymnasts.[8] This number, too, has decreased.

Gymnastics is great fun for the very youngest toddlers, who start out jumping, rolling, and somersaulting. Most girls, at whatever age they start, usually take group lessons at a gymnastics club or other local youth program, such as the YMCA or a community recreation center. As girls continue in gymnastics, they stay with a club program because they can practice and perform all year round. "I love swinging up and over the bars and flipping through the air. It feels like I'm flying," says club gymnast Tory Moreno. In her area, there is no high school program.

If your high school does have a gymnastics program, and you want to try out for it, coaches say it is advantageous to take some lessons in advance to learn the fundamentals. While some schools welcome beginners, in others, particularly if your high school has a fairly competitive program, you will be at a disadvantage if you are totally inexperienced. High school coaches say girls should work on their overall fitness level to increase strength and flexibility. While gymnastics is an anaerobic sport, cardiovascular training, such as running, jumping rope, bicycling, and inline skating, help to raise your general fitness level. A weight-training program that focuses on strengthening the upper body, particularly the arms, shoulders, and back, is helpful but should only be done under the supervision of a qualified instructor. Gymnastics is movement specific, so an overall program should include climbing, swinging, and pulling exercises. Flexibility is extremely important, and stretching before a workout loosens up tight muscles and increases oxygen and blood flow. However, to truly increase flexibility, stretching exercises should be repeated at the end of a workout when the muscles are already warmed up.

Another form of gymnastics is rhythmic gymnastics, which some sports experts say is the sport of the future in the schools. Rhythmic gymnastics combines gymnastics techniques and dance-like movements, only instead of the equipment used in artistic gymnastics, athletes use a ball, hoop, rope, clubs, or ribbons in their routines. Other variations of the sport include general gymnastics and sports acrobatics.

USA Gymnastics is the national governing body for the sport under the United States Olympic Committee. For more information about gymnastics, write to USAG, Pan American Plaza, Suite 300, 201 S. Capitol Avenue, Indianapolis, IN, or call 1–800–345–4719. The website is www.usa-gymnastics.org.

LACROSSE

Lacrosse is exciting, fast-paced, and high-scoring. The women's game combines speed, agility, and creativity. It is very different from the men's game, using more finesse and less physical contact. Two teams of 12 players each compete outdoors on a rectangular field, a little longer than a football field, with goal cages at either end. The object of the game is to shoot the ball past the goalkeeper into the net for a score; each score, or goal, counts as one point. The game is practically nonstop, and players run around the field, using a stick (called a crosse) with a pocket on the end to carry (cradle), pass, and shoot the ball in the air.

Lacrosse is the oldest North American sport. Invented and played by American Indians before Christopher Columbus landed in the New World in 1492, and called "baggataway," the stick and ball game was rough and strenuous. Often used as a training exercise for war, it was frequently violent, and many disputes between tribes were settled by contests that would last for days and include hundreds of players. French Canadians, who took up the game, gave it a new name. They thought the stick the Indians used looked like a bishop's long, hooked staff called a "crosse" in French; hence, the name "lacrosse."

The first known women's game was played in 1886, although it wasn't until the early 1900s when a separate set of rules was developed for women, removing much of the roughness by the elimination of body checking. In 1926, Rosabelle Sinclair, the first woman to be inducted into the Lacrosse Hall of Fame, introduced the game to Bryn Mawr College and clubs and high schools in the Baltimore area. The United States Women's Lacrosse Association (USWLA) was founded in 1931 and was in existence until 1998, when it became part of United States Lacrosse (USL), the sport's national governing body. Today, over 4,000 athletes compete in lacrosse at the college level,[9] while more than 20,000 play in the nation's high schools.[10] Lacrosse is not an Olympic sport, and the highest form of competition is the World Cup Championship, held every four years.

Lacrosse games are divided into two 25-minute halves, with overtime periods of six minutes each used in case of a tie at the end of regulation play. Players wear kilts (short skirts) and long or short sleeve shirts. Athletic shoes with rubber cleats on the bottom help players run and turn without slipping on the grass. The goalkeeper, who stands in the path of hard-hit shots, requires extra protection and wears a helmet with a face mask, body pad, neckguard, chest protector, and mouthguard. Thigh pads and shin guards are optional.

The stick, or crosse, is a wooden, aluminum, or plastic stick (from 35.5 to 42.5 inches long) with a pocket woven with leather or synthetic thongs. Sticks come in various sizes to fit the individual and her position, and should be chosen carefully. A lacrosse ball, 8 inches in circumference, is made of hard rubber. Goal cages are pyramid-shaped, 6 feet across the goal front and 6 feet high.

As in other field sports, like soccer and field hockey, there are offensive players who try to get the ball into the other team's goal and defensive players who try to keep the opposing team from scoring. Midfielders are players who are both offensive and defensive, running back and forth the length of the field. Unlike in soccer and field hockey, where the ball is mainly moved on the ground, in lacrosse players move the ball in the air, from the basket of the crosse.

The game begins with a draw, with two opposing players standing in a circle in the middle of the field, with their sticks held horizontal to the ground and the ball held between the two stick heads. When the referee blows the whistle, each girl attempts to direct the ball to a teammate. All other players must be outside of the center circle. There are no pre-set field boundaries; rather, at the beginning of the game, coaches limit the size of the field based on natural boundaries, such as trees, bleachers, or rocky outcroppings.

Play is nonstop except for goals, fouls, and timeouts. When the ball goes out of bounds or a foul occurs during a game, play is stopped and each player remains where she is until the referee blows the whistle to resume play. All scoring shots must be made from outside the circle surrounding the goal cage, called the crease.

Preparing to try out for the high school lacrosse team is similar to getting in shape for any sport that involves considerable running. Girls who work out in advance of the season by running, lifting weights, and practicing individual stick work have a better chance of making the team than someone who comes unprepared. Participation in other sports, such as basketball, soccer, and field hockey, is helpful. If you already know how to play lacrosse, you have an advantage. Beth Stone, lacrosse coach and physical education instructor, however, encourages girls without experience to come out. She says, "If a girl is already an athlete, I can make her into a lacrosse player!"

Lacrosse is a sport growing in popularity at the high school level, but not all schools have teams. Check with your local community park and recreation department or youth organizations, such as YMCA, for lacrosse programs. You might also contact USL, the national governing body for the sport, for programs in your area. USL has a library of videos to help you learn about individual skills and strategy, goalkeeping, and officiating. The organization can be reached at 113 W. University Parkway, Baltimore, MD 21210, or call 410–235–6882. The website is www.lacrosse.org.

SKIING

Sliding across the snow on boards that are strapped to your feet—that is the basic description of skiing, but it is so much more. Skiers say skiing is about gliding and racing and swooping and jumping and, even, doing somersaults! It's feeling the wind in your face surrounded by the pure whiteness of the snow and exquisite snow-filled silence on wooded trails. It's a wild dash down the mountain at astonishing speeds. You can ski for recreation and leisure or race competitively. At the high school level, skiing is divided into two groups: alpine and nordic, also known as cross-country.

The speed events in alpine skiing can be compared to sprint races in track, while nordic skiing is more like long-distance running. Alpine skiing events take place on downhill slopes and include downhill, slalom, giant slalom, and Super-G races, although not every high school competes in all these events. Nordic skiing takes place over a variety of distances and terrain.

Skiing is not a new activity. Cave and rock drawings as early as 3000 B.C. show that skis were originally used for work and transportation. The first ski poles may have also been used as spears for hunting. Skiing as a sport was developed by people from the Telemark area of Norway in the early 1700s; however, organized competitive skiing did not begin until the 19th century. Norwegians are also credited with introducing skiing to the United States in 1841. The first skis had boots attached at the toes only, with the heels free to move up and down, much like present-day nordic skis. The growing popularity of alpine skiing in the 1930s, mainly due to the invention of the ski lift, brought about a change in equipment. Most notably, boots were mounted to skis at both the toe and the heel, allowing the skier to ski faster and with more control on steeper slopes.

Cross-country skiing and ski jumping made their Olympic debut at the first Winter Games in 1924. It wasn't until the 1948 Olympics in St. Moritz, Switzerland, however, that the first alpine ski events were introduced. While it was not uncommon for women to ski in the 19th century, their entry into Olympic competition did not occur until 1936. A boom in competitive and recreational skiing took place following World War II and has continued, despite the fact that skiing can be an expensive sport.

At the high school level, there are over 4,200 girls competing in alpine skiing and more than 5,000 girls involved in nordic skiing.[11] In colleges, 455 women participate in alpine skiing.[12] While the NCAA does not sponsor nordic competition, there is nordic skiing at many colleges throughout the country.

Because skiing takes place in cold, winter climates, clothing is designed to keep athletes warm and dry. Skiers wear stretch suits or stretch pants and sweaters, sometimes with overpants. Some teams have team jackets or vests. Gloves and sometimes hats are worn. Helmets and goggles are required at high school alpine (but not nordic) ski competitions. For slalom races, skiers sometimes wear padding on forearms and knees to protect them when they bump the gates.

Alpine skiers wear hard, durable plastic boots that fasten with buckles. Nordic skiers wear a lightweight, comfortable, shoe-type boot. Skis, ski bindings, and poles differ, depending on the type of skiing. Many coaches advise beginning skiers to rent equipment. After beginners gain experience, they usually buy their own. Skiers should seek the advice of coaches or ski specialty shop personnel before purchasing equipment.

You may be surprised to learn that much of the preparation and practice for skiing is done on dry land. Coaches advise girls to do stretching exercises; activities to increase aerobic fitness, including biking, cross country, track, inline skating, and aerobic classes; and strength-building activities, especially for the upper body, including tennis and weight training. An alpine ski race is short, a "minute of your life," says Judy

Hunter, high school alpine ski coach, and so training should include short-time, high intensity work, like sprinting.

In alpine skiing, some schools limit their events to the slalom and giant slalom. Slalom racing requires skiers to make short, quick turns around as many as 60 "gates" as they speed downhill toward the finish line. The giant slalom course is longer in distance, with the gates set farther apart.

Nordic ski races take place in designated ski areas and, oftentimes, along trails in natural, wooded areas. In high school competitions, races are anywhere from three to seven kilometers long, and sometimes even longer. A 5k race takes about 15–30 minutes, depending on the skill of the skier and weather and snow conditions. Nordic skiers start a race singly or two abreast at intervals. The object is to cross the finish line in the fastest possible time. Two different techniques are used in nordic skiing: the classical and the freestyle, or skating, style. Athletes must learn and compete in both styles.

To train for the ski season, usually December through February, athletes need to prepare in advance. Nordic skiing requires endurance, much like cross-country running. Roller blading, biking, soccer, basketball, and running are excellent activities for increasing cardiovascular strength and endurance. Roller skiing, ice skating, and roller blading are activities that work on specific muscle groups needed for nordic skiing, especially for the skating technique.

If your high school does not have a ski program, you might be able to participate though a ski club or youth organization in your community or find out about programs sponsored by the United States Ski Association. Contact USSA at P.O. Box 100, Park City, UT 84060, or call 435-649-9090. Check out their website at www.uskiteam.com.

NOTES

1. National Federation of State High School Associations 1998 Participation Survey.

2. National Federation of State High School Associations 1998 Participation Survey.

3. National Collegiate Athletic Association 1997–98 Participation Study.

4. United States Golf Foundation.

5. Carole A. Oglesby, *Encyclopedia of Women and Sport in America*, Phoenix, AZ: Oryx Press, 1998.

6. National Federation of State High School Associations 1998 Participation Survey.

7. National Collegiate Athletic Association 1997–98 Participation Study.

8. National Collegiate Athletic Association 1997–98 Participation Study.

9. National Collegiate Athletic Association 1997–98 Participation Study.

10. National Federation of State High School Associations 1998 Participation Survey.

11. National Federation of State High School Associations 1998 Participation Survey.

12. National Collegiate Athletic Association 1997–98 Participation Study.

Chapter 11

Breaking the Barriers: Male-Dominated Sports

Hockey goalie Libby Witchger is one of the growing number of girls who are breaking down the barriers of male-dominated sports. Photo courtesy of the Witchger Family Collection.

Girls are branching out into sports that have generally been reserved for boys—sports such as football, wrestling, baseball, water polo, and ice hockey. These sports have been mainly off limits because they have the reputation of being too rough for girls. Remember, it was not so long ago that females were considered too weak to run the length of a basketball court, jump over hurdles, swim competitively, or engage in any other taxing physical activity. It was believed that she would injure herself, become less feminine, and in the extreme, compromise her reproductive system.

Overcoming those stereotypes has taken generations, so it's not difficult to understand how much resistance there was—and still is—to girls engaging in sports involving physical contact. Besides having to overcome the historic objections to girls participating in rough, physically strenuous sports, pioneers in each of these sports have had to prove that they are able to compete with and against males.

Ice hockey, lacrosse, and water polo are experiencing a steady growth of opportunities for girls and women. Sports such as baseball, football, and wrestling, however, are just beginning to include girls, albeit reluctantly, in most cases. After reading this chapter, you will have a clearer idea as to whether or not you might like to participate in any of these sports and how you can get involved: by joining the high school girls' team, trying out for the boys' team, or starting your own school team.

Most experts believe that playing on a girls' team (that has resources equal to that of the boys' team) is the best environment for girls, but not all high schools sponsor girls' teams in all sports. Also, not all girls' leagues receive the same resources as the boys. Sometimes, talented girls choose to play on a boys' team in order to gain access to better competitive opportunities and resources, such as coaching, practice times, facilities, and officials. There are two main reasons why girls request permission to participate on a boys' team in an individual sport traditionally reserved for males, and both relate to the lack of equal opportunities for girls. One is the absence of a girls' team at their high school. The other is that the girls' team or league does not have the same resources or it does not offer the same opportunities for talented girl athletes as it offers to boys.

FOOTBALL

Football is a game of strength, speed, and skill. It is bodies slamming into one another, long spiraled passes, high-arcing kicks, spectacular sprints, and dramatic touchdowns. Football is traditionally a male sport. Very few high school girls play the game, and if they do, they play on a boys' team. While the physical nature of the sport can lead to injury for any of its participants, for females who are usually smaller than their male counterparts, the potential for getting hurt is a very real concern. While a burly physique and bulging muscles are considered hallmarks of the sport, there are positions on a football team that call for quickness and special skills rather than brute strength and brawn. These are the positions in which athletes with slighter builds, both boys and girls, have the most success. While girls fill few of these slots today, their participation in the past was unheard of.

The game of American football, which began in ivy league universities during the 19th century, was a combination of soccer and rugby union football. The game was often violent and produced many injuries, even fatalities. Rules adopted to make the sport safer also made it more widely accepted, and by the end of World War I football was played throughout the United States, always by males. Football today is still played by men only at the professional and collegiate levels. In high schools, there are over 700 girls participating, all of them on boys' teams.

Football is played on a rectangular grassy (or artificial surface) field. The object of the game is to score points by crossing the opponents' goal line with the ball or by kicking the ball between the other team's goal posts. Each team attempts to move the ball up the field toward the other team's goal in a series of plays, called "downs." The ball can be moved by carrying, kicking, or throwing it to another player. Games are 48 minutes of actual playing time, divided into four quarters. Goals (or sides) are changed at the end of the first and third periods.

The ball is oval-shaped, with pointed ends, and is covered with "pebbled" leather, making it easier to grip and throw. A team consists of 11 players on the field, and an unlimited number of players can suit up for a game. Players often play either offense or defense or in special situations.

Football is one of the most, if not *the* most, aggressive of all sports, and games have been compared to battles, with teams strategically advancing and retreating. Because of football's intense physical contact, protective gear is worn to minimize injury. Players wear hard plastic helmets with face masks and padded uniforms to help make the sport safer. Players must also wear mouth guards.

High school coaches hold conflicting opinions about whether girls should play football at all, much less with boys. On one hand, they recognize that girls have the right to try out for the team, since there are no girls' football teams at the high school level, but they have special concerns about girls playing. They worry about injuries, especially in major collisions between usually lighter-weight girls and heavier, stronger boys. While the injury factor exists between boys with a wide difference in size, too, there are other potential problems when girls play. Coaches report they have to watch that girls are not harassed by either their own teammates or boys on opposing teams. They sometimes encounter interference from parents and fans who object to girls playing. They also must contend with privacy issues when girls join the team, such as providing separate restrooms and dressing facilities, along with supervisory personnel.

Girls express different reasons for wanting to play football. Faith Matranga, a member of her high school's junior varsity team during her senior year, said she wanted to play football to challenge herself, to "see if I could do it," while long-time soccer player Kim Henry "just loved kicking the ball." Matranga almost quit during the dreaded "double days," the twice-a-day practices held in late summer to prepare for the fall season, but she was encouraged by her coaches to keep going. She says she is glad she did because she enjoyed her experience and said one of the best parts was the camaraderie she built with the boys on her team. "A few gave me strange looks the first time I came out, but after that, they were great." Matranga, who at 6 feet tall was as big or bigger than some of the boys, played a line position, which is even more of a rarity among girls who play football. Most play positions like kicker, defensive back, or receiver—positions that call for speed and agility rather than size and strength.

Henry, who is just over 5 feet tall, was invited to come out for football after a varsity football player saw her kick in a "Powder Puff" football game during homecoming week of her sophomore year. She played on the junior varsity in 11th grade and on varsity as a senior. She says playing football was definitely one of the highlights of her high school experience. Her coaches and teammates treated her like any other player, and she was required to do all the same things other kickers did. When she was heckled by opposing players, her teammates reacted by being "very protective."

Matranga's experiences with opposing teams were also mainly positive. In fact, it wasn't until the very last game of the season that a few players from the other team tried to intimidate her verbally. Both she and Henry say they were never singled out for extra rough treatment on the field, but that is not every female player's experience. Some girls report being treated harshly, physically and verbally, by opposing team members. Some say they were ostracized by players on their own team as well as made fun of by nonplaying schoolmates.

Due to increased interest of girls in playing football, in some areas of the country "Powder Puff" football teams have formed. Most of these teams play "touch" football rather than the traditional game in an effort to minimize the risk of injuries. A few other schools have organized teams for intramural play or even one-time game opportunities. In Healdsburg, California, the annual girls' spring football game is a popular event. Each year the number of participants has increased. Girls practice for a month in advance, coached by the high school football coaching staff. They wear the boys' team uniforms, including full pads, and play tackle football in front of a packed stadium.

Most high school administrators and coaches do not believe football will ever become a girls' interscholastic sport. Besides the problems they perceive, they also do not see strong enough interest on the part of girls to play the game, especially in light of the increased opportunities for girls to play other sports. Football calls for a large squad—11 players on the field at a time—plus many more to make up a competitive team. If a girl wants to play football, she should consider the strength of the high school program. If the school is large and the program highly competitive, she probably will not have much of a chance to make the team. However, some coaches say they do not cut anyone and welcome everyone who turns out. Many programs have junior varsity teams and even freshman/sophomore teams where a girl might have a better chance to get started.

Coaches say that previous football experience (in Pop Warner or other youth programs), good overall body conditioning, speed, agility, and strength are all precursors for success in making the football team for boys or girls. Many high school coaches offer a spring training program and recommend a conditioning program for the summer months, which includes weight training, running, and overall conditioning. Additionally, it is especially important for girls to have a strong interest in the game and a determination to play because they will undoubtedly have to make psychological adjustments to being perhaps the only girl on the team and maybe the only girl in the league.

ICE HOCKEY

Ice hockey offers almost unlimited excitement to players and fans alike. The fastest team sport in the world, ice hockey is a game of skating speed, demanding skill, and agility. Although it might seem that ice hockey would be popular only in areas of the country where winters are cold and frozen lakes and ponds are numerous, indoor rinks provide access to the sport everywhere, even in California and Florida.

No one knows exactly how ice hockey began. Some legends claim it started in Europe when children on skates used a tree branch to hit rocks across the smooth ice. Others credit Canadian soldiers for adapting the game of field hockey so they could play during the winter months. One thing is for certain: Americans were playing ice hockey by the late 1800s. Ice hockey became an Olympic men's sport in 1920, but it took almost 80 years before it became an Olympic medal sport for women. In that inaugural year, at the Winter Olympic Games in Nagano, Japan, the U.S. women's team brought home the first-ever gold medal in women's hockey.

Today more and more high schools, colleges, and universities are adding ice hockey to their roster of sports for women as a solution to meeting Title IX requirements. According to the NCAA, there are more than 600 women playing intercollegiate ice hockey[1] and many more playing on the club level. More than 2,500 girls participate on teams for their high schools, many of them on boys' or "student" teams.[2]

Ice hockey is played on a rounded rectangular sheet of ice between two teams. Players wear ice skates and carry sticks with which they move a hard rubber disk called a puck. The object of the game is to score points by shooting the puck into the opposing team's goal. The team that scores the most points—games consist of three 20-minute periods—is the winner.

Although a team often consists of as many as 20 players, only six players per team are on the ice at a time. When the two teams face off, the six players on the ice are three forwards, two defenders, and one goaltender (or goalie) per team. Each player suits up in protective gear including shin pads, hockey pants, shoulder pads, elbow pads, gloves, helmet, and face mask. Goalies wear special, more protective equipment that can weigh up to 30 pounds, as they must use their bodies to keep the puck from entering the net.

Short shifts, approximately 45–90 seconds, with many substitutions are unique to the sport of ice hockey. The term "changing on the fly" means forwards and defensive players come on and off the ice as play continues. This keeps the game fast-moving and exciting.

Ice hockey rinks are rectangular with rounded corners. Goals are positioned in the center of goal lines set near the end lines. Similar to field hockey, players can play the area behind the goals. Boards surround the rink, with players' benches placed behind the boards. Hockey is a fast sport, and even though body checking is not allowed in the women's game, players do make physical contact and rule infractions occur. When they do, players are penalized by being withdrawn from the ice to serve time out from two to ten minutes, depending on the infraction, on the penalty bench. This creates a problem for the team because they have to play short-handed during the time-out period. The opposing team attempts to take advantage of the other team's shortage by stepping up their offensive game.

Ice hockey skates differ from figure skates in that the blade is curved along the bottom, and there are no "teeth" on the front. Skaters use an L-shaped, wooden stick. The puck, a 1 inch thick by 3 inch diameter disk of vulcanized rubber, can be shot at speeds up to 100 miles an hour!

Because ice hockey is a very physical sport, high school administrators have been reluctant to let females participate. Many girls who started playing on neighborhood ponds at an early age continue to play ice hockey as they grow up, usually with the boys, and fall in love with the game. Libby Witchger is one of those girls. Witchger, now assistant women's ice hockey coach at University of Minnesota, began playing with her two older brothers and tagged along to their competitions. She started playing on a boys' team when she was six, then worked her way up through the age groups. Each time she tried out for the next level of competition, she faced objections, mostly from parents of boys who said it was unfair for a girl to take a place on the team away from a boy. Her parents, though, were supportive. "They were glad I found a sport I liked," she says.

There was no girls' team at her high school, and she was not encouraged to try out for the boys' team. "Although I didn't make the team the first year, I was determined not to quit," Witchger says. But, she survived the cut in her junior year and was one of two goalies who played. "It was one of my greatest experiences," she says. Even though she made varsity in her senior year and practiced daily with the team, she was hardly allowed to play. During most games, she was not allowed on the bench. Instead, she sat in the stands and kept statistics for the team. While she was not satisfied with the amount of game time, she didn't quit the team. Witchger went on to play four years of Division I women's varsity ice hockey at Brown University. Today, as a college coach, she is still involved with the game.

Girls ice hockey is still scarce at the high school level, yet opportunities to play are increasing rapidly. For girls interested in trying out for either a girls' or boys' team, coaches suggest pre-season training to improve their chances. Work on increasing endurance, strength, and agility—all important aspects of the game. Improve cardiovascular endurance and ice hockey skills by playing as much as possible in the pre-season. A good way to increase strength is to get into a weight-training program. Talk to an expert trained to instruct you on the proper use of weights to prevent injury and maximize your workout.

The game of ice hockey is played in short bursts, so doing interval training during the pre-season is a good way to maximize your sprinting ability. Agility drills, including jumping rope, are also important. So is improving eye-hand coordination. Juggling or throwing a tennis ball against a wall alone or with a partner is helpful.

If ice hockey is not offered at your high school, there may be a youth hockey league in your area. For more information about local leagues, contact USA Hockey at 719–599–5500, or through their website at www.usahockey.org and/or call a local ice arena.

BASEBALL

Baseball has been "America's national pastime" for almost 140 years, yet it only became an official Olympic sport in 1996. Although baseball has long been a popular spectator sport for both genders, participation has been almost exclusively limited to males. An important exception, however, occurred during World War II, when a women's professional baseball league was formed because many big-league players went into the armed forces and team owners wanted to keep the game alive. The All-American Girls Professional Baseball League, featured in the movie *A League of Their Own*, enjoyed great popularity and gave talented female athletes a chance to play. Unfortunately, the league folded several years after the war ended and the men returned home. More recently, the Colorado Silver Bullets, a women's professional team, was organized in 1994, but they have since disbanded.

There has probably been less pressure on the game of baseball to include women because most girls and women play softball, a close relative of baseball. Some females prefer the overhand pitching and smaller ball used in baseball, so, while baseball is not a girls' sport at the high school level, there are some girls who now play on boys' teams.

Julie Croteau was not one of them. She was not allowed to play on her high school team because she was a girl, even though the varsity coach told her she was good enough. Croteau went on to become the first woman to play men's college varsity baseball at St. Mary's College in Maryland and coach a men's NCAA baseball team. She experienced frustration, was harassed, ostracized, and criticized for wanting to play a boys' sport. Even when she was hired as coach of the Division I baseball program at University of Massachusetts, she encountered skepticism about her abilities and motives. "People stared and there was some harassment," she says. "It was a hard job, but I reminded myself that men do this all the time. I could, too."[3]

While the exact origins of baseball are unknown, it probably came from a game called rounders. English immigrants who came to America in the early 1600s brought the game, which involved hitting a pitched ball with a stick or bat and trying to score runs. By the 1800s a version of the sport called town ball became popular, and later in the century, Ernest Lawrence Thayer wrote what was probably the first poem to baseball (and maybe to any sport), "Casey at the Bat." In the early years stakes were used instead of bases and the fielding team threw the ball *at* the baserunner to get him out. Moreover, there were no set fielding positions, and an unlimited number of players were allowed on the field. By 1900 baseball had developed uniform rules and was very similar to today's game. Baseball is now enjoyed by people in over 100 countries around the world.

A bat, a ball, and a glove are the main equipment baseball players use. Bats come in various lengths and weights and can be made from either wood or aluminum. Leather gloves, used to protect the hand and to improve catching ability, also come in a variety of sizes. A baseball is smaller than a softball and weighs about 5 ounces. It has a cork center wrapped with string and an outer leather cover.

Players wear uniforms that consist of a cap; a jersey with the team name and player's number on it; baseball pants; and a pair of stirrups that are worn over athletic socks. Shoes with cleats or bars on the soles help players maintain their footing. Batters and baserunners wear helmets to protect them from a thrown or batted ball; catchers wear special equipment to avoid injury, such as a helmet, face mask, chest protector, and leg guards.

A baseball field is called a diamond because it looks like a square turned on its edge with a base located at each corner. The infield is smooth surfaced, while the outfield is usually close-cut grass or a similar-looking artificial surface. A fence surrounds the field, and one of the most exciting sights in baseball is when a batter hits the ball over the fence for a home run. Even more exciting is when a "grand slam" is hit: a home run with the bases loaded.

The object of the game is to score runs (points) by hitting the ball and advancing runners around the four bases. The team that scores the most runs wins the game. Games are made up of seven innings at the high school level. In each inning a team bats until three outs are made, then the opposing team gets its turn to bat. The goal of the batting team is to hit the ball, get on base safely, and score by crossing home plate. The goal of the team in the field is to keep the other team from scoring and retiring the side (making three outs).

Baseball has fairly complex rules and a colorful vocabulary, with terms such as *catch a fly, pop up, wild pitch, steal a base, texas leaguer, doughnut,* and *bull pen.* It is a game of power and grace, of hitting, throwing, running, and sliding. It takes a lot of skill to play baseball. Exquisite eye-hand coordination, balance, and strength are hallmarks of a good hitter. Throwing the ball fast, accurately, and sometimes for long distances are skills a fielder works to develop. Physical skill alone is not enough, however. Players need to learn the strategy of the game and to be able to make split-second decisions.

While in some school districts girls try out for boys' or student teams, in other areas girls are restricted from baseball because softball is considered an alternative sport for girls. The number of girls playing baseball in high school is 1,262.[4] According to the NCAA, there is no intercollegiate baseball for women, and with the demise of the Silver Bullets in 1998, there are currently no professional women's baseball teams.

Coaches advise girls who want to try out for a spot on the high school baseball team to prepare in advance by learning as much as possible about the game and getting in condition. Experience in youth baseball is advantageous. Since 1974, Little League teams have been accepting female players, so girls coming up through Little League or other youth baseball programs definitely have an advantage over girls who have had limited or no training.

Increasing overall fitness is essential. Girls benefit from running to build up cardiovascular fitness. Participation in other sports, such as basketball, soccer, track, cross country, field hockey, or other running-based activities, build endurance, too. Weight training helps increase strength, and coaches often will offer suggestions on how to train. Trainers in weight rooms or at gyms and health clubs can also set up a program that will help build your strength safely.

Coaches say the most effective way to learn baseball skills is to practice hitting, throwing, and catching a ball. You can join a club or recreational team, practice with friends and family, go to clinics, or sign up for a class at your local community college. Learn as much about the game as possible. Watch baseball being played, read up on the rules, talk to baseball players and coaches about baseball strategy. If you have a good sense of the game, this will be obvious at tryouts, and it will give you an edge. You can contact USA Baseball for information about programs in your area. Call 520–327–9221, or check out the web site: www.usabaseball.com.

WATER POLO

When you hear the word polo, you might think of riders on horseback, but water polo has nothing to do with horses. Instead, it is a team sport played in a pool combining swimming with ball handling. Water polo is a strenuous, often rough, sport that takes strength and stamina. While water polo is one of the oldest team sports in Olympic history (since the 1900 Games in Paris), it is not yet an Olympic event for women, even though women have been playing for years.

Water polo originated in the rivers and lakes of England in the mid-19th century, an aquatic version of rugby football. Players carried the ball through the water and placed it onto a floating dock to score a goal. The goalie, who could stand on the dock, would jump on top of players who tried to score! Often a dangerous game, a 1911 contest between teams from Illinois and New York resulted in four players being carried from the pool unconscious.[5]

By the 1880s rules were instituted to make the game safer and water polo moved to indoor pools. When, at about the same time, water polo began in the United States, it more closely resembled a game of American football in water. Generally regarded as the roughest game in the world, the U.S. version came under pressure to become more civilized, and by 1914, American clubs agreed to play under international rules.

Woman played water polo at the club level until 1926 when the sport fell into disfavor as being too rough for females. A revival began in the early 1960s, and in 1976 the U.S. Women's National Team was formed to compete at the international level. Only recently has women's water polo achieved intercollegiate status, and today over 660 women compete at colleges.[6] In high schools across the country it is an even newer sport. While girls' teams are increasing (10,800 girls now play in high schools),[7] most girls still play on boys' teams.

The object of water polo is to throw a soccer-like ball into a cage (goal). The ball is moved around the pool by swimming with it or throwing, passing, and catching it. Each team has seven players: six field players and a goalie. Players tread water for the entire game and may not touch the sides of the pool or stand on the bottom. The goalie is allowed to stand on the bottom and to use two hands, all other players are allowed to use only one.

The length of a varsity high school water polo game is 28 minutes of actual play (four periods of seven minutes each). There is a two-minute interval between periods for changing sides and a five-minute half-time. The ball is put into play by a referee throwing it onto the center line. Players from both teams, lined up on each side along the pool wall, then sprint to the ball. The team who gets control goes on the offense and tries to score a goal. There is an offside rule. Offsides is when one or more offensive players are within two meters of the goal when the ball is outside those two meters. If the ball is within two meters, any and all players can be in there.

Penalties are awarded for fouls and other rule infractions. Ordinary fouls are penalized by a free throw for the fouled team, while major fouls call for a free shot or cause the offending player to be ejected for 20 seconds, depending on where the foul takes place. If a player is ejected three times, she is eliminated from the game, and a substitute is allowed to replace her.

Women's water polo is ideally played in a 25 meter pool, with a recommended depth of 6 feet, 6 inches and marked with lines of different colors. Goals must be rigid, perpendicular, and painted white. Each goal is enclosed by a net.

Players wear double swim suits—thicker suits made of wetsuit-like material. Caps, which tie under the chin and are fitted with ear protectors, are mandatory. Each team needs two caps: one white and the other a dark color. The home team always wears dark caps.

Georgina (Georgy) Whyte coaches girls' water polo at her former high school, where she was the first girl on the boys' team during her school days. A swimmer, she started out practicing with the boys just to keep in shape for swim season; she then went on to play for the team. She says she met resistance at first but worked hard and gained the acceptance and respect of her teammates. Whyte had a harder time with the boys on opposing teams, some of whom tried to pull off her swimsuit under the water or rough her up. Others made passes at her. She says one boy threw a ball at her head purposefully, stunning her. She almost quit but "my mom instilled in me never to quit what you start, so I stuck with it." She's glad she did because she loves the sport and says she gained confidence from her experience. She played on a women's team in college and now feels the players she coaches in high school are lucky to be playing on a girls' team rather than trying to break the barriers on a boys' team as she did. "Physically guys are just stronger than women, especially in the water. It's a rough sport. When you look at guys playing it's like alligators rolling over and wrestling with each other." Whyte says water polo, while still a strenuous, physical game, is more equitable when girls play on an all-female team.

Coaches recommend girls begin playing water polo before they get to high school, if possible, though the sport for girls is so new that many don't have the opportunity to get involved earlier. While it helps to have a swimming background, other girls come from sports such as basketball or soccer. In fact, because in water polo players are vertical much of the time, good ball skills are especially advantageous. If there is youth water polo in your area, sign up for lessons or for the team. If there is none, coaches suggest girls join a recreational or club swim team, take swim lessons, and/or swim laps at a local pool. Playing keep-away with others in a pool is a good way to get used to handling a ball in the water. It helps to learn the fundamentals of the sport, too, so watching water polo being played either firsthand or on video and reading up on the rules is helpful.

Because water polo is such a physically demanding sport, working on cardiovascular conditioning is essential. Running for endurance, sprinting, and interval training for the short bursts needed in games and cross-training with other sports such as cycling, basketball, volleyball, field hockey, and soccer are all valuable pre-season activities. Weight training is also recommended, especially to strengthen areas such as the back, legs, and triceps.

For information about programs near you, contact USA Water Polo at 719–634–0699, or visit their web site: www.uswp.org.

WRESTLING

High school wrestling is a far cry from the wild and crazy form of professional wrestling seen on television. It is a serious competitive sport, a one-on-one test of physical strength and mental acuity. Wrestling is one of, if not the most, basic form of competition between two individuals.

Egyptian cave drawings as far back as 2,600 B.C. show individuals grappling with an opponent. Wrestling later became the most popular sport at the ancient Olympic Games, where unarmed athletes struggled hand to hand, with each attempting to subdue or unbalance the other. Two versions of the sport emerged: freestyle and Greco-Roman. Both spread throughout Europe and then to the United States by the 1800s. During the Civil War, troops engaged in wrestling for sport and entertainment. While men's Greco-Roman wrestling, in which contestants cannot use their legs, became part of the modern Olympic Games in 1896, freestyle did not make its debut until 1904.

Women's involvement in wrestling is very recent. At the international level, since the late 1980s females have competed in their own world championships; nationally, the governing body, USA Wrestling, has developed programs for women and girls. However, females competing against other females is still in its infancy in the United States and is not yet widely accepted at the college or high school levels. According to the NCAA, there is no intercollegiate competition between women's wrestling teams, although in 1995 University of Minnesota–Morris became the first college in the nation to sponsor a women's varsity team (they wrestle teams from Canada, where the women's collegiate wrestling program is more extensive). While there are some girls-only teams at the high school level, most girls who wrestle (over 1,900) do so on boys' teams.[8] In high schools and colleges, folk-style (similar to freestyle) rules are used.

Wrestling is a highly intense contest in which each of two opponents tries to throw or force the other to the ground. The rules for wrestling do not allow using the fists or certain holds on the body. Wrestlers compete in weight classes, so they are matched up with opponents of the same weight. Wrestling takes place on a rubber or spongy synthetic mat. Matches are three rounds of two minutes each. Wrestlers attempt to outscore an opponent by using holds to gain technical points and/or by holding the opponent's shoulder blades to the mat for two seconds. Matches begin with wrestlers standing and facing each other. At the beginning of the second and third periods, a coin is tossed to determine which wrestler gets the choice of starting position: top, bottom, or neutral. Wrestlers receive points for certain moves, such as *takedowns, near falls, reversals, rides,* and *escapes.* They also receive points when their opponent commits a penalty. The match ends when one wrestler pins the other or builds a lead of 15 points. If neither occurs, the wrestler with the most points at the end of the match wins.

Wrestlers wear a singlet, a brief, one-piece uniform that is tight-fitting and made of stretchy material. Girls normally wear a shirt under the singlet. High-topped sports shoes that close firmly around the ankle and are without a heel or any metal parts must be worn. Nylon caps are worn by girls (or by boys with longer hair). Head gear is required for all high school wrestlers.

Perhaps more than any other sport, wrestling seems to be the one most difficult for girls to break into and stay involved with—at least on a boys' team. An example is Carla Traube. Traube is not wrestling for her high school boys' team this year, even though as a junior she has two years of experience behind her. Traube decided, however, that she doesn't need the pressure or aggravation of trying to compete against boys in a sport that doesn't really welcome girls. Her own teammates accepted her, she says, but she often faced opposition, harassment, and derision from competing wrestlers, and even their coaches and parents. Some wrestlers refused to wrestle against her. "I love wrestling," says Traube, "but I think I've gone as far as I can, and it's time to do something else." Traube, who is also a cross-country runner, decided to give wrestling a try after being encouraged by a schoolmate who was on the wrestling team. She made the freshman/sophomore team in her first year, then moved up to junior varsity where she was selected as team captain. She enjoyed the pure physicality of the sport, plus the mental aspects—the strategy and concentration—but she did not like the problems she encountered.

According to girls who wrestle, one dilemma is the outfit. In a sport such as football, the uniform provides total coverage and is bulky. Uniforms for wrestling are form fitting and skimpy. Most girls wear a T-shirt underneath; although a girl's model, cut more modestly, has recently become available but is more expensive. The revealing uniforms, along with the basic wrestling moves, subject athletes of both sexes to more than a little discomfort and embarrassment.

Another problem is that boys and girls are ambivalent about winning and losing to each other. In a society where most boys have been taught to not hurt girls, they now find it hard to physically manhandle girls, especially on a one-on-one basis. At the same time, there is a certain stigma to losing to a girl. Some parents, too, are uneasy or downright negative in response to their boys wrestling against girls—some to the point that they forbid it. Coaches say they have had to forfeit matches in response to a boy's or his parents' objections.

In spite of these concerns, girls who want to wrestle need to get in shape just like the boys. High school wrestling coach Dan Brand says, "When girls come out, I tell them I'm going to treat them like the boys; they have to make the team and they won't get special favors." He tells wrestlers there are five keys to wrestling success: strength, speed, skill, strategy, and stamina. He advises them to join a summer club program to learn and to get some experience wrestling before they try out.

Weight training is vital to increase strength, especially for girls, who are usually not as strong as boys, especially after puberty. Contacting a trainer or getting instruction from the coach is important, not only to maximize benefits of weight training but also to avoid injury. Running, wind sprints, and stretching for flexibility are also recommended. "Wrestling is extremely demanding," says Brand, "mentally as well as physically." Wrestlers have to know how and when to use their strength and balance, what to do in certain situations, and what the best strategy is for taking down the opponent. All that comes with preparedness and experience.

Female wrestlers also advise girls to come to tryouts mentally as well as physically prepared. "You have to be self-confident and determined," says Carla Traube. "You have to really want to wrestle." In recent years, women have become increasingly active in wrestling and today have their own world championships. For more information about women's wrestling, contact USA Wrestling at 719-598-8181, or visit their web page: www.usawrestling.org.

NOTES

1. National Collegiate Athletic Association 1997–98 Participation Study.
2. National Federation of State High School Associations 1998 Participation Survey.
3. Alexandra Powe-Allred and Michelle Powe, *The Quiet Storm: A Celebration of Women in Sport*. Indianapolis: Masters Press, 1997.
4. National Federation of State High School Associations 1998 Participation Survey.

    5. Neil, Cohen, ed. *The Everything You Want to Know about Sports Encyclopedia.* New York: Bantam Books, 1994.
    6. National Collegiate Athletic Association 1997–98 Participation Study.
    7. National Federation of State High School Associations 1998 Participation Survey.
    8. National Federation of State High School Associations 1998 Participation Survey.

Chapter 12

The Young Female Athlete: Dealing with Special Issues

A popular television ad campaign features elite female athletes and begins with a girl's voice saying, "If you let me play sports. . . ." Then in each commercial she concludes with a different ending, such as: "I will like myself more. . . . I will have more self-confidence. . . . I will learn what it means to be strong." These and other ads by companies selling products from athletic shoes to automobiles show young women in action: going up for a lay-up, kicking a soccer ball into the goal, diving from a platform into a pool, and sprinting across the finish line. They look intense, they look fit, they look radiant—each one a testimonial to the pleasures and benefits of sports. These commercials, as well as televised women's games and events and programs about women's sports, are exciting. They represent all that is good in sports for females.

Along with the good things, however, some women and girls encounter special issues that take away from the pure joy of their sports experience or, at least, cause them anxiety and concern. While some of these issues are merely annoying or bothersome, others are far more serious. Becoming aware of these issues shouldn't discourage you from participating in sports, because most girls report that their sports experiences are overwhelmingly positive. In the event that you run into any of these situations as you play sports, you will be aware that they exist, that other girls have gone through similar experiences, and that there are ways to deal with the problems. Not surprisingly, many of these issues are not limited to sports but might occur in other areas of your life.

When asked about problems they have encountered in sports, girls most frequently cite seven troublesome areas: bias toward girls playing sports, overtraining, problems with coaches, trouble with teammates, nutrition, drugs, and over-involved parents.

BIAS TOWARD GIRLS PLAYING SPORTS

Girls encounter bias even before they begin to play sports and in subtle ways. So subtle, in fact, that they are often unaware of it. Boys traditionally have been encouraged to engage in vigorous and boisterous activity, to take risks, to compete with others, to be strong and independent, while girls have been conditioned to be less active, to avoid conflict and competition, to be "sugar and spice and everything nice!" They have often been protected because of the notion that they are the "weaker sex." This overall stereotyping just naturally carries over into the sports arena.

For some girls the bias they encounter is not disguised at all, but rather, the message that sports are not as acceptable or not as important for girls is loud and clear. Parents, grandparents, teachers, or school officials may openly discourage them from participating. Play opportunities in their communities may be limited. Girls may even be called unfeminine for participating in a sport, particularly if they excel at it. They may be told they are not strong enough, that only certain, non-contact sports are acceptable, or that they have no right to try out for a traditionally male-dominated team. They may encounter teasing, resistance, or even exclusion by nonathlete friends and male athletes.

Whether they have been exposed to subtle or more direct forms of bias in sports, girls notice. Some who shared their experiences cited:

- A lacrosse player whose boyfriend told her he did not like girls who sweat.

- A soccer player and her teammates who thought sweating was considered unfeminine took diuretics before each game (a very dangerous practice) to inhibit perspiration.

- A girl trying out for the high school ice hockey team (there was only a boys' team) was told by a parent that she shouldn't be there because, "You might be taking a place on the team away from a boy."

- A high school athlete noticed that there were inequities between the boys' and the girls' programs. "The baseball team had newer uniforms and were assigned the best times for practices. The girls' softball team practiced after the boys finished, and for most of the season we had to cut practice short because it got dark."

- A swimmer said the weight room at her high school was male dominated. She was told she could work out, but she did not feel welcome. "The coach helped the boys but ignored the girls," she said.

- A girl decided not to try out for the high school softball team after being told that the players were all lesbians.

- A volleyball player, whose games were often at the same time as her brother's football games, says her parents rarely came to see her play. She concluded that they considered her brother's sports involvement more important than hers.

More and more parents, physical education teachers, coaches, and school administrators today believe that girls have as much right to play sports as boys, and bias is lessening. One thing that has helped is that today girls have role models, athletes they can to look up to and in whose footsteps they can follow. These young women didn't let prejudice prevent them from participating and excelling in their sports. Soccer's Mia Hamm, basketball's Rebecca Lobo, skiing's Picabo Street, track's Marian Jones, gymnastics' Dominique Dawes, volleyball's Gabriella Reese, and softball's Dot Richardson are examples of high-profile elite athletes who girls can see and dream of being. Years ago, if women had sports heroes, they were male. Today's girls have strong, talented, and feminine sports heroes that look like them.

PROBLEMS WITH COACHES

Most coaches help young athletes, teaching and influencing them in positive ways. However, with even the finest coaches, difficulties occasionally arise. Girls say that having a problem with a coach is similar to having a problem with just about anyone in authority—a parent, teacher, or employer. You may not like their personality or the way they teach. You may think they play favorites or don't know very much. You may think they talk down to you or make you work too hard. You just may not see eye to eye with them. Many girls recommend that you "don't sweat the small stuff," but rather, overlook personality differences and enjoy your teammates and the overall sports experience. But what if that doesn't work?

Talking directly to the coach about your concerns is usually beneficial and can clear up misunderstandings. If that feels too intimidating, you can talk with someone else on the coaching staff. You can also seek advice from another adult, such as a teacher or the athletic director at your school. They might even talk to the coach on your behalf or sit in on a discussion between you and the coach. Coaches say they would prefer a player who is upset or angry to talk directly to them rather than to keep quiet and let their unhappiness fester or to complain to their teammates or others who are not in a position to help resolve the problem.

Sometimes you and your coach will have a personality clash or differences of opinion that cannot be reconciled. If you absolutely cannot resolve your differences, and they are spoiling the sports experience for you, consider finding another place to play your sport or consider switching sports.

One girl quit her high school soccer team, joined a club team, and had a satisfying experience. This happened after her high school coach told her that she was never going to get much playing time if she did not play a more physical game against girls on the opposing team. He told her to slide tackle to get the ball and take the other girls' legs out from under them at the same time. He told her to physically intimidate her opponents by pushing and playing roughly. She was uncomfortable with that style of play and ended up quitting because, "We just didn't have the same philosophy."

If team members share a common problem, then it is a good idea to meet as a team and relate your feelings to the coach. This gives girls a chance to express themselves and allows the coach to hear their concerns and respond. If, however, the problems persist or you feel like your concerns are being ignored, consider talking with the athletic director.

While differences of opinion are one thing, abuse or mistreatment is something else. Anytime you believe a coach is mistreating you, either verbally or physically, you must tell another adult right away—your parents, a teacher, a counselor, or the athletic director. Verbal abuse includes calling you names; making degrading remarks about you, either in private or in front of your teammates or to others; swearing and/ or making inappropriate remarks or suggestions. Physical harassment is grabbing, hitting, shoving, or in any way touching your body roughly or inappropriately, as in a sexual manner. These kinds of behavior are absolutely wrong and must not be tolerated.

Some girls are afraid to tell someone when a coach is abusive. They worry that nothing will be done, that they will just make the coach mad at them, and that they won't be able to play, or that the coach will pick on them even more. They may wonder if they did something wrong to cause the coach to treat them badly. Any coach who harasses a female athlete should be removed from his or her position of power.

When an athlete reports a coach for mistreating her, school officials will sometimes issue a warning to the coach, depending on the severity of the situation. Oftentimes, a warning will cause coaches to change their behavior, especially if they have been unaware that their actions are harmful. If, however, they continue to be abusive or retaliatory, players should report them and keep reporting them until someone listens and takes action.

One high school sprinter's male coach told crude jokes and commented on the size of her breasts. She tried to ignore him, then told him that she didn't like the way he was talking, but he didn't stop. Although she thought about quitting the team because she felt so uncomfortable, she talked to her parents. They went with her to the athletic director, and, after the situation was looked into, the coach was fired. "I felt a little guilty, at first," the girl said, but other girls told her they were relieved he was gone, because they had also been upset by his inappropriate comments.

TEAMMATE TROUBLES

Having problems with teammates is similar to having problems in the classroom, in clubs and organizations, or with your girlfriends. Personality conflicts, differences of opinion, misunderstandings, and hurt feelings can take place whenever people interact. On a team, where the atmosphere is often intense, tempers get frayed, emotions surface, and girls get mad at one another. Most girls try to overlook slight annoyances or quick outbursts, realizing that in the heat of competition, these things are commonplace. A basketball player said she has had to apologize more than once for yelling at a teammate. "Sometimes I think I'm shouting encouragement, but then I'll play it back to myself, and it sounds like I'm criticizing."

Talking about an ongoing problem with a teammate directly rather than talking about her to other players works best for most girls. If that doesn't solve the problem, bring in the team captain as an intermediary or ask the coach to help.

One team did just this and not only resolved a problem, but became a more cohesive group. Two girls had a bad attitude according to their junior varsity volleyball teammates. "They were bringing down the whole team and acting like we were beneath them," said one of the players. Finally, after talking to the coach, the captain called a team meeting, and the players told the two girls how their attitude was affecting everyone. The girls admitted they were extremely disappointed that they hadn't made the varsity team, and they guessed they were letting that show. They apologized to their teammates and, as one of the players reported, they "completely turned things around and became part of the team."

Sometimes girls with superior skills and a more competitive spirit sense jealousy from teammates. This happened to one of the catchers on a freshman softball team who was an especially talented player. She started every game, while the other catcher came off the bench only occasionally. The second-string catcher started a rumor about the starter. When it got back to the starter, she was hurt. She confronted her teammate, who denied responsibility. When the girl continued to talk about her, however, the starter told her mother and they arranged a meeting with the other girl and her parents. "It wasn't a pleasant experience for anyone," relates the catcher, "but the girl stopped, and that's all I wanted." They are not close friends, but they are still on the same team and work together cooperatively.

OVERTRAINING

Overtraining—practicing and exercising excessively—can be physically and psychologically damaging. It is also nonproductive. Richard Ball, author of *Sports Injury Concerns: The Female Athlete*, calls overtraining, the "law of diminishing returns." By overtraining the athlete stops improving at some point and either becomes burned out or gets hurt. Burnout, which occurs when the athlete starts losing concentration and interest in the sport, develops from practicing and working out excessively and for too long. The overly tired body is more likely to sustain injuries caused by fatigue and overuse.

Stress fractures can occur with overuse in both girls and boys. For female athletes, overtraining can cause the body to produce too little estrogen, the hormone responsible for healthy bone growth, thus causing numerous problems, including stress fractures. Failure to produce estrogen inhibits healthy bone growth. Additionally, girls can stop having their periods or fail to start menstruating when they participate in extended periods of intense physical exertion.

If you feel as if you are burning out, either physically or mentally, or if you are trying to play through pain, experts recommend taking a break from the sport, easing up on your workouts, and seeing a sports trainer or physician about the physical discomfort and/or fatigue you are experiencing. Also, talk to your coach about how you are feeling. If your coach is not responsive, be sure to talk to your parents. You could seriously injure yourself by overtraining.

Female Athlete Triad

Female athletes who compete in sports requiring a pre-adolescent body build for success or emphasizing low body weight for competition are prone to a medical condition known as the *female athlete triad*. Eating disorders represent the first factor in the triad. Amenorrhea (absence of menstruation) is the secondary phase. The third component is the loss of bone mass (osteoporosis).

Highly competitive athletes are the most prone to the female athlete triad, but all girls are at risk. The reasons for the condition are complicated, but experts say the pressure to excel, a desire to win at all costs, and the pursuit of perfection are leading factors. According to the American College of Sports Medicine, certain sport activities predispose the participant to the condition:

- Sports using weight categories for competition (rowing, martial arts, wrestling)
- Sports dependent on subjective scoring (figure skating, gymnastics)
- Endurance exercise (long-distance running, cycling)
- Sports emphasizing a prepubertal body build (figure skating, gymnastics, diving)
- Sports requiring contour-fitting clothing for competition (volleyball, track, swimming, diving, cheerleading)[1]

Female athlete triad is a serious but preventable disorder that affects athletes for both the short and long term. Intervention and treatment by qualified professionals are necessary.

NUTRITION

The body is like a machine. It needs to be properly maintained so it can perform smoothly and efficiently. Feeding your body is like fueling your car. If you don't fill up your car's tank with high-grade fuel, it performs poorly and eventually runs out of gas. In the same way, if you don't fill up your body with healthy, nutritious food, you won't reach peak performance and, ultimately, you will run out of energy. Muscles begin to starve and the entire system begs for the nutrients it needs. If you deprive it too long, it can break down.

For athletes, improper nutritional practices raise an even greater risk than for other girls. Athletes use up more calories and need more food. Food is more than just a filler that stops your hunger. A soft drink can do that. So can a candy bar. Keeping your body running strong takes foods that contain the nutrients essential for creating optimal health and top performance. Young athletes, often pressured by lack of time and influenced by fads and peer pressure, don't always eat well. A nutritional diet for everyone, and especially athletes, contains six basic nutrients: carbohydrates, fat, protein, vitamins, minerals, and water.

Planning ahead is a key to eating well. Some girls do better when they plan their meals and snacks. Fixing food to take with you to school, rather than grabbing something at the snack bar or at a fast food restaurant to fill up, helps. Some girls either shop for themselves or ask their parents to keep stocked up on fruit, bread and sandwich fillings, energy bars, cut up vegetables, juices, and yogurt. They pack these things as well as other tasty, nutritional foods, and bottled water, and take them to school for before and after practice.

Girls who want to make sure they are eating well can educate themselves about proper nutrition. Books and videos are available at libraries or bookstores, and you can talk to your coach, although it should be noted that many coaches and physical educators are not very well informed about nutrition. You can also seek advice from nutritional experts or your family doctor.

Besides eating healthful foods, girls need to eat enough to replenish the calories they use up in physical activity. But many girls, and not just those involved in sports, are worried about their weight and don't want to get fat. Society puts immense pressure on females of all ages to be thin, often abnormally so. This pressure can lead to girls becoming dissatisfied with their bodies. Even in some sports, there is pressure to be unusually thin. With emphasis on thinness and slogans like ''there's no such thing as being too thin," some girls become so obsessed about their weight that they starve themselves and develop eating disorders. While studies show that female athletes have a better and more realistic body image than nonathletes as well as more confidence in the way their bodies looks, there is some evidence that with the increasing competition in girls' sports, eating disorders among female athletes are on the rise.

Coaches say they stay alert to symptoms of eating disorders in the athletes they coach. One coach recently worried about one of her runners. She had lost almost 15 pounds from the beginning of track season. When the coach called her in and talked with her, the athlete denied having a problem. The girl insisted she was too fat even though her appearance did not confirm this. The coach consulted with the school nurse and arranged a meeting with the girl's parents to discuss the problem and find a way to solve a potentially very serious problem.

The most prevalent eating disorders are bulimia and anorexia. Bulimics often diet rigidly, then overeat, suffer remorse, and induce vomiting to rid themselves of the food and guilt. This can lead to a vicious and dangerously unhealthy cycle of binging and purging. Anorexia nervosa is self-imposed starvation. In its early stages, a girl loses weight and becomes thin; at its most extreme, she eats so few calories over a prolonged period that her body weight decreases until medical intervention or death occurs.

If you think you might be suffering from an eating disorder, you should talk to your parents or another adult, a coach, counselor, or teacher right away. If you know of someone whom you think is anorexic or bulimic, you need to tell an adult. The problems surrounding eating disorders usually do not go away by themselves. They almost always require expert help.

DRUGS

As female athletes become more competitive, they look for ways to improve their performance. Besides intensifying their practices and workouts, eating right, drinking enough liquids, and getting adequate rest, some girls use drugs. There are two kinds of drugs of concern to female athletes: performance-enhancing drugs and so-called recreational drugs.

Recreational drugs, both legal and illegal substances, including alcohol, marijuana, cocaine/crack, and heroin, are banned in high school athletics. The use of tobacco is discouraged. There are six main categories of performance-enhancing drugs: anabolic steroids, pain suppressants, stimulants, beta blockers, diuretics, and peptide hormones. While each type does something different, they all are used in an effort to improve athletic performance: to increase strength; allow quicker recovery from fatigue; reduce pain; increase endurance; decrease anxiety; and eliminate fluids for quick, temporary weight loss.

Performance-enhancing drug use is illegal in high school athletics, as well as unethical. Besides giving athletes an unfair advantage, performance-enhancing drugs are banned because they also have long-term, negative side effects, including heart and liver problems. They can also become addictive. Dr. Deborah B. Moore, assistant commissioner for the Ohio High School Athletic Association says, "Using drugs is cheating—cheating oneself, cheating the game, cheating the entire sports experience."

Some girls do not realize these drugs are so potentially dangerous, and out of curiosity, peer pressure, or the desire to excel at their sport they may think about taking a performance-enhancing drug. Health officials as well as most coaches and athletes advise against it. A long-distance runner learned the hard way when, after hurting her knee, she took pain suppressants given to her by a "friend" so she could begin training for track season. While her doctor had not released her to run, she was anxious to get started. When she ran, she couldn't feel the pain that would ordinarily have warned her to stop. Ultimately, she did considerable, possibly permanent, damage to the knee, forcing her to sit out her entire senior season.

Drugs are not the only substances out there claiming to increase athletic performance. Baseball superstar and home run record-holder Mark McGwire brought national attention to the use of food supplements for enhancing sports performance when he readily admitted using them. The National Federation of State High School Associations, in response to questions about the of use of food supplements said, "even natural substances in unnatural amounts may have short-term or long-term negative health effects." Recently, Robert F. Kanaby, NFHS executive director, stated:

> In recent days, the Associated Press has quoted Mark McGwire as speaking favorably of androstenedione and creatine. We do not presume to second-guess Mr. McGwire's statements about what may be appropriate for a professional athlete in his 30s; however,

drugs are not harmless and are not free of consequences when ingested by student-athletes of high school age.

I strongly urge that high school student-athletes, parents, coaches and school administrators thoroughly investigate short-term and long-term health consequences before ingesting, or allowing the ingestion of, any performance-enhancing substance.[2]

Experts strongly advise adolescents whose bodies are growing and changing, to avoid taking any substance without first discussing it with their parents and a physician. Studies are being done on many of these substances, but the jury is still out on their effects—whether negative or positive. Any time you are told there is something you can take to make you bigger, faster, or stronger, take a step back.

OVER-INVOLVED PARENTS

Most girls play sports for fun. They love being active, staying in shape, learning new skills, challenging themselves, competing against others, and being with their friends. Girls say sports give them courage and confidence and that they feel happy when they play. Yet, some girls report that their satisfaction with sports is lessened, or sometimes even ruined, by their parents.

Parents don't start out to make their daughters' sports experience miserable. Most parents are interested in their girls, enjoy being involved in their activities, and want to support them. Yet, sometimes, they become too intensely involved, and support turns into pressure. Parental involvement frequently starts when their daughters are young. They take them back and forth to practice and events; they may volunteer to coach, work in the snackbar, organize carpools, help with fundraising activities. At events they act as referees, judges, timers, and scorers. They stand at poolside, sit in the bleachers, or along the side lines and cheer their daughters on. Youth sports need a high level of parental involvement. But by high school the level of parental participation usually decreases, although girls still need their support. Sometimes parents have a difficult time accepting their daughters' desire for independence and realizing that someone else is in charge.

One softball mother had coached her daughter Kelly's youth team since she had begun playing the sport. When she learned the high school coaching position was open, she was delighted and wanted to apply. Kelly, however, didn't want her mother to "follow me to high school."

"It's not that she wasn't a good coach . . . she was. It's that I wanted her to just be a mom, and I wanted someone else for a coach." It was tough for Kelly to say this to her mom, but she did, and her mother took it well.

Girls say they appreciate their parents' interest and encouragement. They like for their parents to respond when they ask for help and they appreciate parents coming to their games and encouraging them. What makes girls unhappy, though, is when parents take over and support becomes pressure. One volleyball player said, "It stopped being for me and became my dad's thing."

Some coaches hold pre-season meetings for the team and their parents. These meetings help everyone get acquainted and give the coach a chance to explain his or her philosophy and goals for the season. They sometimes talk about parental involvement. Most of them request that parents let the coaches coach and players play and that they cheer and offer encouragement, rather than complain or yell negative comments. Girls say they want that too. One soccer mom, who had played and coached for years, called out what she thought were encouraging comments to her daughter from the side lines. During one game, her daughter Denise, hearing her mother's voice perhaps once too often, stopped, looked over, and said with exasperation, "Mom, you can cheer, but don't coach!"

Most parents who get carried away on the side lines, participate more than their children want them to, or make suggestions even when they're not asked are motivated by their love for their children and their desire to see them succeed. Others, though, become too focused on their daughter's performance, pressuring her to play up to their own expectations. One basketball player said a teammate's father called out instructions to his daughter during games. He stood as close to the court as he could get, waved his arms, and yelled loudly. Not only did he distract her, but he annoyed the entire team. Many times during the season the referee had to warn him about his behavior; several times he was asked to leave the gym.

Experts suggest that girls who feel their parents are too involved or are putting too much pressure on them talk to their parents away from the sport, when everyone is calm. They say it usually works best if you express your appreciation for their interest and concern, but then let them know that their involvement is bothering you. Let them know what you need from them and what they are doing that is pressuring you or making you unhappy. In most cases, parents do not realize how you are feeling; they certainly don't mean to upset you. Being honest in your communications with them usually solves or lessens the problem.

If this doesn't work, you might consider discussing the situation with a sympathetic adult: your coach, another parent, a teacher, the athletic director. It sometimes takes a third person's observations or comments to make parents aware that their behavior is irritating or even harmful.

One swimmer spoke about her friend who had quit the team because her dad wouldn't leave her alone. "The minute she finished her event, he told her everything she did wrong. He compared her technique and times with other swimmers." She talked to him, but he denied he was being negative. Another parent even tried talking to him. The athlete eventually chose to quit swimming rather than deal with her father's interference.

While some girls who play sports encounter special—sometimes bothersome and even painful—issues, the majority have fun, get fit, learn new skills, and enjoy the camaraderie of their teammates. The opportunity to participate and the benefits of sports clearly outweigh the possible problems. In fact, some girls say the challenges they faced were as valuable as the game itself.

NOTES

1. Robert M. Otto and John Wygand, "Coaches Should Be Aware of Dangers Related to Female Athlete Triad," *Interscholastic Athletic Administration*, 25, no. 1 (fall 1998): 8–9.

2. August 31, 1998 news release, "NFHS Takes Position on Androstenedione," National Federation of State High School Associations, Kansas City, MO.

Chapter 13
Pursuing Sports Beyond High School

You don't have to turn in your athletic gear along with your cap and gown when you graduate from high school. You may think your life as an athlete must end when your high school days are over, but it isn't true. Whether you were new to sports in your senior year or a veteran who's played since kindergarten, there are opportunities for you to continue on in sports practically forever.

The next stop for girls furthering their education is college sports. If you have talent and better-than-average skills, you can earn an athletic scholarship at the intercollegiate level. Or you can play intramural sports: competition between clubs, dormitories, or other groups on campus. Intramural sports are usually recreational, allowing girls to meet new people, stay in shape, and have fun.

Few females go on to play professional sports, mainly because opportunities are limited. Still, there are many places for women to continue to compete or to pursue fitness after college and on through their lifetimes: in community recreation programs, club sports, and activities sponsored by the national governing bodies of individual sports, such as tennis, track and field, volleyball, softball, and swimming.

COLLEGE SPORTS

One of the places Title IX—the law mandating gender equity for women—has made a huge difference is at the college level. Not only have universities and colleges added women's sports to their athletic programs, but scholarships have made it possible for many female athletes to continue to play their sport in college and to help pay for their education, too. It may be hard to imagine, but in 1972, when Title IX was enacted, there were few intercollegiate sports available for women and athletic scholarships were virtually nonexistent. Things are very different today. Title IX and changes in attitudes about females and sports have made it possible for just about every woman to participate in some sporting activity while she's in college. University gyms offer recreational sports such as volleyball, badminton, and basketball, while weight rooms are open for workouts; outdoor tracks and courts are lit up at night for joggers and tennis players; and grassy fields welcome pickup games of flag football, rugby, and lacrosse.

Many colleges require freshmen to live in on-campus housing, and each dormitory or apartment complex usually forms teams to compete against each other. College "club" teams also offer opportunities to play sports. They are usually less competitive than intercollegiate sports teams (although they may not agree!). Club teams usually receive little, if any, funding from the athletic department.

Intercollegiate sports are sponsored by the colleges, and most expenses are paid through athletic department funds. Teams play against teams from other colleges in their conference or league. The level of competition varies from school to school and often depends on the division the team is part of.

You may hear about Divisions I, II, and III and wonder what these designations mean. Colleges belong to athletic associations that organize and administer all areas of intercollegiate athletics, including recruiting. The National College Athletic Association (NCAA) is the largest and most well known of the associations, but there are others, such as the National Association of Intercollegiate Athletics (NAIA) and the National Junior College Athletic Association (NJCAA). Each of the associations is divided up into divisions. Division I is usually the most competitive, and there are other differences (see Table 13.1).

The opportunities to play intercollegiate sports have increased dramatically, and so has the athletic skill level of high school girls, many of whom have competed in sports from a young age. Consequently, the competition to make the college team or participate in an individual sport is keen. Sports scholarships are awarded to female student-athletes who are the most highly regarded or sought after by a college coach.

Close to $200 million is awarded each year to college female athletes. Although that is only about 33 percent of the total dollars awarded to all college athletes, it is a tremendous amount of money to help young women with their college expenses. Most girls, though, are confused about finding a college where they will fit in both academically and athletically. They may have heard about recruiting but don't really

Table 13.1
NCAA Divisions

Division I	• Typically very competitive • Mostly comprised of major colleges and universities • Athletic scholarships awarded
Division II	• Often less competitive • Sometimes comprised of smaller colleges and universities than Division I • Athletic scholarships awarded
Division III	• Often less competitive • Comprised of smaller colleges and universities than Division I • No athletic scholarships awarded

know how it works. They notice that some student-athletes are vigorously recruited by college coaches while others—not necessarily less talented—are ignored. They assume that if they are skilled enough, coaches will automatically know about them. They also believe that only superstars win sports scholarships.

In truth, only 1 percent of the nation's high school athletes are superstars, or "blue-chip" athletes. So, college coaches must look to the other 99 percent of highly skilled, though less spectacular, female athletes to fill out their rosters. This opens the door to thousands of girls playing high school softball, basketball, field hockey, and soccer—just four of the more than 20 sports awarding scholarships to women athletes—to compete for full or partial scholarships for colleges throughout the country (see Table 13.2).

For girls to assume that college coaches will know about them if they are good enough is a myth that leaves girls standing on the side lines if they wait for college coaches to contact them. There is no computer data base of the almost 2.5 million girls playing high school sports for coaches to scroll through to find the right athletes for their programs. So, most coaches never hear about the vast majority of girls who would love to go to their college and who could contribute greatly to their sports programs. No matter how valuable you are to your high school team, no matter how much local publicity you get, it is most likely that

Table 13.2
College Sports for Women

Archery*	Skiing
Badminton*	Soccer
Basketball	Softball
Bowling*	Squash*
Cross Country	Swimming and Diving
Fencing	Synchronized Swimming*
Field Hockey	Team Handball*
Golf	Tennis
Gymnastics	Track, Indoor
Ice Hockey*	Track, Outdoor
Lacrosse	Volleyball
Rifle	Water Polo*
Rowing	

*Emerging sports for women

the only coaches who will see you and recognize your talent are those who live and coach nearby.

What can a girl do to draw the attention of college coaches and get recruited? What she can't do is sit back and wait to be noticed. Instead, it is up to the high school athlete to market herself, to introduce her talents to college coaches and catch their interest. Anne Goodman James, assistant athletic director and swimming coach at Northern Michigan University, advises girls to "call the coach and express interest. Once the contact has been made, all the appropriate materials will be sent. This will start the recruiting process."[1] Coaches are glad to hear from student-athletes interested in their program. However, coaches are looking for the student-athlete who is just that: a student *and* an athlete. Coaches want accomplished students. In fact, the NCAA, as well as other athletic associations have eligibility rules colleges must follow, and athletes who do not meet minimum academic requirements cannot play at their member colleges.

Few coaches want to take a chance on the barely eligible student no matter how talented she is athletically. That's because they know that the mediocre student, like the marginal player, will have a tough time jumping up to college-level competition in academics as well as in athletics. They don't want to recruit a girl and give her a scholarship only to have her spend her time on the bench because she's ineligible to play due to failing grades.

Many girls say they don't know where to begin the search for colleges. Check your school and public library for college guides that describe two-year and four-year colleges and universities. Most colleges today have their own websites to help familiarize you with each campus and curriculum. Counselors advise girls to first consider the overall experience when looking at colleges. After making a preliminary list of schools that interest you, check to see if those schools offer your sport, if they award athletic scholarships, and in which division they compete. There are several athletic guides that describe sports programs at colleges throughout the country.

Next, write to coaches at the schools on your list and ask for information about the colleges and their sports programs. This is the first step in the recruiting process. After you receive their packets, study each school's information to decide whether or not you are interested enough to continue. If so, send the coach a letter or résumé about your sports and scholastic background. This will bring you to the attention of coaches at colleges you are interested in and enable them to start a file on you. From this point forward, recruiting is a two-way street: you will want to learn more about the school and sports program; the coach will want to know more about you.

Don't be afraid to be persistent if you are truly interested in a school. Follow up to find out more about the program and to get to know the coach better. Visit the campus during the school year to see firsthand what the school is like, to meet the coach in person, and to talk to other students, especially your prospective teammates. This way you can get a feel for the atmosphere of the college and get to know the people you will be closely involved with if you attend that school.

Not all athletic programs have the same amount of scholarship dollars to award. Most of them want to see the money distributed among as many girls as possible, so they offer partial scholarships. Scholarships can be divided up in different ways, such as tuition and room and board; or tuition and books; or room and board only. Sports scholarships are based on skill and talent and are usually not "need based." That means it doesn't matter what your family finances are; you are being offered the scholarship to induce you to go to a particular school and to help you pay expenses.

Sometimes partial athletic scholarships are combined with other forms of financial aid. Every college has a financial aid office that helps students who need assistance to gather the resources necessary to attend college. Financial aid officers guide students in locating a job and applying for scholarships, loans, and grants. Many times a girl will be offered a partial athletic scholarship along with an academic scholarship (another advantage for girls with higher grade point averages) to create an acceptable financial aid package that will enable the girl to go to that school. Many girls hope for a full-ride scholarship, a scholarship that pays all expenses. Each college determines the amount based on how much it costs to go to the individual school. But a full-ride scholarship never pays more than college expenses; girls still have to have their own money for clothing, entertainment, and extras.

Even when coaches think a girl will fit into their program, they might not offer her a scholarship. Maybe there aren't enough to go around, maybe the school doesn't budget much money for that sport, or maybe the coach wants to see the athlete perform with the team before making a commitment. Whatever the reason, coaches will sometimes ask you to "walk on" (try out for the team) after you are admitted to the college, with the possibility that you will earn a scholarship later if you do well.

Playing intercollegiate sports is a big change from playing high school sports. Intensity, time commitment, and living away from home for the first time are just a few of the factors college athletes must deal with. In fact, juggling sports, studies, socializing, and sleep may be the biggest challenge you face in college. Here is what some athletes say about college sports:

> "Be prepared for long practices and road trips and staying up late to study."
>
> "Prepare to spend more time involved with your sport than most other students do by working a part-time job."
>
> "You have to approach your sport as you would a job, with the same intensity and time commitment."
>
> "Juggling college classes with sports and being away from home is a revelation. It would be hard enough without the sports."
>
> "Time management is the key to success for the college student-athlete. Balancing the three major areas—academic, athletic and social—is a challenge."[2]

Along with their admonitions, most student-athletes enjoy participating in college sports. One girl sums up the feeling of many: "It was the best experience of my life. I made lifelong friends while having the time of my life.''

PROFESSIONAL SPORTS

For most women, college athletics are the pinnacle, the highest level of competition they will face. But in some cases, females go on to become professional athletes. Although the number is very low because the availability of professional sports for women, especially in the United States, is limited, there are some professional opportunities out there for the most elite female athletes. Sports such as tennis, golf, archery, bowling, figure skating, track and field, and basketball have professional leagues or events. Volleyball, softball, and soccer are considering starting up professional leagues within the near future. There are also opportunities to play sports in other countries, and talented women who want to continue playing but are not able to do so in the United States often spend years in other countries getting paid for playing. Two women's basketball leagues started up in the past few years, the American Basketball League (ABL) and the Women's National Basketball League (WNBA). In late 1998 the ABL disbanded, but the WNBA continues to allow women who formerly had nowhere to play in the United States to stay home and play their sport. The Women's World Cup is the precursor to professional women's soccer, while the great interest in 1996 gold medal winning U.S. softball team has encouraged supporters to start moving toward a professional league.

OTHER PLACES TO PLAY SPORTS

In most communities there are recreational sports and fitness programs for all ages, while club sports exist for the more competitive players, often by age group. These programs allow everyone to participate at their own skill level with people their own age. Your sports life can go on as long as you remain healthy and fit, and one way to remain healthy and fit is to participate in sports!

At the World Games in Portland, Oregon, during the summer of 1998, an 81-year-old California woman won gold medals in swimming in her age division, and many other seniors run, ride bicycles, shoot baskets, and play softball regularly. While this is a very high level of competition, many other organizations and clubs have programs for the more casual or ''weekend'' athlete. Contacting your local park and recreation department or chamber of commerce can usually reveal what is available in your community. There are also classes, camps, and clinics offered for adults who want to learn a sport or increase their skills, and adult leagues usually offer weekend competitions. The national governing body of a sport is a good resource for finding out where there are programs near you. These are listed in the Resources section at the end of this book.

Some athletes who never played sports as children became interested as adults. Monica Hilcu, who "dabbled" in high school sports, didn't consider herself an athlete until she went to college and discovered rowing. She joined the crew team and rowed throughout college. Today, she works for a computer software company and rows after work and on weekends for a club team. "It's my passion," she says.

STAYING INVOLVED WITH SPORTS

Women sometimes discover sports in their adult years, while other, long-time athletes take up new sports, become avid spectators, help organize sporting activities, or work in some capacity just so they can be around their sport. Mothers of young athletes often coach, become team mothers, organize carpools or the team telephone tree, help with fundraising, and take kids back and forth to games both at home and away. They get involved with league management, help develop policy, and schedule the facilities and officials. Some women become referees or umpires, scorekeepers, or equipment managers. Others help during the registration process, call in schedules and scores to local newspapers and television stations, or organize swaps so girls can buy used sports equipment and clothing at a discount.

Other women are introduced to sports or learn a new sport in their adult years. One group of women, all 30-something, played recreational tennis in a women's league. One day they were approached with the idea of starting a women's soccer team. Most of them were mothers of young soccer players who thought it looked like fun. They formed a team that became the nucleus for the first women's soccer league in their area. Today, their league has dozens of teams in various age groups.

CAREERS IN SPORTS-RELATED FIELDS

Besides playing, many women who want to stay involved with athletics choose careers in sports-related fields. Women are moving into sports medicine, management, marketing, and manufacturing and many other sports-occupational areas. It hasn't always been this way. If you were a young woman with a passion for sports in 1972, you had few options available. Unless you were one of a handful of elite tennis players or golfers, there were no women's professional sports. Few women made their livings as sports broadcasters, athletic directors, or sports trainers. Not surprisingly, this was a sign of the times: women in general were not doctors, lawyers, or engineers, either.

Women first gained entry to sports-related careers by teaching physical education, coaching, and doing athletic administration—segments of the employment scene men did not view as attractive career options because of relatively low pay and little status. By 1992 sports had grown into a more than $60 million industry, providing new opportunities in sport-related careers. The tremendous surge in participation of women in sports, combined with the growth of careers in the sports industry, opened the door for women to enter.

Male domination in sports-related careers still exists, but there have been changes. Smart, savvy women have risen to the top of many fields. Women own major league baseball teams and sporting goods companies, lead major college athletic departments, and set policy for multimillion-dollar sports businesses. You see them anchoring sporting events on television and read stories with women's bylines on sports pages of newspapers. Females race cars and horses, play professional basketball, and perform with gold-medal perfection at the Olympic Games. A woman has served as the chief medical officer of the United States Olympic Committee and another has been president of the NCAA.[3] Women may be scarce at some levels and in some areas of sports, but they are no longer oddities.

Judith Sweet, athletic director at the University of California at San Diego, grew up in the 1950s and majored in physical education in college because that was the only area available to women who had sports interest. Sweet went on to break the glass ceiling and become one of the first women to direct a combined women's and men's college athletic program and the first female president of a major athletic association, the NCAA.

In part because of women like Sweet, who have helped pave the way for subsequent female athletes, women today have almost unlimited choices. Jennifer Walter, educational services manager at the Women's Sports Foundation (WSF), played intramural volleyball and basketball while pursuing a psychology degree in college. She went on to get a master's degree in sports psychology and landed the job at WSF, which she says is "perfect" for her. Among her other duties, she oversees the internship program with as many as 16 interns at one time working for the organization. Walter gets to use her psychology and sports backgrounds in her work. "I love what I do every day," she says, "I talk to the interns about their personal as well as their professional lives."

Sports psychology is another career option for women. Other sports fields in which women are making an impact include medicine, sales, broadcasting, manufacturing, recruiting, officiating, journalism, photography, coaching, administration, and field and equipment maintenance. While many of these areas need special education or training—some require a college and/or graduate degree—others can be learned on the job or after a specialized training course. The passion for sports and an athletic background can be combined with just about any area of interest and, together with the appropriate credentials, make a woman supremely qualified for just about any job in the sports field.

Many formerly male-dominated sports-related companies now actively seek female athletes. Vivian Langley, former volleyball and softball player and coach, and current director of membership for the American Volleyball Coaches Association, says that she has noticed an increasing trend in companies to contact college coaches in their search for prospective employees. "Finally, they are realizing that the very qualities that make women successful in sports make them top employees," says Langley. The qualities of good athletes—persistence, time management, leadership, and teamwork—are all assets for the workplace. Add a knowledge and enthusiasm for sports, and the applicant has a decided advantage over other job seekers lacking a sports background. Employing women in sports-related fields is good business for companies. Women of all ages are participating in sports in record numbers. Companies such as Nike, Danskin, Reebok, and others now design equipment, clothing, and accessories exclusively for the female athlete. In doing so, these and other savvy businesses are not only meeting a need but filling a void and making a profit as well.

Women are the biggest buyers of sports-related products not only for themselves but for their families. The surge of sports interest among women, together with their increased buying power, has created the demand for more products. Hence, more jobs have also been created for clothing and equipment designers, account executives, sales professionals, accountants, and public relations directors. Today, many of these positions are filled by women. Table 13.3 is a partial list of sports

Table 13.3
Sports-Related Careers

Massage therapy	Sports medicine
Physical education	Sports nutrition
Physical recreation	Sports photography
Public relations	Sports promotion
Retail sales of sporting goods products	Sports psychology
Sports administration	
Sports architecture	*Women also work as:*
Sports broadcasting	Acupuncturists
Sports equipment management and	Clothing designers
maintenance	Curators in sports museums
Sports facilities management and	Equipment designers
maintenance	Personal trainers
Sports information	Physical therapists
Sports journalism	Professional athletes
Sports law	Professional or college scouts
Sports management	Sports officials
Sports marketing	Statisticians

career opportunities for women. In some areas the window of opportunity is just opening; in others, it is open wide and women are equal participants. Additionally, women are athletic directors, fitness instructors, sports agents, sports artists, sports camp directors, sports cartoonists, sports historians, sports illustrators, and sports entrepreneurs. Women not only make a living in these careers, but they excel at what they do. Below are just a few of these jobs with suggested education and/or training requirements for breaking into the field.

Sports Journalist

Sports journalists report the news of the sports world to the public. Prerequisites to enter the field usually include a four-year degree in journalism and/or equivalent writing experience. Job opportunities exist in newspapers and magazines, radio, and television. Most women enter the field as interns on college newspapers, radio, or television stations or as general reporters on small-town newspapers. Curiosity, writing, and interviewing skills and the ability to work within deadlines are characteristics of successful journalists.

Joan Ryan, a nationally known sports columnist for the *San Francisco Chronicle* newspaper and winner of many awards for excellence in sports writing, has combined her passion for sports with a degree in journalism. She is also the author of two books about women and sports.

Sports Agent

A sports agent acts as a professional athlete's representative in negotiating contracts, salaries, endorsements, and other business arrangements. Education includes a four-year college degree in business or a related major, often followed by a law degree. Negotiating skills, sales ability, and ability to work under stressful conditions, often in a male-dominated environment, are all traits of the successful sports agent.

Ellen Zavian is one of the first female sports agents in the United States. She interned with the National Football League during law school, then became a paid employee upon graduation. Today Zavian, who has been a competitive body builder, runner, and triathlete, is an agent representing more than 30 professional athletes and entertainers.

Professional Athlete

Careers for professional women athletes are extremely limited and highly competitive, but opportunities are greater than they were 20 years ago. Today there are women professionals in auto racing, basketball, beach volleyball, billiards, bowling, cycling, equestrian sports, figure skating, golf, racquetball, skiing, sled dog racing, sports climbing, squash, surfing, tennis, triathlon, and water skiing. Plans for professional volleyball, softball, and ice hockey leagues are currently being discussed.

Becoming a professional athlete takes athletic talent and many years of training. Most athletes hone their skills in youth, high school, and college athletic programs. Talent and determination to succeed, as well as luck and timing, are essential for success.

Julie Foudy is the co-captain of the United States Women's National Team. A former high school and Stanford University All-American, Foudy is a ten-year veteran of the U.S. team and played a major role on the 1996 Olympic gold medal team and the 1999 Women's World Cup Championship team. Foudy is also a television sports commentator.

College Coach

College coaches are responsible for getting athletic teams ready to play in competition. In smaller schools they may coach several sports, while in larger colleges or universities they will usually be responsible for just one team. Their duties include recruiting players, developing game strategies, and teaching skills. Most college coaching positions require a minimum of four years of college. A college coach may begin her career track as an athlete, followed by becoming an assistant coach at the high school or college level.

> **Deanne Vochatzer, head track and field coach at the University of California, Davis, started out as a hurdler in high school and college. In addition to her duties as head coach of both the men and women at her college, she was the Women's Track and Field Coach for the 1996 Olympic Games.**

Exercise Physiologist

An exercise physiologist studies how the stress of exercise affects the body. There are a variety of arenas in which exercise physiologists work. Generally it is in the area of prevention (teaching people healthy lifestyle habits) or in the rehabilitative area (after a debilitating injury or heart attack). They may be director of a wellness center or involved in research. Most positions require a minimum of a master's degree with an expertise in exercise physiology or a Ph.D. along with a national certification from organizations like the American College of Sports Medicine.

> **Beth L. Kelley, M.S., ran track and played soccer throughout high school. She earned her undergraduate degree in physical education with an emphasis in athletic training and her master's degree in exercise physiology. Her company, Kelley Concepts, provides educational seminars for companies and professionals in the health and fitness industries. She is a consultant to the California Governors Council on Physical Fitness and Sports and is a college instructor.**

Sports Administrator

A sports administrator oversees an organization's athletic program, business, or association, including budget and staff. Some administrators

represent their organizations at public events. Prerequisites are a four-
year college degree in a business-related field, often followed by a graduate degree. Organizational and motivational skills, attention to detail,
and good verbal and written communication skills are highly recommended.

> **Lori Hendricks is the educational outreach program coordi-
> nator for the National College Athletic Association (NCAA). A
> cross-country and track runner from seventh grade through
> college, she earned her undergraduate degree in politics and
> economics. A special program offered through Harvard Uni-
> versity took Hendricks to South Africa where she worked in
> a program teaching physical education to young people. She
> subsequently earned a master's degree in sports management
> at Ohio State University. An internship at the NCAA led to her
> current position.**

NON-SPORTS-RELATED CAREERS

Women with a background in team or individual sports are not limited
to sports-related careers. They are often perceived to be strong candi-
dates for employment overall. While a woman's athletic career may
cease once she finishes high school or college, she takes many of the
skills she has acquired through sports along with her. Lessons learned
on the playing field transfer superbly to the job market. Regardless of a
woman's area of interest, a sports background can give her that extra
edge in a competitive job market. Many people believe that American
business is based on the sports model. Donna A. Lopiano, Ph.D., executive director of the Women's Sports Foundation, states, "Sports is one
of the most important socio-cultural learning environments in our society and, until quite recently, has been reserved for boys and men."[4]

Women who have not participated in sports and so have not learned
the "rules" of sports often are at a disadvantage, especially in decision-
making positions and other positions of power. Many employers say that
they view prospective employees with an athletic background as highly
desirable in the work place, especially those who have played at the
high school and collegiate level. Employers are impressed that these
student-athletes have been able to excel in both the classroom and in
sports, two very difficult and competitive arenas. They believe their
participation demonstrates that these young women know how to man-
age their time, have acquired self-discipline, and are highly motivated—

just a few of the traits employers seek in prospective employees. According to a study by the University of Virginia, 80 percent of women identified as key leaders in Fortune 500 companies participated in sports during their childhood and identified themselves as having been "tomboys."[5] Besides leadership, other highly prized traits common to successful athletes include:

Self-confidence

High energy

Physical strength and agility

Ability to work in a team setting

Assertiveness

Competitiveness

Persistence

Ability to focus

High motivation

Civil engineering major and former member of the Stanford University women's soccer team, Jennifer Caven, says she has frequently been asked about her athletic background during job interviews. "The fact that I participated in sports, especially at the collegiate level, definitely seems to make me more desirable to prospective employers. I have been complimented on being able to maintain high grades in a tough technical major while successfully competing on a Division I sports team. I think it sets me apart and gives me an extra dimension." The CEO of an east coast job recruiting service concurs. "When I look at a person who has actively participated in sports over the years, I know that he or she must have learned important lessons that will help them on the job." Four skills learned through sports that employers value most are discipline, time management, teamwork, and leadership.

Discipline

An athlete learns to make tough choices. She learns to sacrifice short-term pleasures for long-term goals. One of those pleasures is sleep. Often it was late evening by the time Caven was able to begin studying after a long day of classes, weight training, and a grueling soccer practice. "But I had to get re-energized and apply myself to the books," Caven says. Many times it was tempting to forget about studying and just go to bed, but self-discipline marched her to her desk and kept her there until sometimes the early morning hours.

Time Management

Time management is another skill developed by many athletes. Because their schedules are so full, they learn to control their time by setting goals, establishing priorities, and working efficiently. These are also talents that transfer to job performance and attract employers.

Teamwork

In most jobs, the ability to work as part of a team is important. In athletics, getting along, cooperating, helping out, negotiating, and sharing the glory as well as the responsibility are keys to success. These are also characteristics of the team player within a company.

Leadership

Leadership skills are often learned through the sports experience. According to Kathryn Herrfeldt, director of international marketing for a computer software firm and former collegiate ski team captain, "When someone gives me a tough project, I know I can do it, and I can help motivate others to do the same. Sports taught me that."

You may not choose a career in sports, but your athletic background will benefit you throughout your lifetime. The benefits will continue to grow as long as you continue to participate in sports and fitness activities. Why stop once you graduate from high school when the opportunities to play sports are available to women of all ages? Studies prove that women who stay physically active are healthier and happier. They look better and feel better about their bodies; they have more energy and confidence to face life's challenges; and they have fewer health problems. Most of all, women who continue to play sports have fun!

NOTES

1. Penny Hastings and Todd D. Caven, *How to Win a Sports Scholarship*, Los Angeles: First Base Sports, 1999.
2. Penny Hastings and Todd D. Caven, *How to Win a Sports Scholarship*, Los Angeles: First Base Sports, 1999.
3. Women's Sports Foundation, Career Packet, 1994.
4. Donna A. Lopiano, "Why Women Should Learn How to Use Sport for

Business," speech given at the Women's Sports Foundation Conference, May 1996.

5. L. K. Bunker, "Lifelong Benefits of Youth Sport Participation for Girls and Women," paper presented at the Sport Psychology Conference, University of Virginia, Charlottesville, June 22, 1988.

Resources

BOOKS

General

Cayleff, Susan E. *Babe: The Life and Legend of Babe Didrikson Zaharias*. Urbana: University of Illinois Press, 1995.

Cohen, Neil, ed. *The Everything You Want to Know About Sports Encyclopedia: A Sports Illustrated for Kids Book*. New York: Bantam Books, 1994.

Condon, Robert J. *Great Women Athletes of the 20th Century*. Jefferson, NC: McFarland, 1991.

Drummond, Siobhan. *Grace & Glory: A Century of Women in the Olympics*. Washington, DC: Multi-Media Partners, Ltd., 1996.

Greenberg, Judith E. *Getting into the Game: Women and Sports*. New York: Franklin Watts, 1997.

Guttman, Allen. *Women's Sports: A History*. New York: Columbia University Press, 1991.

Hine, Darlene Clark, ed. *Facts on File Encyclopedia of Black Women in America: Dance, Sports, and Visual Arts*. Vol. 3. New York: Facts on File, Inc., 1999.

Holohan, Maureen. *The Broadway Ballplayers Series*. Wilmette, IL: Broadway Ballplayers, Inc., 1998.

Johnson, Anne Janette. *Great Women in Sports*. Detroit, MI: Visible Ink Press, 1996.

Kraemer, William. *Strength Training for Young Athletes*. Champaign, IL: Human Kinetics, 1993.

Layden, Joe. *Women in Sports: The Complete Book on the World's Greatest Female Athletes*. Los Angeles: General Publishing Group, 1997.

Lindop, Laurie. *Athletes (Dynamic Modern Women)*. New York: Twenty First Century Books, 1996.

Macy, Sue. *Winning Ways: A Photohistory of American Women in Sports*. New York: Henry Holt and Co., 1996.

Moran, Gary. *Cross-Training for Sports*. Champaign, IL: Human Kinetics, 1997.

Nelson, Mariah Burton. *Are We Winning Yet? How Women Are Changing Sports and Sports Are Changing Women*. New York: Random House, 1991.

————. *Embracing Victory: Life Lessons in Competition and Compassion*. New York: William Morrow and Company, 1998.

Oglesby, Carole A., ed. *Encyclopedia of Women and Sport in America*. Phoenix, AZ: Oryx Press, 1998.

Peterson, James A. *Strength Training for Women*. Champaign, IL: Human Kinetics, 1995

Pipher, Mary. *Reviving Ophelia: Saving the Selves of Adolescent Girls*. New York: Ballantine Books, 1994.

Plowden, Martha Ward. *Olympic Black Women*. New York: Pelican, 1995.

Powe-Allred, Alexandra, and Michelle Powe. *The Quiet Storm: A Celebration of Women in Sport*. Indianapolis: Masters Press, 1997.

Rapoport, Ron, ed. *A Kind of Grace: A Treasury of Sportswriting by Women*. Berkeley, CA: Zenobia Press, 1994.

Riley, Dawn. *Taking the Helm*. Boston: Little, Brown and Co., 1995.

Roberts, S., and B. Weider. *Strength and Weight Training for Young Athletes*. Chicago: Contemporary Books, 1994.

Rutter, Virginia Beane. *Celebrating Girls: Nurturing and Empowering Our Daughters*. Berkeley, CA: Conari Press, 1996.

Sandoz, Joli, ed. *A Whole Other Ball Game: Women's Literature on Women's Sports*. New York: Noonday, 1997.

Smith, Lissa, ed. *Nike Is a Goddess: The History of Women in Sports*. New York: Atlantic Monthly Press, 1998.

Steiner, Andy. *A Sporting Chance: Sports and Gender*. Minneapolis, MN: Lerner Publications, 1995.

Summitt, Pat, with Sally Jenkins. *Reach for the Summitt: The Definite Dozen System for Succeeding at Whatever You Do*. New York: Broadway Books, 1998.

Willard, Frances E. *How I Learned to Ride the Bicycle*. 1895. Sunnyvale, CA: Fair Oaks Publishing, 1991.

Woolum, Janet. *Outstanding Women Athletes: Who They Are and How They Influenced Sports in America*. Phoenix, AZ: Oryx Press, 1998.

Zimmerman, Jean, and Gil Reavill. *Raising Our Athletic Daughters: How Sports Can Build Self-Esteem and Save Girls' Lives*. New York: Bantam Doubleday Dell, 1998.

Basketball

Blais, Madeleine. *In These Girls, Hope Is a Muscle*. New York: Atlantic Monthly Press, 1995.

Corbett, Sara. *Venus to the Hoop*. New York: Doubleday, 1997.

Kessler, Lauren. *Full Court Press: A Season in the Life of a Winning Basketball Team and the Women Who Made It Happen*. New York: Penguin USA, 1998.

Lieberman-Cline, Nancy, Robin Roberts, Kevin Warneke, and Pat Summitt. *Basketball for Women: Becoming a Complete Player*. Champaign, IL: Human Kinetics, 1996.

Lobo, RuthAnn, and Rebecca Lobo. *Home Team: Of Mothers, Daughters, and American Champions*. New York: Kodansha International, 1996.

Miller, Faye, and Wayne Coffey. *Winning Basketball for Girls*. New York: Facts on File, 1992.
Ominsky, Dave, and P. J. Harari. *Basketball Made Simple: A Spectator's Guide*, 2d ed. Los Angeles: First Base Sports, 1998.
VanDerveer, Tara, and Joan Ryan. *Shooting from the Outside: How a Coach and Her Olympic Team Transformed Women's Basketball*. New York: Avon Books, 1997.

Field Hockey

Anders, Elizabeth. *Field Hockey: Steps to Success*. Champaign, IL: Human Kinetics, 1998.
Axton, W. F., and Wendy Martin. *Field Hockey*. Indianapolis: Masters Press, 1993.
French, L. *How to Play Hockey: A Step-by-Step Guide*. Norwich, CT: Jarrold Publishers, 1991.

Soccer

Bonney, Barbara. *Soccer: Rules of the Game*. Vero Beach, FL: Rourke Press, 1997.
Crisfield, Deborah. *Winning Soccer for Girls*. New York: Facts on File, 1996.
Dewazien, Karl. *FUNdamental Soccer Guide*. Clovis, CA: Fun Soccer Enterprises, 1995.
Ominsky, Dave, and P. J. Harari. *Soccer Made Simple: A Spectator's Guide*, rev. ed. Los Angeles: First Base Sports, 1999.

Softball

Babb, Ron, and the Amateur Softball Association. *Etched in Gold: The Story of America's First-Ever Olympic Gold Medal Winning Softball Team*. Chicago: Masters Publishers, 1997.
Nitz, Kristin Wolden. *Fundamental Softball*. Minneapolis: Lerner Publications Company, 1997.
Richardson, Dot, with Don Yaeger. *Living the Dream*. New York: Kensington Books, 1997.
Wolff, Virginia Euwer. *Bat 6*. New York: Scholastic Press, 1998.

Swimming and Diving

Gill, Janet. *Fly 'n' Free*. New York: Camelot, 1997.
Laughlin, T. *Total Immersion: The Revolutionary Way to Swim Better, Faster, and Easier*. New York: Fireside Books, 1996.
Rouse, Jeff. *The Young Swimmer*. New York: DK Publishing, 1997.
Tarpinian, Steve. *The Essential Swimmer*. New York: Lyons & Burford, 1996.

Tennis

Gould, Dick. *Tennis, Anyone?* Mountain View, CA: Mayfield Publications, 1992.

King, Billie Jean. *We Have Come a Long Way: The Story of Women's Tennis*. New York: McGraw-Hill, 1988.

Sanchez Vicario, Arantxa. *The Young Tennis Player*. New York: DK Publishing, 1996.

Seles, Monica. *Monica: From Fear to Victory*. New York: HarperCollins, 1996.

Track and Field

Jackson, Colin. *The Young Track and Field Athlete*. New York: DK Publishing, 1996.

Joyner-Kersee, Jackie. *A Kind of Grace: The Autobiography of the World's Greatest Female Athlete*. New York: Warner Books, 1997.

Samuelson, Joan Benoit, and Gloria Averbuch. *Joan Samuelson's Running for Women*. Emmaus, PA: Rodale Press, 1995.

Tricard, Louise M. *American Women's Track and Field: A History, 1895 through 1980*. New York: McFarland and Company, 1996.

Ward, Tony. *Track & Field*. Des Plaines, IL: Heinemann Library, 1997.

Volleyball

Crisfield, Deborah. *Winning Volleyball for Girls*. New York: Facts on File, 1995.

Kilkenny, Bernard. *Volleyball Rules: A Player's Guide*. New York: Sterling Publishing Co., 1997.

Neville, William. *Serve It Up: Volleyball for Life*. Mountain View, CA: Mayfield Publishing Co., 1993.

Reece, Gabrielle, and Karen Karbo. *Big Girl in the Middle*. New York: Crown Publishing, 1997.

Viera, B. L., and B. J. Ferguson. *Volleyball: Steps to Success*. Champaign, IL: Human Kinetics, 1996.

Other Sports

Badminton

Girce, William. *Badminton: Steps to Success*. Champaign, IL: Human Kinetics, 1996.

Baseball

Berlage, G. I. *Women in Baseball: The Forgotten History*. Westport, CT: Praeger, 1996.

Macy, Sue. *A Whole New Ball Game: The Story of the All-American Girls Professional Baseball League*. New York: Henry Holt, 1993.

Golf

Burnett, Jim. *Tee Times: On the Road with the Ladies Professional Golf Tour*. New York: Scribner, 1997.

Sheehan, Patty, and Betty Hicks. *Patty Sheehan on Golf*. Dallas, TX: Taylor Publishing, 1996.

Gymnastics

Bragg, Linda Wallenberg. *Fundamental Gymnastics*. Minneapolis: Lerner Publications Company, 1995.

Feeney, Rik. *Gymnastics: A Guide for Parents & Athletes*. Lincolnwood, IL: NTC/ Contemporary Publishing Co., 1992.

Green, Septima. *Going for the Gold: Shannon Miller*. New York: Avon Books, 1996.

Jackman, Joan. *The Young Gymnast: A Young Enthusiast's Guide to Gymnastics*. New York: DK Publishing, 1995.

Quiner, Krista. *Dominique Moceanu: A Gymnastics Sensation*. East Hanover, NJ: Bradford Book Company, 1997.

Skating

Blair, Bonnie. *A Winning Edge*. Dallas, TX: Taylor Publishing, 1996.

Brennan, Christine. *Inside Edge: A Revealing Journey into the Secret World of Figure Skating*. New York: Scribner, 1996.

Kwan, Michelle, as told to Laura James. *Michelle Kwan: Heart of a Champion*. New York: Scholastic, 1997.

Skiing

Gaskill, Steven. *Fitness Cross-Country Skiing*. Champaign, IL: Human Kinetics, 1998.

Guillion, L. *Nordic Skiing: Steps to Success*. Champaign, IL: Human Kinetics, 1993.

Yacenda, John A., and Timothy R. Ross. *High Performance Skiing*. Champaign, IL: Human Kinetics, 1998.

Football

Hawkes, Dwight D. *Football's Best Offensive Playbook*. Champaign, IL: Human Kinetics, 1998.

Ominsky, Dave, and P. J. Harari. *Football Made Simple: A Spectator's Guide*, 3d ed. Los Angeles: First Base Sports, 1998.

Renner, Bill. *Kicking the Football*. Champaign, IL: Human Kinetics, 1997.

Hockey

Diamond, Dan, ed. *The Spirit of the Game: Exceptional Photographs from the Hockey Hall of Fame*. Chicago, IL: Triumph Books, 1996.

Ominsky, Dave, and P. J. Harari. *Ice Hockey Made Simple: A Spectator's Guide*, 3d ed. Los Angeles: First Base Sports, 1998.

Stewart, Barbara. *She Shoots . . . She Scores!: Complete Guide to Girls' and Women's Hockey*. New York: Firefly Books, 1998.

Lacrosse

Tierney, Bill. *Lacrosse*. Indianapolis: Masters Press, 1995.

Trafford, B., and K. Howarth. *Women's Lacrosse*. Ann Arbor, MI: Crowell House Pub. Co., 1990.

Wrestling

Savage, Jeff. *Wrestling Basics*. Minneapolis, MN: Capstone Press, 1996.

Sinelli, J. *There Is a Girl in My Hammerlock*. New York: Aladdin Paperbacks, 1993.

Special Issues

Ball, Richard T. *Sports Injury Concerns: The Female Athlete*. North Palm Beach, FL: The Coalition of Americans to Protect Sports, 1992.

Cahn, Susan. *Coming on Strong: Gender and Sexuality in Twentieth Century Women's Sport*. New York: Free Press, 1994.

Clark, Nancy. *Nancy Clark's Sports Nutrition Guidebook*. Champaign, IL: Human Kinetics, 1997.

Festle, Mary Jo. *Playing Nice: Politics and Apologies in Women's Sports*. New York: Columbia University Press, 1996.

Nelson, Mariah Burton. *The Stronger Women Get, the More Men Love Football: Sexism and the American Culture of Sports*. New York: Harcourt Brace & Company, 1994.

Ryan, Joan. *Little Girls in Pretty Boxes: The Making and Breaking of Elite Gymnasts and Figure Skaters*. New York: Doubleday, 1995.

Salter, David F. *Crashing the Old Boys' Network: The Tragedies and Triumphs of Girls and Women in Sports*. Westport, CT: Praeger, 1996.

Smith, Kathy. *Kathy Smith's Getting Better All the Time: Shape Up, Eat Smart, Feel Great*. New York: Warner Books, 1998.

After High School Sports

Cassidy, Daniel J. *The Scholarship Book*. Paramus, NJ: Prentice-Hall, 1998.

Hastings, Penny, and Todd D. Caven. *How to Win a Sports Scholarship*. Los Angeles: First Base Sports, 1995.

Karlin, Len. *The Guide to Careers in Sports*. New York: Careers & Colleges, 1997.

Pasternak, C. *Sports: Cool Careers for Girls*. San Luis Obispo, CA: Impact Publications, 1999.

Schlachter, Gail. *Directory of Financial Aid for Women*. El Dorado Hills, CA: Reference Service Press, 1997–1999.

Walker, Ron, ed. *Peterson's Sports Scholarships & College Athletic Programs.* Princeton, NJ: Peterson's, 1998.

VIDEOS

Videos about female participation in sports are increasingly popular. Check out public and school libraries and video rental stores. Most national sports governing bodies and other athletic organizations have video libraries. Also see publications about your favorite sports. Most list videos for purchase.

WEBSITES

Amy Love's Real Sports Magazine	www.loves-real-sports.com
CBS Sportsline	www.cbs.sportsline.com/u/women/index
Go, Girl Magazine	www.gogirlsmag.com
Her Heritage	www.plgrm.com/heritage/women/athletes
Just Sports for Women	www.justwomen.com
Sports Illustrated Online	www.cnnsi.com
Women in Sports	www.makeithappen.com/wis
WomenSport International	www.per.ualberta.ca/wsi
Women's Sports Foundation	www.womenssportsfoundation.org
Women's Wire	www.womenswire.com

ORGANIZATIONS

Amateur Athletic Foundation
2141 West Adams Boulevard
Los Angeles, CA 90018–2040
213-730-9600
www.aafla.org

Canadian Association for the Advancement of Women and Sport and Physical Activity
1600 James Naismith Drive
Gloucester, ON K1B 5N4
613-748-5793
www.caaws.ca

Girl Scouts of the USA
420 Fifth Avenue
New York, NY 10018
212-852-5732
www.gsusa.org

Girls Incorporated
30 East 33d Street
New York, NY 10016
212-689-3700
www.girlsinc.org

Melpomene Institute
1010 University Avenue
St. Paul, MN 55104
651-642-1951
www.melpomene.org

National Association for Girls & Women in Sport
1900 Associate Drive
Reston, VA 22091
703-476-3450, or 800-321-0789
www.aahperd.org/nagws/nagws

National Collegiate Athletic Association (NCAA)
6201 College Boulevard
Overland Park, KS 66221-2422
913-339-1906
www.ncaa.org

National Federation of State High School Associations (NFHS)
11724 NW Plaza Circle
P.O. Box 20626
Kansas City, MO 64195-0626
816-464-5400
www.nfhs.org

Tucker Center for Research on Girls and Women in Sport
University of Minnesota
203 Cooke Hall
1900 University Ave., SE
Minneapolis, MN 55455

612–625–7327
www.kls.coled.umn.edu/crgws

United States Olympic Committee (USOC)
One Olympic Plaza
Colorado Springs, CO 80909
719–578–4833
www.olympic-usa.org

Women's Sports Foundation
Eisenhower Park
East Meadow, NY 11554
516–542–4700
www.womenssportsfoundation.org

YWCA of the USA
Empire State Building, Suite 301
350 Fifth Avenue
New York, NY 10118
212–273–7800
www.ywca.org

Index

About the Author

PENNY HASTINGS is a professional writer and public relations consultant. She is a nationally syndicated newspaper columnist and the coauthor of *How to Win a Sports Scholarship* (1995).